The PERENNIAL GARDEN

The PERENNIAL GARDEN

Color Harmonies through the Seasons

Jeff and Marilyn Cox

Rodale Press, Emmaus, Pennsylvania

To the First Source and Center

Illustrations by Pamela and Walter Carroll.
Photographs by T. L. Gettings, John P. Hamel, Derek Fell, Mitchell T. Mandel, Pat Seip,
Jerry Pavia, Joanne Pavia, and Donna Hornberger.
Book design by Linda Jacopetti.

Library of Congress Cataloging in Publication Data

Cox, Jeff, 1940–
    The perennial garden.

    Includes index.
    1. Perennials. 2. Color in gardening. I. Cox,
Marilyn, 1951–   II. Title.
SB434.C68 1985   635.9′32   85-14192
ISBN 0-87857-573-1 hardcover

   6 8 10 9 7 5   hardcover

*At any season one only sees part of the symphony,
just one movement. Flower gardening is an ephemeral art,
like music and dance.*

—Jim van Sweden

Contents

Photography Credits

T. L. Gettings: photos 3, 7, 8, 9, 20, 22, 23, 24, 25, 26, 27, 28, 29, 38, 39, 40, 41, 42, 43, 44, 45, 46, 47, 48, 49, 50, 51, 52, 53, 54, 55, 56, 59, 72, 73, 74, 75, 78, 79, 80

John P. Hamel: photos 6, 33, 34, 35, 60, 61, 62, 63, 64, 65, 66, 67, 68, 69, 70, 71

Derek Fell: photo on page 66; photos 1, 2, 5, 14, 15, 16, 17, 18, 32, 57, 77

Mitchell T. Mandel: photos 10, 11, 12, 13

Pat Seip: photos 4, 30, 31, 36

Jerry Pavia: photos 21, 76

Joanne Pavia: photos 19, 37

Donna Hornberger: photo 58

Acknowledgments

We'd like to thank Elizabeth Baas, who shared her love of flowers with her grandchildren, including Marilyn.

Special thanks go to those wonderful gardeners who allowed us to visit and learn from them: Martha Barnet, Harland Hand, Jane Lennon, Ruth Levitan, Fred and Maryanne McGourty, Florence Reynolds, Joanna Reed, Grace Rose, Bob and Cindy Seip, Sir John Thouron, and Elsie Yarema. Much of the beauty in this book was created by them.

Among institutions that were always helpful to us, we'd like to thank the staff of the Pennsylvania Horticultural Society, Dr. Darrell Apps at Longwood Gardens, Carl Totemeir at Old Westbury Gardens, and the kind folks at White Flower Farm, who allowed us to visit and photograph and answered our letters of query about the flowers they grow so well.

Cliff Russell of Russell Gardens gave us great help in preparing the chart of perennials.

Hundreds of growers and horticulturists around the country took the time to answer our query letters also, and we hope that they individually understand the necessity for thanks en masse.

We'd like to thank the photographers who found the color harmonies and captured them for us. At Rodale Press, our thanks go to Tom Gettings, John Hamel, Mitch Mandel, Alison Miksch, and Pat Seip, and to their secretarial staff. And thanks to our freelance photographers: Derek Fell, Donna Hornberger, and Joanne and Jerry Pavia. Thanks also to illustrators Pamela and Walter Carroll.

We'd also like to thank Anne Halpin and Barbara Emert for their help in editing and preparing this book.

Plant Hardiness Zones

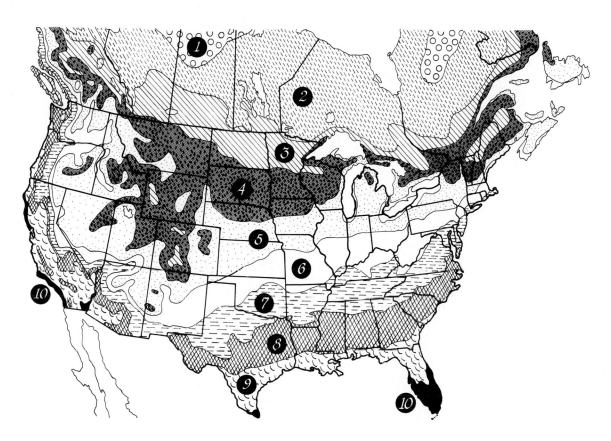

Average Minimum Temperatures for Each Zone

Zone 1	below -50°F		Zone 6	-10° to 0°
Zone 2	-50° to -40°		Zone 7	0° to 10°
Zone 3	-40° to -30°		Zone 8	10° to 20°
Zone 4	-30° to -20°		Zone 9	20° to 30°
Zone 5	-20° to -10°		Zone 10	30° to 40°

A Note on Perennials

But time remembered is grief forgotten.
The frosts are slain, the flowers begotten,
And in green underwood and cover,
Blossom by blossom,
The spring begins.

—Algernon Charles Swinburne

For plants flowers perform an essential function—they exist to lure the pollinating insects. For foraging bees, flowers' cups and trumpets brim with nutritious dew and pollen, necessary food that's there for the taking. But for people, flowers are just for beauty, an exalted concept reserved for humanity's appreciation, but present in the flower nevertheless. For us, they are sheer adornment, nature's evanescent jewelry, and far more gorgeous than they have to be for their practical duties alone.

We read a benign intent in the world through the language of flowers. And how could this intent be better conveyed than by the endless variety of the fragile, living shapes and colors that so please us, and yet don't even have to be? What is intended is our pleasure.

Those of us who live in the temperate parts of North America are therefore sorely tried by the circling seasons that annually destroy the gardens of pleasure we've so carefully tended. Like it or not, we are witness to the melancholy autumn, whose ever-more-ferocious frosts slay the flowers and freeze the leaves from the trees. Gardens so carefully prepared and nurtured slowly wither and fall to ruin each year. Summer's creations are dashed by cold rains and broken by snow, scoured of color until all is murk and shadow, sunk into sunless winter.

We know what the world would be like without flowers, for we endure such a world for part of every year: It would be bleak and hopeless. It is for good reason that we set flowers near the sick, so they can be cheered and given hope by the sight.

Although the winter tries us, it's then that we can truly say of our perennial flowers, "They are gone, but they are not dead." When they return in spring, they are renewed, with fresh foliage and new blossoms—old friends resurrected; old loves aflame again. They are at once different—for this is new growth we see—and yet the same plants we put into our gardens in past years.

Each year I go out into my garden and paint the same clump of daylilies. I set my easel in the same place and always start in the morning when the golden-orange blossoms are backlit by the eastern sun. The artist, the paints, and even the brushes are the same, yet every painting in this series is completely different, exploring new aspects of the flowers and finding new techniques to express them. I realize, as I paint, that not only the daylilies have been renewed since my last painting of them; the passing year has also given me fresh eyes. I know what I knew last year, but also something else. Last year's experience has been subsumed and nurtures me now in the ever-renewing moment. And so it is with my subject. The leaves and stalks I painted last year have fallen to the soil and, in their decay, nourish the flowers I paint today.

The purpose and meaning of flowers for people—no matter what their other functions—have to do with our capacities for higher perception. Flowers are thoroughly communicative of these meanings, speaking to our senses with their scents, shapes and colors, to our minds with their geometries and biology, and to our hearts with their messages of hope and cheer. And their yearly return adds still more meaning and attraction to perennials. What a miracle of promise is the first blossom of the year—

an ordinary little snowdrop, perhaps—that viewed alongside delphiniums and tritomas would be insignificant, but viewed against nature's blank canvas is appreciated more than any other flower.

In the youthful spring, most perennials make exuberant foliage growth. In their young adulthood, they flower. In the fullness of their maturity, they ripen fruit and seed. And in their cold decline, they cast the seed and then fall protectively upon it.

This apparent death does not reach the root. Buried away under the detritus of past years, out of sight and in secret, the living core persists. Some day a bird will call, and a warming sun will loosen winter's frosty claws. The root will stir, and from the crown new growth will reach toward the light. It emerges into a new world, made fresh by winter's rains and ruins, with new life and a chance to give again.

All this—and we haven't even spoken of the effect of perennials' beauty on the sensitive soul. But perhaps words are not the way. The best way is to experience the glory and renewal of a perennial garden you have created and know intimately. To do that, information and inspiration are needed. Hence this book.

CHAPTER 1

A Place for Flowers

When the dinosaurs shrieked in the primordial night, and the world's highest law was to eat or be eaten, there were no flowers. Angiosperms—flowering plants—hadn't yet appeared. The advent of human beings lay 130 million years or so in the future.

Angiosperms suddenly appeared 125 million years ago, in the early to mid-Cretaceous Period, and in great quantities. Our modern magnolia tree most closely resembles the first angiosperms, with its large, brightly colored flowers and primitive construction. Angiosperms signaled a new era on the earth, and at the end of the Cretaceous, about 65 million years ago, the dinosaurs disappeared, and the age of flowers and mammals and insects, called the Tertiary Period, began.

At first, flowering plants were all dicots—plants that have two seedling leaves, a network of veins in their leaves, and flower parts that use the numbers four and five to build their lovely temples. The world was cooling off during this period, and angiosperms developed several ways of coping with cold stress. Some plants found they could survive cold spells by dropping their leaves, their woody, aerial parts remaining alive to push out new leaves and flowers when warmth returned. We call these plants woody perennials. Other plants with green and juicy herbaceous stems died back to the ground each year, but the roots stayed

alive to push out new growth in the spring. We call these herbaceous perennials. Still other plants set seed and then died entirely during cold weather, relying on a coming spring to germinate the seed and continue their line. We call these plants annuals. Finally, some plants mixed modes and formed an herbaceous plant the first season after germinating. Like an herbaceous perennial, this kind of plant died back to the ground in winter, with a live root. The following year, the plant put forth new leaves and also sent up a flower stalk. When the flowers set seed, the plant died away like an annual. These plants are called biennials.

After the dicots were established, a new variation appeared: monocots. These angiosperms differed from dicots by having only one seedling leaf, parallel rather than networked leaf veins, and flower structures based on the numbers three and six. Palms, grasses, lilies, and orchids are monocots. With a few exceptions, all other flowering plants are dicots.

Since these early epochs of angiosperm history, the trend of evolution has been toward simpler structures, reduced flower parts, and especially the clustering of many tiny flowers into composite heads that look like one flower, such as sunflowers and dandelions. Another trend has been toward flowers built to insure that foraging insects will brush against pollen-bearing structures before they reach the stigma and the nectaries. One pollen grain will enter the stigma and travel down the style to the ovary, fertilizing a potential seed. Some orchids grow very elaborate flower architectures to keep insects moving the way they want them to. Among the dicots, snapdragons have also come up with a flower that insures pollination.

Another hand besides nature's has begun manipulating the angiosperms of late—the human hand. Since the dawn of agriculture, people have been saving strains of seeds and plants that they find valuable for food or for the beauty of their flowers. Over the past few thousand years, constant selection has led to crops that can't survive without man, such as hybrid corn, and to flowers with colors chosen for man's eye, not the bee's.

The Focus of This Book

So many thousands of varieties of woody and herbaceous perennials, biennials, and annuals—trees, shrubs, herbs, flowers, and food crops—have been saved over the years, it would take an encyclopedia just to list them all. To focus this book of flower harmonies, we'll concentrate on herbaceous perennials—although we'll mention woody plants, biennials, and annuals when we put the perennials in living contexts.

Herbaceous perennials form the basis for a garden of flowers that will return and increase year after year, until they fill your flower beds with a succession of color, form, foliage, and sweet smells that begins with the pale, late winter sun and ends in the cold glories of the fading fall. You will come to know many of them intimately, the way you know your children or your friends.

While you don't have to restock a bed of herbaceous perennials with new plants each year, you will be moving them around, dividing them, and working over the years toward plant groupings that will accomplish the following:

- Reliably return year after year, a sure indication the plants like where you've planted them.
- Show flowers in all seasons.
- Offer a pleasing arrangement of shapes and leaf textures.
- Naturalize and grow into mature beds that tend to shade out weeds.
- Juxtapose colors in harmonious and interesting ways.
- Require a minimum of maintenance.

Such a bed's satisfying picture, upon close inspection, resolves into marvelously subtle and thoughtful combinations of colors and textures. The overall view of a perennial bed is only one aspect of its beauty. The real treasures are to be found when one sits in the garden and focuses on just a few square feet. Last May, for instance, I was weeding one of our beds when I noticed, just 2 feet in front of me, a place where pink and blue *Phlox subulata* spilled over a rocky ledge. A few inches below this small ledge, Johnny-jump-ups grew and, in one exquisite little place, hung their flowers directly in front of the phlox. The broad brush strokes of pink and blue were picked up by the Johnnies and in them were reduced, intensified, and distilled to their essence ... and dangled in front! In addition, the Johnnies' centers were smeared with the most intense buttery gold for an accent and homage to the sun.

The Purpose of This Book

Planning a perennial flower bed of pleasing colors is a lot like creating a painting. Each choice as to color, shape, arrangement, and so on expresses the artist's aesthetic sense. It's our hope that the information in this book will help you choose perennials that express not our conception of beauty, but yours. To do this, we'll give you the information you need to please your own sensibilities and to make choices you'll be happy with every time you look out the window.

The Origin of Garden Perennials

The sheer multitude of perennials available to us today is due to the efforts of our forebears, who brought them home to Europe and America from travels all over the world. The beautiful *Belamcanda,* or blackberry lily, for instance, was brought to England in 1823 from China. Above all nations, it was the seagoing English with their penchant for gardening who soon had the British Isles flourishing with exotic plants. North and South America were fertile reservoirs of new plant material for the English, who took the plants home and improved them, whereupon they found their way back to the Americas as horticultural specimens. Native North American asters, for instance, were taken to England in the early eighteenth century, where they were called Michaelmas daisies. Centuries of crossing and breeding work done there have given North American gardeners their pick of *Aster ericoides* in pastel shades that range from pale blue through creamy yellow to lilac-pink and white.

Other flowers are true natives, brought into North American gardens from the wild and improved here.

Because our garden perennials have come from all over the world, one would suspect they'd be rather finicky about their soil, light, and water requirements, and would grow best in conditions approximating those of their ancestral home. With some plants this is absolutely true, but others thrive just about anywhere and in a great range of soils. Look what happened to daylilies when they escaped from our ancestors' gardens—now they happily line our roadways. Or to purple loosestrife (*Lythrum salicaria*), a British native that took to the fields and roadsides of northeastern North America with such a vengeance that it's considered an invasive weed. But what a weed! When dry August comes and the floral spectaculars of June have long faded and the fields are boring shades of white and yellow, along come the strong, tall, magenta spikes of loosestrife.

Probably the most important condition of a plant's origin is the soil in which it developed. It probably still likes that soil condition. We'll be describing the plants' soil needs in the chart in chapter 7.

The Use of Horticultural Latin

The Latin names by which plants are classified are a superb invention of Carolus

Linnaeus, an early eighteenth century Swedish explorer and scientist who created the taxonomic system that we use today. Modern horticulture could hardly exist without these names, for they are the lingua franca of the plant world, the names everyone has agreed to use so that plants don't get mixed up. Of course, some still do get mixed up, but Linnaeus's system effectively contains most of the damage. Almost all our flowers have common names, such as purple loosestrife for *Lythrum,* or daylily for *Hemerocallis,* or balloon flower for *Platycodon.* People found early on that common names change drastically from one locality to another, and my balloon flower may be your summer bells, my goatweed your goutweed, and what you call goosefoot, I may call Good King Henry. Latin (and occasionally Greek) names efficiently clear all that up. It's good to use them. We have no trouble saying *Chrysanthemum,* which is the proper scientific name for that plant, and so we shouldn't really have any trouble with a name like *Campanula*—except, is it pronounced *kam-PAN-you-la* or *kam-pan-OO-la?* We'll help with this, too, by putting a phonetic rendering of the plant's genus name after its correct spelling in the chart in chapter 7.

Specific information about a plant can be found in its scientific names, if you know some Latin. As an example, let's look at *Platycodon* more closely, specifically *Platycodon grandiflorus* 'Mariesii'. The word *Platycodon* is the genus name, based on the Greek for "broad pods," and refers to any kind of *Platycodon* (and there are several very different kinds). The word *grandiflorus* is Latin for "large flowered" and is the name of a particular species of this plant,

with the common name of balloon flower. 'Mariesii' is the cultivar name, referring here to a cultivar that's early and somewhat compact, and that was developed in 1884. The telltale double "-i" on the end usually means it's named for the developer of the cultivar. An "-ae" ending means the developer was female, and "-iana" means that the flower name commemorates the personal name it's attached to, such as Sieboldiana. Sometimes cultivars are named as a commemoration of someone, such as *Scabiosa caucasica* 'Clive Greaves'. The species name here tells us that the plant is native to the Caucasus region of Europe, while the cultivar name commemorates Mr. Greaves.

Cultivars, then, are names for varieties within a species that are developed by people. There are also natural variations within species.

Genus includes all the species of a certain kind of plant. And there are family names that include several genera. Family names usually end in the suffix "-aceae," such as Rosaceae, Liliaceae, or Campanulaceae, and are usually in Roman type placed within parentheses when used in the name.

There is a particularly nice shell pink platycodon that we love, and here is its full botanical name, including family, genus, species, and cultivar: *Platycodon grandiflorus* 'Mother of Pearl' (Campanulaceae). An English translation of the name tells us that this is a large-flowered platycodon of shell pink color, a member of the campanula, or bellflower, family.

While it helps to know the Latin names to insure proper plant identification, and especially when you're writing to someone, common names remain commonly used. It's just easier to say red-hot poker than *Kni-*

The Meaning of Latin and Greek Plant Names

The Latin, and sometimes Greek, names for plants used by botanists all mean something specific. They may name a genus for figures from mythology, such as Narcissus, or they may in some way describe the plant. Here's a sampling of botanical names and what they mean.

Botanical Name	English Meaning
Acanthus mollis	*Acanthus* = thorny; *mollis* = soft.
Achillea millefolium	*Achillea* = named after Achilles of the Homeric legend, supposedly used by him for healing; *millefolium* = thousand leaved.
Arenaria species	*Arenaria* = grows in a sandy place (from the Latin word *arena*, meaning "sandy place").
Aster macrophyllus	*Aster* = star; *macro* = large, *phyllus* = leaf.
Campanula glomerata	*Campanula* = bell flowered; *glomerata* = clustering.
Ceratostigma plumbaginoides	*Ceratostigma* = horned stigmas; *plumbaginoides* = like a plumbago ("-oides" means "somewhat resembles").
Chrysanthemum coccineum	*Chrysanthemum* = golden flowers; *coccineum* = deep red.
Cimicifuga cordifolia	*Cimicifuga* – bug chaser; *cordifolium* = heart-shaped leaf.
Convallaria variegata	*Convallaria* = pertaining to the valley (*Convallaria* is lily-of-the valley); *variegata* = has mottled or variegated leaves.
Delphinium elatum	*Delphinium* = dolphin-like (referring to shape of the individual flowers); *elatum* = tall.
Hemerocallis fulva	*Hemera* = day, *Kallos* = beauty: beauty for a day, referring to the life span of a single flower; *fulva* = tawny.

phofia, or obedient plant than *Physostegia*. Long familiarity with the Latin names tends to lead one to use them, however. And of course, for positive identification, we'll be using Latin names in this book.

Sources of Inspiration

As I write this, I'm looking out a window of the small building where I have my study onto a rather wild part of our property, the wood's edge into which our home is tucked. At various times we've had it cleaned up, and Marilyn has put in plants, but this year we've neglected it in favor of gardens more central to the outdoor living areas. And yet, as I look at it, I realize that the scene is a study in unstudied elegance. Fifty feet from the window, mature trees reach up and overarch the view, glowing light yellow-green in the sky. Beneath them is a deep pool of black—the black roof of our springhouse, its edges broken up to my view by sprays of yellow birch leaves. There's a path on the left, leading from the springhouse up toward the big house, flanked on its left by an old stone wall. The wall is lined with tall ferns that Marilyn planted. In the middle of the scene is a gorgeously curled and arched Japanese plum tree that I planted eight years ago to replace an old apple that had toppled in a severe ice storm. Between the plum tree and the springhouse, August lilies are in full bloom, perfuming the air with sweet scents and throwing out masses of pure white trumpets. Volunteer phlox waves its light lavender panicles down near the springhouse. Weeds fill in with infinite varieties of green.

The scene is wild and unkept, yet exquisite. I wish our carefully tended new gardens looked like this—an arrangement by a master colorist with a very restrained hand. Its appeal is due in great part, I must admit, to the fact that we've let it alone back here, and nature had a chance to create beauty. She always does, as the overwhelming beauty of wilderness attests. We want our other beds—the ones we care for—to achieve that grace and informal elegance that nature lavishes on her wild creations. If we are to bring plants in from the wild and cultivate them, then we must give them enough rein to do pretty much what they want to in the space allotted for them. Too many gardens are antiseptically weeded and kept. Not enough are big, sprawly affairs that form little pockets of wild beauty on their own, without a human planner. Marilyn has a description of herself that I think gets to the heart of creating a garden like that. "I'm not a great weeder," she says, "but I am a great planter." She plants up a space until there really isn't a lot of room for weeds. Still, they are represented in most of our gardens, and often welcome.

Inspiration for designing flower gardens can come from almost anywhere—from a painting in a museum to a swamp with its wild reeds and grasses. Our job is to drop our preconceptions and open our eyes. Then we'll see the beauty. And then we can bring it home.

America's Unused Potential

We live in Berks County, Pennsylvania, a well-watered, verdant part of the Northeast that's suited to a great variety of perennial flowers. And yet, as we drive to town from our country place, past properties where owners have plenty of elbow room, I see very few beds or borders of herbaceous perennials. Yes, in the spring everyone seems to have a few daffodils or tulips. But after the bulb season, most people seem content with a foundation planting of evergreens, or perhaps some borders of annual marigolds, red salvia, impatiens, and petunias.

I've noticed that in neighborhoods someone will plant a bed of petunias, and for several houses around, there will also be petunias. Obviously the neighbors have admired the flowers and followed someone's lead. Perhaps the person with the petunias shared some knowledge of how to grow them with his or her friends. We'd like to see more people try perennials. We're sure it wouldn't take long before neighbors were asking for cuttings and clumps. There's enormous unused potential in the yards of America. Rare is any planting of herbaceous perennials, and rarer still a well-thought-out garden of perennials.

In England, it's a different story. The gardeners are ferocious there, and every plant has its society and its adherents (and detractors). It's common to find beds of gorgeous perennials there, and this intense interest has made English gardens and gardening books among the best in the world. Unfortunately for North Americans, England has a sheltered, wet climate, with moderate summers and winters softened by the warm Gulf Stream. The English have a whole category of half-hardy perennials that just don't work very well in the United States, except for rare spots in the South and along the Pacific Coast. While absolutely wonderful, English gardening books are English, and they can be very misleading for Americans.

Also, some of the best English works, such as those by Gertrude Jekyll, presuppose an army of gardeners to carry out one's whims, setting out hundreds of plants, moving them each year, putting in and taking out whole beds to achieve the desired effects.

In this book we're going to assume that American perennial gardeners will be doing the work themselves, and that maximum effect for minimum effort is what we're after. We'll not be talking about landscaping acres as much as creating small but excellent gardens—ones that can be managed by people who only have some small part of their spare time to devote to the task. To create masterpiece gardens over even one acre of property will take a gardener 30 hours a week during every week of the growing season, which is fine if your time and enthusiasm run that far. But we want to scale down the time and labor so that your property has areas of brilliance, and you still have time to take the kids to the movies.

However, Americans are doing more flower gardening now than ever before. In fact, flower gardening passed vegetable and

house plant growing as the major interest of gardeners in the early 1980s. Perennial growers I've spoken with all report expanding business. Still, for all that activity, a cruise down most American streets and byways reveals that most yards have few flowers. Our destiny as a nation of flower growers still awaits us.

Your Kind of Garden

Some folks just can't stand Johnny-jump-ups and others hate pachysandra. Some people want beds for cut flowers; others want beds and borders to see through the windows or from a patio. Still others are away for the summer months, and so they plant for spring and fall bloom. We've found from reading the perennial authorities that one will advise you to plant your whole property with your favorite flowers, while another will warn against planting too much of the same thing. The contradictions bother some people, but we take them as personal opinion, not immutable law. Our advice is to listen to all reasonable ideas, sprinkle them all with grains of salt, and then design and create the gardens that you want, for the reasons you want, with the plants you like.

Assessing Your Property for Perennial Plantings

To design a perennial garden, the first questions you have to answer are: Where should you put the plantings, and what size and shape should they be?

We realize that readers of this book will have all kinds of situations—small suburban rectangles, large country estates, bulldozed subsoil around a new house, an overgrown jumble that was once well-planted, even established flower gardens. In addition, readers' climates will vary from coast to coast and North to South. Yet the principles of placing perennial plantings to take advantage of the natural climate, geography, and environmental conditions are the same everywhere. These principles are built on the following factors.

What's Your Zone?

According to the U.S. Department of Agriculture's (USDA) map of hardiness zones (see page xiii), we live in Zone 6, with an average annual minimum temperature of from -10° to 0°F. And yet, twice in the past four years, we've had blasts of December air that reached to -25°F. Although it may average out to just 10 below, we must anticipate winters where the minimum temperatures go much lower. Keep that in account when choosing plants that are supposedly hardy in your zone—some may die out under local conditions. The margin of error in the zone chart goes the other way, too. Although liriope, for example, isn't supposed to be hardy much north of Washington, D.C., it has been grown farther north in recent years with good results. It just needs a good mulching to carry it through winters in Zone 6 and in favored sheltered spots in Zone 5.

These USDA zones are determined by the average annual frost-free days and minimum winter temperatures, and they're in a general way accurate. They are not *specifically* accurate, however. If you're near the border of your zone, or live on a high hill and face north, it's likely you are ac-

tually in the next colder zone, while someone a few miles away in a sheltered south-facing part of the valley floor near a lake could be in the next warmest zone.

Besides local variations, there are national variations. A look at the zone map shows that Zone 6 starts along the westerly part of the Maine seacoast, includes the Boston to Philadelphia corridor, strikes out across Appalachia to the heart of the Midwest, then runs down through the plains to Amarillo, Texas, whence it dips almost to the Mexican border, then rises through Arizona and Nevada to ride the Sierras and Cascades up the coast into British Columbia. Zone 6, therefore, is as diverse as Maine and Nevada. Eastern Zone 6 is subject to lots of rain, and plants that like it moist will do well there. But the same plants may not do well at all in Nevada, where the land is thousands of feet above sea level and dry as dust. Just because a catalog says a plant grows in Zone 6 doesn't mean it grows everywhere in that zone. It means that if the plant likes the local conditions, it won't freeze out—usually.

Use the zones as a general measure of plant hardiness, rather than as a climate guide. You know your local climate, rainfall patterns, and environmental conditions better than any map. However, some generalizations can be made about the different characteristics of various zones.

In cold and wet climates, such as along the northern border of the United States from Minnesota to Maine, decayed organic matter tends to build up in the soil. In fact, in the very far North, we encounter peat bogs dozens of feet thick. On the other hand, in the hot, wet climates of the Southeast, organic matter tends to burn out of the soil faster than nature can replace it. In the tropics, the soil has very little organic matter; it's all aloft in the stems, trunks, and foliage.

From Zone 5 south, there tend to be two flowering seasons—spring and fall—separated by a hot, dry period during summer when the garden just hangs in there. The farther south you go, the more pronounced are these dual seasons, until you reach the subtropical zones, with their whole range of unique plants growing throughout the year.

In the West, winter conditions are often more influenced by elevation above sea level than by latitude, and that's why the zone map looks so jumbled up in that mountainous region.

The northern latitudes get more hours of sunlight during the growing season than the southern latitudes. The sun stays abroad longer in July in Wisconsin than it does in Dallas. Since solar radiation is one of the prime determining factors for budding and flowering, the same plants will flower at different times in different latitudes.

Most of the flowering times given in this book are for regions from 35 to 45

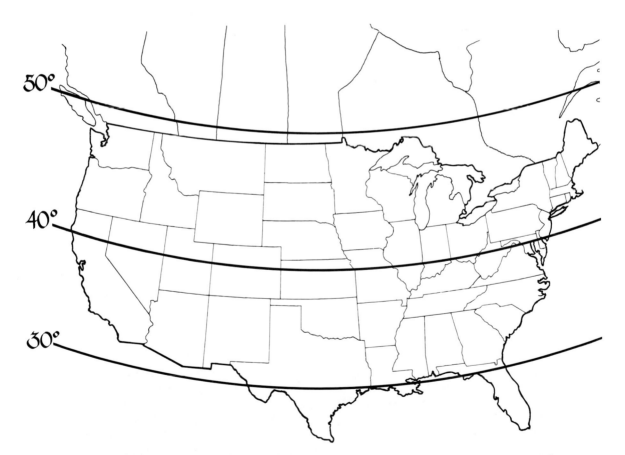

Most of the blooming periods given in this book are accurate for 35 to 45 degrees north latitude. Plants will bloom about three weeks earlier for every 5 degrees south of 40 degrees, and three weeks later for every 5 degrees north of 40 degrees.

degrees north latitude, which covers a great deal of the most populated parts of the United States. Perennials will flower earlier in the South and later in the most northerly regions. There's no room to give flowering times for all perennials in all regions, but we can give you a rule of thumb to follow: Just advance the flowering time about three weeks for every 5 degrees of latitude south of 40 degrees, and delay it three weeks for every 5 degrees of latitude north of 40 degrees. This is only a rule of thumb, and a lot depends on the flowering habits of the plants.

The very best ways to determine flowering times in your area are to keep a sharp eye out for them on your journeys close to home, to visit nurseries and ask growers, and to take perennial garden tours given by horticultural societies and garden clubs. There's much for all of us to learn about plants' local adaptations. Take along a notebook on your travels. Simply by jotting down what's blooming when, you'll soon be working with planting times that are perfectly accurate for you. It will help immensely when, in future years, you're choosing perennials to bloom together. In the meantime, the flowering times given in this book can be a general guide and will serve for most varieties you'll plant.

What Are Your Property's Environmental Conditions?

Plants respond to various environmental conditions that you must take into account when choosing perennials to grow well together.

Shade, Partial Shade, or Full Sun

The amount of sunlight reaching the garden site will partially determine which plants to grow. Some *must* have full shade, others full sun. Some can tolerate almost any degree of shade or sun. Look at the shadow patterns on your property in the morning, at noon, in the afternoon, and in the evening. These will vary from spring to fall, too, so watch throughout the growing season. The purpose is to know for sure which areas get no sun, which get sun for just an hour or two each day, which get three to six hours, and which get a full sun exposure all day long.

In the chart of perennial varieties that appears in chapter 7, a light requirement of full shade means just that—usually an area under a closed tree canopy. Partial shade may be an area under a tree that stands alone, or under a few trees, which gets no more than a few hours of dappled sun during the course of the day. Partial sun usually refers to an area that gets three to five hours of sun, and full sun means six or more hours every day. Sun-loving plants may grow in the shade, but they'll set fewer blooms and won't reach their growth potential.

Shade is a factor you can do something about if it's caused by overgrown or thick stands of trees. If old trees are hemming you in and you want sun near the house, boldly consider removing any or all of them. It costs nothing to imagine them gone. When it comes to opening up an overgrown area to light, however, be conservative. Big trees are priceless creatures. They cool the air around the house, reduce noise, form the focal points of the landscape, produce leaves that are valuable for mulch and compost, harbor birds, and otherwise soften the land. First remove diseased or misshapen trees, then see what you've got. At our place, the back end of the house is in the woods, and a huge white ash arches over the house. When we built a deck out back a few years ago, we built it right around that beautiful ash. It's better than a six-ton air conditioner. The front of our place looks out on two cleared acres of lawn and gardens, with woods' edge visible beyond them.

Shade gardens are often among the most beautiful of perennial gardens, possibly because the choice of plants limits the gardener's palette somewhat, which adds to coherence, but more possibly because shade-loving plants run to types, and these mix well.

There will be shade thrown by objects you won't want to do anything about, such as the house. House shade tends to be less intense than foliage shade, because leaves soak up sunlight and don't scatter it, whereas the light walls of houses scatter a lot of it. Full shade from a house can often support plants needing light shade or partial sun.

Southeastern to southern slopes get the most sunlight, while northern and north-western slopes get the least. In northern regions, a south slope might be good for perennials that may need some protection from the intense sun in southernly regions. The same plants would do better in the south on an eastern or northern slope.

Regarding sunlight, there's a difference in quality between morning sun and after-noon sun. Morning sun is less intense, after-noon sun somewhat more intense. An area that gets just a few hours of morning sun would be a candidate for plants needing "some sun," and perhaps plants needing light shade.

Even if all you have is full sun, you can create conditions of partial shade by planting behind or beneath bigger plants or land-scape plantings of ornamental trees, and by using the shade thrown by structures like houses and walls.

In addition, your shade may be wet—such as in a low spot where the water table reaches to the surface. Or it may be of normal, water-holding capacity. Or it may occur in an elevated or rocky part of the property that drains quickly and stays dry. Where tree roots feed near the surface, the soil is much drier than where no such roots occur, and that's often a shady spot.

Wet, Normal, or Dry

A spot that's constantly wet (except because the septic tank's drain field is there) may provide the makings of a water garden. There are many beautiful perennials that can turn a small pond into a fanciful garden. Or the spot may simply remain moist, which again limits the perennials you can plant, but not your ability to create a beautiful garden, since many fine plants like "wet feet."

Where the soil drains normally, it will hold water for about a week in the summer until it needs more. It needs a total of about an inch a week. Rainwater will not stand in such areas, but will quickly drain away. These areas are ideal for the great mass of perennials. Dry soils are found under trees with surface roots, such as maples, and in rocky and elevated areas.

Soil Type

Soil is usually characterized as sandy, clay, or silty, or as the mixture of all three, which is called loam. Loams are the best kind of base soil for a perennial garden, but soils that are loose and sandy can be made better with the addition of lots of decaying organic matter. Clay soils are heavy and thick and form great, hard chunks when dry. These are the poorest soils for most perennials and must be improved with additions of rotted organic matter and sand to get them fertile, loose, and loamy. Silty soils also need organic matter and perhaps a little sand to loosen them.

To find out what kind of soil you have to work with, take some moist—not wet—soil from various spots around the property where you might put the perennial bed. Squeeze a handful of it into a ball in your fist. Now strike the ball sharply with a finger. If it doesn't crumble much at all, slick the side of it with your thumb. If it makes a smooth but crumbly path, it contains moderate amounts of clay or possibly silt. If it makes a shiny, slick path, it's mostly clay.

If the ball in your fist crumbles apart into large agglomerations of soil with a crumb-like structure, you've got a loam, and a good soil for your garden.

If the ball crumbles easily apart into a pile of sandy dirt, it's too sandy.

All soils will respond to organic treatments, but improvement will take work and time, and you may want to place a first bed into the best soil you've got, if it's in a suitable spot.

Soil pH

PH measures the acidity or alkalinity of your soil. It's measured on a scale of 0 to 14, with 7 indicating neutral. Zero is an acid so strong it will eat through glass, and 14 is an alkaline so caustic you can turn fat into soap with it. Preferred soils are in the 6.0 to 7.0 range for most perennials. A few, however, like it much more acid, and some like it alkaline. In much of the Southwest, soils are alkaline from salts deposited when water evaporated from the surface. These soils can have pH values that range above 8.0.

Soil pH tests are available commercially from laboratories. The cheapest way to get your soil pH tested is to call your county agent, listed in the phone book under U.S. Government, Department of Agriculture, and ask for a pH test. The agent will have bags to hold soil samples, and the service costs only a few dollars. In addition, the test usually tells you whether your soil has adequate amounts of nitrogen, phosphorus, and potassium, since soil tests are usually done for farmers checking fertility levels.

Very acid or alkaline soils may tolerate only a limited number of perennials that prefer those special conditions. It's possible to sweeten acid soils with lime and reduce alkalinity with gypsum. In some cases, you may have a neutral soil and want to plant an acid-loving flower. In such cases an acidic mulch of pine needle duff would keep things comfortable for the plant.

Generally, low, boggy areas with moss growing on the ground and an abundance of wild strawberries indicate an acid soil. Neutral soil grows most everything that's suited to the climate. Some cacti and sages indicate an alkaline soil. Whatever the pH of the soil you're starting with, organic treatment will tend to bring it toward neutral.

Soil Profile

Before putting in a bed, it's important to know what's under the surface. Though you may dig the beds deeply, an area of hardpan (a hard layer below the surface that resists water and root penetration), underlying rock, or a spring that brings the water table too close to the surface, all present difficulties. Hardpan or compressed layers must be broken up to allow free water and root movement. If the hardpan is 3 feet down, we're talking about a big job involving a great deal of digging, if done by hand. You can tell if you have hardpan or subsurface rocks by digging a hole 2 feet deep and inspecting the sides of the hole for hard, compacted soil. Bedrock or large rocks too close to the surface means roots will not be able to reach deeply into the soil, and these areas will dry out more quickly. A high water table means that shallow-rooted plants may be okay, but deep-rooted plants will have wet feet during the winter—a prime cause of lost perennials where drainage is poor.

Prevailing Winds

The winds tend to come from different directions in summer and winter, so check for both when you call the local weather service or airport and ask for prevailing wind directions in your area.

In summer, and in flat or very windy areas, you'll need to find places where flower beds will be protected from gusty thunderstorms and windy, cool frontal systems. Tall, herbaceous perennials, such as delphiniums, are prone to wind damage. Staking is a lot of work, and a sheltered spot may eliminate the need for it. In winter, be aware of the direction from whence come the frigid blasts or the dry winds off the desert. These winter winds can cause lots of damage to your woody ornamentals and fruit-bearing plants. Although your herbaceous perennials may be frozen back to the ground, they often need a good mulching to protect their crowns from searing winter winds.

Your Local Ecosystem

Look carefully at your surroundings. If there are lots of woods, and the sun doesn't reach your clearing until 11:00 A.M., stay away from meadow plants that require lots of sun. Use your perennial beds to augment, rather than to replace, your local environment, and if you live in a swamp, go with swamp plants. It helps to know the wildflowers native to your region. Often you can find cultivated varieties (cultivars) of these same species or genera, which are more showy or colorful than the wildlings, but which continue to share their fondness for the area's climate. I grew up in the Pocono Mountains of Pennsylvania, and the August fields there were always covered with wild lilac bee balm (*Monarda fistulosa*). Were I to be gardening there now, I'd feel confident about planting any of the bee balms, especially the cultivars of *M. fistulosa,* such as 'Magnifica' and 'Prairie Night'.

Think, too, about the visual qualities of your region. The Japanese influence in gardening fits perfectly with the wind-swept pines and rocks of California's central coast. In the meadows of New England and the Middle Atlantic states, the English influence in garden design seems more appropriate. Look at how other gardeners in your area approach design and placement, and get a feel for the cultural factors that influenced their choices. These can be the greatest inspiration for a perennial gardener. We're not suggesting that a Japanese garden is wrong for the East, of course. It simply may be harder to achieve a believable example of such a garden there than in Monterey, because the climate and native plants are so different.

The View from the House

The best time to think about landscape design in the temperate regions is in the dead of winter, when the landscape is stripped to its bare bones and the major movements of the land and woody perennials are visible. Is your property well-designed at this time of year? Look out all the windows of your house and see what you like and don't like. Now decide which windows will get the most viewing time, and which ones especially lend themselves to viewing—such as a bay or picture window.

Let's say that the kitchen window looks out on an edge of the yard where only a few large trees grow now. You spend a lot of time glancing out that window, and you definitely want to have a garden somewhere in view. No matter what the season, imagine that it's January. What will you see? If the trees are not clumped, but are planted in a row, maybe one or more could come out to give some rhythm to the picture.

On the other hand, things could be a clogged-up mass of old, overgrown border plants, in which case you'd visualize what would happen if you took out some things and pruned back others to a responsible size.

Maybe there's a wall or fence with nothing but grass around it, or a wild area you'll clean out entirely. In that case, and also in places where you simply see an empty stretch of grass or field, you can plan evergreen and tree plantings from scratch. Before describing how to plan for these, let's

Trees can be placed to create rhythm and interest in the landscape. The drawing at left shows a static row of trees. At right, several trees have been removed to create rhythm.

A neglected landscape can be opened up by getting rid of excess growth. The drawing at left shows an overgrown border. At right, the border has been much improved after some plants have been pruned and others removed entirely.

consider some additional factors to be taken into account before planning begins.

Planning Paths

Anything you plant, from annual flowers to oak trees, must fit in with the natural pathways of your property. If the shortest way to the vacant lot and the corner market is between the rhododendron bushes, you can bet there'll be a pathway there, used chiefly by kids and dogs, which is only blocked at your plants' peril.

Where do the kids and dogs travel on your property? Where are the existing paths?

Which way do most people climb the slope to the upper garden? Does your front yard have a nice stone pathway that gently curves to a place nobody ever goes, resulting in a bare area on the lawn where everyone takes a shortcut?

Your paths will work best if you use the big, established pathways that people (and dogs) already use, and design your plantings around them.

The Borrowed Landscape

Forget the boundaries of your property and see what's actually there. Can you see portions of the neighbors' yards, or can you see five miles into the next county? What will be visible in January when the leaves are off? There may be a hilltop a few miles away that makes a shape you can reproduce in miniature on your property, creating a visual echo. Or there may be a tall tree or roofline in a neighbor's yard that dominates your view as well. Use it as an element in your design and you've "borrowed" landscaping from your neighbor. It's a Japanese idea that simply makes sure the designer is taking reality, and not a mental conception of property borders, into account when planning.

The Elements of Landscape Structure

A good landscape composition has major structural lines that are related, with a focal point that relates to all the lines. And it is usually asymmetrical—meaning that the focal point is placed off-center.

The illustration on the opposite page shows a group of compositions based on a row of trees with several removed.

Composition A groups evergreen shrubs around the base of the two clumps of trees. It's an improvement over nothing, but the clumps remain unrelated. Composition B is more tied together. Here again, evergreens are clumped around the trees, but in this composition they extend from the clump with three trees and arc behind, creating a pathway and tying the two clumps together. The pathway disappears around a corner, inviting someone to walk in. Perhaps a garden of shade-loving perennials could be placed back there. The bush marked X is

the focal point of this composition. You'll notice it forms the apex of a triangle, the base of which is formed by the clumps of bushes around the trees. This kind of classic triangle, with the apex at the focal point, is the basis for many of the world's great compositions on canvas.

For an example of bad composition, take a look at composition C. Several evergreens are clumped between the trees, interrupting the path, making the rhythm of the trees awkward, and emphasizing the vertical—which is emphasized enough by the tree trunks. One of the chief compositional functions of evergreens and shrubs is to provide some graceful horizontal lines to relieve the vertical lines of tree trunks.

Composition D shows the trees edged at the base with herbaceous perennials, such as hostas, and bordered in back by a line of evergreen shrubs. This design will be less pleasing when the perennial borders are down in winter. Notice that when the evergreens are used with the trees, as in composition B, the basic compositional structure will remain in winter, no matter where you put perennial beds or borders. Besides, perennials look best when they have dark backgrounds of evergreens, walls, fences, or other visual elements.

Perennial borders should not line every inch of your evergreen shrubs, like lace around a doily. Where the evergreens protrude into view, make the perennials retreat and disappear. Where the evergreens recede, thicken the perennial border. An example based on composition B is shown on page 18. Note that the perennial borders interrupt the continuous line of evergreens, and vice versa. I've placed an area for a freestanding bed or "island bed" of perennials in front of the left-hand clump of

Four compositions with shrubs

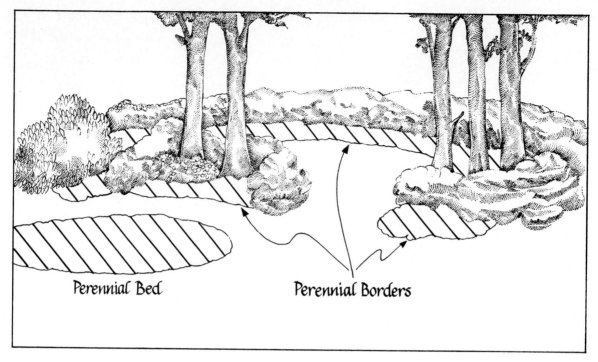

In this landscape, composed in a classic triangular design, perennial beds and borders interrupt the lines created by trees and shrubs and add interest to the scene.

trees. This will create an added pathway and hide the flowers behind it in summer, so that anyone who walks there will discover several intriguing paths, all of which lead to and past flower beds.

Foundation plantings of evergreens can echo, soften, and interrupt the straight lines of buildings, when placed in rhythmic clumps interspersed with areas of perennials. Building or landscape outlines should be broken by shrubs at places where the ratio follows a principle known as the Golden Section. The Golden Section is an ancient Greek discovery used to compose everything from temples to tombs, from classic art to perennial gardens. It is a proven, aesthetically

pleasing proportion, defined as the division of a line so that the shorter part is to the longer part as the longer part is to the whole.

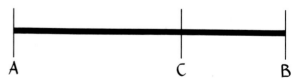

The Golden Section: This diagram illustrates the proportions determined by the Golden Section. Point C is 8/13ths of the distance from A to B. The length of line segment CB relates to segment AC in the same proportion that AC relates to AB.

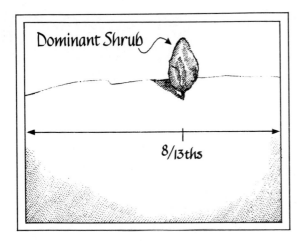

In this landscape view, as seen through a window of the house, the shrub is placed at the Golden Section of the bank.

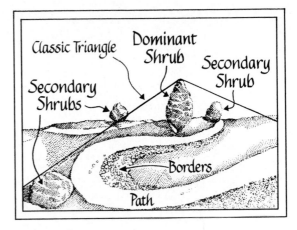

The classic triangle is used to frame other design elements in the landscape.

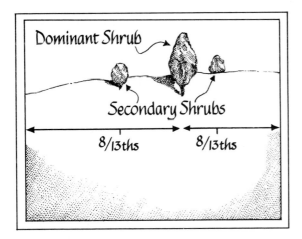

The placement of secondary design elements is also determined by Golden Sections.

If the whole line is given a value of 1.0, then the Golden Section falls at 0.618 on the line, or about eight-thirteenths of its length.

So if you have a view of a bare bank from your window and want to know where along the bank to place the dominant shrub, why not put it eight-thirteenths of the way? The new proportions created can also be reduced by Golden Sections, as is demonstrated in the illustrations.

Such calmly composed vistas are serene, and serenity is a good quality for any garden to have. Vitality is even better. Contrast creates vitality in a basic landscape structure. Line, shape, sun, shadow, and color can be contrasted in your layout to keep the composition active. If you have a rectangular wall, the curvilinear shapes of shrubs and trees can soften and integrate it into the landscape. If you're daring, go beyond vitality to make a few areas of tension. Tension is created by the anticipation of what lies ahead, such as with a path that suggests mystery around the bend, or by unexpected changes in the view or in the regular order of things. Tension is also created when lines and shapes *almost* touch, or when big shapes look like they are about to collide. An area of tension can relieve the serenity of a garden for a moment and cleanse the senses for the next view of quiet beauty.

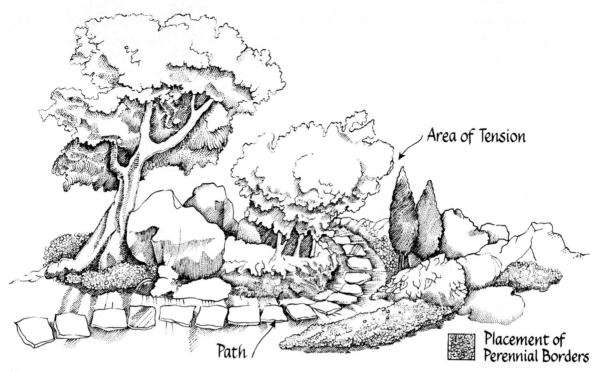

Tension is created in this landscape by two elements: the path that disappears around a bend, and the nearly touching forms of the small trees and columnar evergreens.

With these ideas, draw a quick sketch of how you'd like the views from the windows to look in January, with just the basic elements showing. Now step outside.

The View from Outside the House

Take your sketch of permanent design elements to various spots around the property. Come up the front walk the way you usually do. How will the plantings you've designed look from that angle?

Go to the places where you spend most of your outdoor time. There you'll plant borders or beds that will be in full bloom during the times you use those areas. Sit on the porch or patio and consider your sketch from that perspective.

Down by the pool, think about sites that will be blooming during the hot part of the summer. Hang out by the barbecue pit, or any favorite place you have for sitting. Try to visualize how your designs will look from those angles. You might find that shrubs that look good from the kitchen window will form an awkward arrangement when seen from the patio. Change your plans to create the same sense of vital, aesthetically pleasing composition from places outside the house that you achieved from inside the house. This most often means moving one shrub forward and another back to vary straight lines. Since it's all happening on paper and in your head, it's easy enough to do at this point, but harder to do once the shrubs are in the ground.

Walk the paths between islands of vegetation that will someday be there, and visualize how it will look. Stop along the path and study the lay of the land. Perhaps there'll be a space between two evergreens on a higher level, up a slope. That might be the perfect place to plant a specimen of some particularly gorgeous deciduous tree, such as a flowering crab apple or dogwood. The dark evergreens will flank the view to the tree, and you'll achieve the contrast and exciting view you're after.

When considering design elements, don't limit yourself to plants and trees. Think what it might look like to add some very large rocks, or to excavate an eroding bank into a terrace, or to add a dry wall of native stone. Is there a place for a freshwater pool for water plants, or for a combination toolshed and potting shed, or a freestanding solar greenhouse? Could you build some curvilinear decking right out into the perennial beds and evergreen islands? As long as you're just thinking, why not?

The Purpose of Your Perennial Gardens

If the reason you want a garden is for cutting fresh flowers to bring into the house, I'd suggest you create a garden especially for that purpose. Gardens for show can be cut, of course, but only very lightly without reducing the visual effect of the massed blossoms. I'm assuming that the primary purpose of any of the perennial gardens we're discussing is visual beauty in situ.

There are dozens of secondary reasons why you might want a perennial planting, however. Let me suggest a few to you:

- To grace an area where you plan to live outside during the summer.
- To get some privacy from neighbors or the street.
- To make terraces of flowers out of an overgrown bank.
- To beautify a wooded area or slope.
- To change a low, swampy spot into a water garden.
- To add interest to a small space bordered by a hedge or fences.
- To turn the nondescript path alongside the house into an inviting entrance to the rear yard.
- To enhance a spot for outdoor entertaining day or night.
- To produce flowers of extraordinary fragrance near the house or patio to perfume the air.
- To integrate a vegetable, herb, or fruit garden into the landscape.
- To create a place of beauty in which to relax or read.
- To show off prized specimens of favorite plants.
- To dramatize an entrance to the house or property.
- To camouflage a chunky building or garage.
- To use a space that's too rocky for any other kind of gardening.
- To take advantage of already-existing walls and terraces.
- To create a spectacular view from a balcony or window.
- To have enough plants to sell some from your home.
- To hide the garbage cans, trash-burning fireplace, compost area, or an otherwise unsightly view.

And, of course, there are as many more reasons as there are gardeners.

Making a Final Landscape Design

Now that you've sketched from your windows and looked at the potential sites from all angles outdoors, you're ready to make your final design selections. Remember to design your permanent plantings for *mature* plants. There are no "instant" landscapes. The plants go into the ground when they're little and take years to fill out and grow up. This means that at first, your landscaping will appear a little puny. Ground covers and fast-growing ornamental grasses between shrubs and trees can alleviate some of this look. Mown grass can fill in for a while until the plantings overtake it. Keeping the permanent plants mulched reduces weed competition and helps them grow more quickly. Areas of mulch can take up some of the extra space among evergreen plants, as can perennial flower borders that mature in two to three years. Be prepared to move some perennials to new locations, when the shrubs really start filling in and the trees start throwing dense shade—from five years on.

As with a good landscape painting, the scene you create in your yard will look best with a foreground, middle ground, and background. Your foreground may be perennial flowers or foliage plants that edge the lawn. The middle ground will be tall perennials and shrubs, and the background may be a hedge or fence, shade trees, or large shrubs. In general, areas with magnificent vistas should be kept open and clean looking, so as not to detract from the view, which will be the featured element in the picture. Perennial flowers often look best when they are contained in room-sized areas formed from background plants. Such rooms present their flowers as the featured attraction.

Most of your permanent plantings will be green for most of the time. When choosing landscaping plants for a massed effect, vary the shades of green and the textures of the leaves or needles to add interest to the scene. Lilacs, for instance, look good planted with junipers—in summer, their foliage contrasts so well, and in winter, the starkly dramatic, upward-twisting arms of the lilacs offset the rounded shapes of the juniper bushes. I remember once seeing a group of hollies and rhododendron growing from a bed of pachysandra that made an excellent anchor for a small backyard planted with many types of perennials. All these plants like an acid soil, growing well and looking good together. Similarly, dogwood, junipers, and hollies make an interesting group. Among the hollies, 'China Girl' is one of the hardiest cultivars. There's a nice double-flowered dogwood, *Cornus florida* 'Pluribracteata', and one with variegated leaves, *C. florida* 'Welchii'. The pink-flowered dogwoods can be grown with the lovely Japanese maple, *Acer palmatum* 'Crimson Queen', to combine their big, pink flowers with the deep reddish maple leaves.

The subject of landscaping is an enormous one, and this book can only suggest some basic elements around which you can plant the herbaceous perennials. These permanent plants bring your flowers to life and anchor your flower compositions to the bones of the earth. There are as many how-to-landscape books as there are how-to-paint books, and all are filled with great techniques people have invented for achieving good-looking results. When these techniques were first invented, however, they came from beyond the training—from the artist's inherent conviction that an effect was justified, even though it broke with tradition.

Don't be afraid to follow your instincts when you plan your landscape. In other words, don't do a paint-by-numbers job. Stand where you get a good view of the future garden and feel the earth. Feel the rhythm of the ground as it rises or falls, or its placidity when flat. Work with these feelings. Squint at the space and let your imagination grow shrubbery there. See it, and imagine how it will look. Emphasize the strong features of the land, such as jutting rocks or a steep rise, or create emphasis on an expanse of featureless ground.

Now hold your arms out in front of you with your hands about 15 inches apart. The angle your arms create, projected out to the garden, is the size of the area your eyes can fully grasp. Plan your designs so that they work within that angle, whether you're standing near or far.

A most important part of creating a basic landscape structure is choosing low-maintenance plants. Don't go for the imported or the bizarre. There are hundreds of hardy, time-tested, and beautiful trees and shrubs of all kinds in your area. You want them to be hardy, pest- and disease-free, able to grow well in your soil, suited to your climate, and able to grow quietly through the years without your having to do a lot of pruning and picking at them. Local nursery people can be endless sources of information for you.

Finally, remember that less can be more. One of the most beautiful gardens I've ever seen was a Japanese-style garden in San Francisco that consisted of some gnarled tree roots writhing up from the bare soil, some large round stones set into the soil, and a single broad-leaved plant spreading out behind. This was set in a corner of a yard fenced in with bamboo and shaded by large overarching fronds of bamboo from the other side. Simplicity is a part of any superb design.

For a comprehensive look at woody trees and shrubs, both deciduous and evergreen, ask your local library for copies of *Trees and Shrubs and Hedges,* two volumes in the American Horticultural Society's *Illustrated Encyclopedia of Gardening.* Hundreds of trees and shrubs are grouped in these books by function, such as fall foliage color, shape, winter interest, showy fruit, and so on.

The Size of Perennial Borders

Now that you know where you want to place the perennial borders, consider their dimensions. Borders line walkways, walls, or fences, or they join to permanent plantings. Straight borders give a formal look to plantings, while curvilinear borders that sweep around corners present a variety of differing views as one walks along and create hidden areas that add intrigue and privacy to the property.

Borders may also be peninsular—that is, they join at some part to other plantings, but stand mostly on their own. A sunny rock garden that joins a group of trees and shrubs at its shady corner is an example of a peninsular bed.

The simple masses of dark green shrub borders or neutral fences and walls usually set off a perennial planting better than open space just beyond the flowers. Color clashes happen when, from a distance, the varying color schemes of several borders are seen at once. Unless you're directly going for a coordinated series of borders, tuck your plants into the hollow, concave parts of the shrub or tree borders. Standing where you'll get the farthest full view of the border, again hold your arms out with your hands 15 inches apart. Keep the length of the border within the arc between your hands if you want a feeling of privacy about your perennial plantings. On either end of the border, shrubs or other features of the property can interrupt it. The next hollow promises to show more beautiful flowers and so entices people to walk and look.

But let's say you've got a large area where you want to put lots of perennials for showy spectaculars. If that's what you want, do it. Always rely on your instincts, and you'll eventually develop a style all your own. In garden design as in painting, slavishly following rules leads to reproductions of other people's ideas and rarely to inspiring work.

At Sir John Thouron's beautiful estate in southeastern Pennsylvania, for example, a huge sweep of lawn has been flanked by a 20-foot-wide perennial border that goes for hundreds of feet. Sir John didn't try to create any private little spaces there. He went for dazzle and got it. But then, he needed it. See page 99 for a look at this spectacular garden.

I like borders that curve, tapering into the shrubbery or into the corner of a house at each end, and thickening in the middle. If you're going to edge a length of lawn with perennials, the borders will be in a pleasing proportion when they take up about a third of the combined width of lawn and border.

Suppose there's a length of lawn 60 feet wide that you want to edge with perennials. A third of 60 is 20. If the border is to go on one side of the lawn, make it 20 feet wide. If it is to go on both sides, make each border 10 feet wide. The lawn area will then be reduced to 40 feet. If the border tapers into shrubbery, make its thickest part equal to about one-third of the lawn space that it borders.

Many properties have lots of lawn, however—big stretches of it that would require a border 50 feet thick or more if this one-third rule were used, such as at Sir John Thouron's. Where there's too much lawn to use as a yardstick for proportioning a border, use the height of the background shrubs or trees. And again, a proportion of one-third the height of the background is nice. In a case where the perennial border is backed up by mature shrubbery 15 to 20 feet tall, overarched by a tree canopy, use the height of the mature shrubs as a yardstick, and aim for one-third their height.

These are all general guidelines. In your specific cases, visualize the most pleasing proportions. Most borders will tend to be from 4 to 8 feet at their widest in small areas, and perhaps 10 to 12 feet in larger, more expansive places.

Remember that you must be able to weed, water, mulch, stake, pick off spent blooms, divide and move plants, and otherwise get around in your borders. Given a border 8 feet wide, many gardeners leave a 2-foot path in the back for access. Besides giving you working room, the path also separates the roots of perennials and back-border shrubbery. Thus, the planted area is really only 6 or so feet wide. From the front of the border, the gardener can reach the front 3 feet of the planting, and from the back path, can reach the back 3 feet.

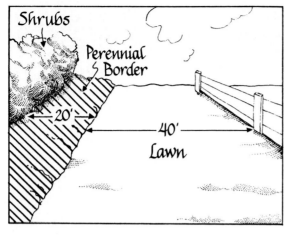

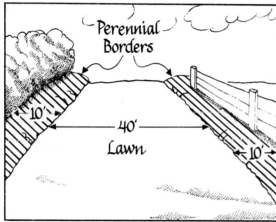

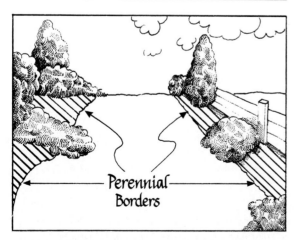

All the borders shown here are in correct proportion to the width of the lawn, but the bottom design works best because the borders curve and are interrupted by shrubs.

There are places where a very wide border of perennials might be used—to anchor a bank, for instance, or along a path to an outside sitting area. In such a case a path itself becomes integral to the border. Some of the nicest borders have lovely curving stone paths, or use rock outcroppings as places to step through the gardens.

The Size of Perennial Beds

Beds are islands of perennials surrounded by lawn or natural growth. They may include woody shrubs and trees as the bones of their design, so that they retain some shape and interest in winter, but these structural elements aren't necessary. In areas where winters are cold, summer islands of flowers can die back to the ground in winter, allowing a longer view of the evergreens or trees behind, or opening up a long, familiar vista that's only visible in winter. In warmer areas, many more evergreens are available to gardeners. Perennials die back during the dry months, but evergreens will "bloom" all year.

Square and rectangular beds give a formal look to a yard. Oval and free-form curving shapes give a casual, more natural look. Does the length of your proposed bed fit in with the other proportions of the gardens around it? If not, scale it up or down accordingly.

You'll achieve the most pleasing effect if the bed is twice as wide as its tallest plants are high. Most of the tallest perennials grow from 6 to 8 feet high, which means the beds need to be 12 to 16 feet wide.

Stand where the bed will be most commonly viewed. The length of the bed should be a little less than half the distance to the bed from the optimum viewing point. Let's say that you're sitting on a patio 50 feet from an island bed across an expanse of lawn. From 20 to 24 feet would be an optimum length for the bed. This gives you a rough oval dimension. Now consider curving the edges of the bed. Make all the curves go the same way. The illustration shows one example of how you might work with this shape.

Because a bed can be seen from all sides, the taller perennials should be planted toward the center so that the flowers mount up to a high point. And it's usually prettiest

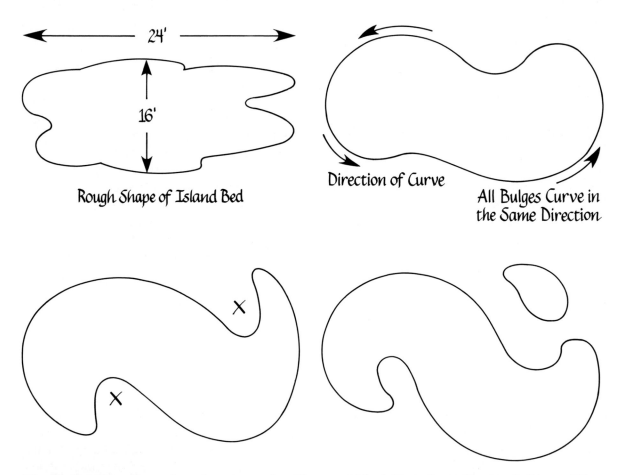

The illustrations above show how to work with an oval bed. First, figure the rough shape of the bed (top left). Next, add some motion to the design (top right). You can continue to add more motion to the design. Pockets for viewing the plants up close are formed at X (bottom left). Even more motion is created if the bed splits into two pieces that follow the same curve (bottom right).

Rotary Shape   Kidney Shape   Egg Shape

Three other pleasing shapes for island beds.

when the bed has one highest point, rather than a ridge of tall plants running down the center.

It's rarely a good idea to plunk the bed smack in the middle of the lawn, even if it looks good from the kitchen window that way. If the bed is moved to one side, it gives more dynamism to the space achieved. Any island bed is going to create two walkways—one around either side—and these will offer more interesting spaces to explore if they are of varying widths.

Beds can be mulched right up to the lawn, or they can be edged with stones, slate, or wooden railroad ties for a raised effect (although easy, flowing curves are hard to get with the straight railroad ties). If the bed is being designed for a hilly or sloping spot, you might consider raising one end of the bed on the downward side of the slope. The raised portion could be formed by a dry wall, bricks, or large rocks.

Large rocks or stepping stones are one good way to get into the center of the bed to work in it. They form a bare-bones composition that can be augmented with shrubs for winter, and they almost disappear when the summer plants are up and growing.

The other way to insure easy access is to keep the beds to only 8 feet across, so that you can reach the center from either side, with a little leaning. For proper proportions, the tallest plants should reach 4 to 5 feet at the most. If the bed is roughly twice as long as it is wide—that is, it's about 15 feet long—it can be fully appreciated and its composition grasped from an optimum distance of about 30 feet. Those rough proportions: 8 feet wide, 15 feet long, 5 feet high, pulled and curved into an interesting shape that capitalizes on rocks and other features of the property; this is a perfect size for most lawn and yard situations. Such beds are easy to care for and their relatively modest size allows the gardener to select a limited group of plants for an integrated, cohesive look that still contains several passages of related colors.

Tall perennials are best planted toward the center of a bed with the flowers mounting up to a high point (left). For the best display, have a single high point, rather than a ridge of tall plants running down the center of the bed (right).

Where is the best place for an island bed? It's rarely a good idea to plunk the bed down smack in the middle of the lawn, even if it looks good from the kitchen window that way, as shown in the illustration on the right. If the bed is moved to one side, as shown in the center illustration, it gives more dynamism to the spaces achieved. Any island bed is going to create two walkways—one around either side—and these will offer more interesting spaces to explore if they are of varying widths. Consider how the shape of the bed will blend in with features seen as you walk around both sides.

As shown in the top illustration, beds can be mulched right up to the lawn, or they can be edged with stones, slate, or wooden railroad ties for a raised effect (although easy curves are hard to get with ties). On the downward side of a slope (bottom), you might consider raising one end of the bed. The raised portion could be formed by a dry wall, bricks, or large rocks.

Walks and Paths

Allowing people access to the little places within a bed or border is a friendly touch. And if somebody takes the time to walk up into a garden, it's nice for them to have a place to sit and look at the beauty bursting all around them.

Big, broad walks encourage people to enter the garden; small walkways, such as stepping stones, don't. Depending on your purpose, choose the kind of walk that will invite everyone in or keep almost everyone out.

Walks are sometimes simply beaten paths through the garden, and they can be quite nice as long as there's enough foot traffic to prevent weeds from growing. They are not particularly encouraging to the visitor, however.

Mulched paths are more encouraging, as you obviously intend people to walk there. Two good-looking mulches for paths are shredded bark and wood chips. Forget white pebbles: They look chintzy and weeds tend to take them over. Also, after a short while, pebbles tend to sink down into the mud when people tread on them in wet weather.

Walks can be kept in mown grass, but grass pathways create the visual effect of splitting beds into two parts, since the grass lawn is the base material out of which the beds and borders emerge. To maintain a coherent design, avoid grass paths in your perennial beds.

Probably the best materials for walkways are flat stones, such as flagstones, cobbles, or slate. Stone paths can be made to undulate through the gardens, leading the viewer along from one small view to another. To prevent heaving in the winter, it's best to dig out the walkway to a depth of 6 to 8 inches, lay down a bed of finely crushed stone or fine gravel or sand, then set in the stones and sweep more sand or fine gravel between them. The sand or gravel lets water drain away quickly, so that during cold weather, ground water that freezes will have plenty of room to expand without rolling the stones aside.

Establishing fine mosses, mother of thyme (*Thymus serpyllum*), and other tiny creepers between the stones gives them the appearance of floating in a sea of green—and this is probably the prettiest effect of all.

Native stone—being the color of local rocks and outcroppings—is least conspicuous and usually most appealing. It gives garden paths the softest and most natural look.

Walkways can also be done in brick, which positively encourages—even demands—people to walk on them. Like stones, bricks must be set in 6 to 8 inches of sand or fine gravel—preferably sand—or they will heave out of place during the winter. Even in areas where the ground doesn't freeze, a layer of sand underneath the bricks helps water drain away quickly.

There are many beautiful patterns for brick walkways. The illustrations on the opposite page show a few examples.

Straight walks are formal looking, and curved walks are the more natural looking, especially if they curve out of sight around sweeping borders of flowers and shrubs.

The upper garden path at our house is made of slates, laid by Marilyn to form an easy S-curve toward an arbor over a featured garden rock. We chose slates because she found them offered inexpensively in our local newspaper. We also used bricks that were salvaged from a building that was being torn down. On our property there's no end of stones, and I used them to lay a dry stone wall along the bottom of our display garden. Your choice of path materials will probably be similarly made for you by what's readily available.

Mark the placement of straight paths with a taut string, as you would to mark garden rows. For a curved path, take the garden hose and lay it along the curve you

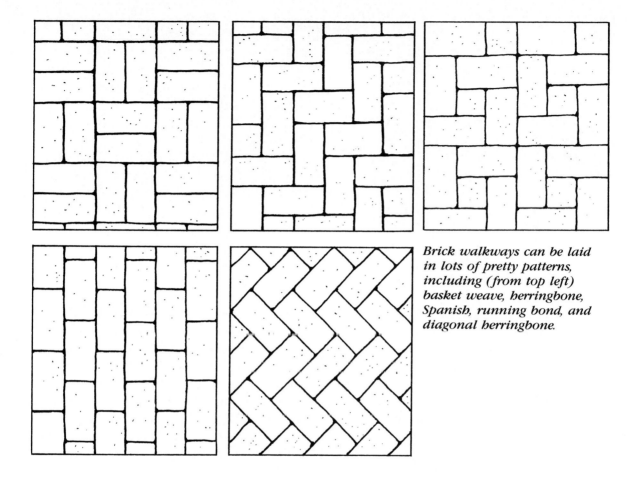

Brick walkways can be laid in lots of pretty patterns, including (from top left) basket weave, herringbone, Spanish, running bond, and diagonal herringbone.

want, then dig a small trench to mark the curve. This gives you one side of the path. To be accurate with the other side of the path, begin by laying the garden hose to follow the same curve as the trench. Check the work by holding a string across the path at right angles to the trench. It takes two people. One holds the string just above the trench; the other holds it across the path just above the garden hose. Both walk along outside of the path, always keeping the string at right angles to the curve. Adjust the garden hose so it's always under the point where

the string is being held. Make the second trench along the garden hose and you've outlined your path.

Dig out the pathway to a depth of 6 inches. Get the soil in the bottom as smooth, even, and level as you can, then tamp it down hard. Lay 3 inches of gravel over this and again, smooth and tamp. Then lay down 3 inches of sand, and smooth and level it. Set the hose on mist and thoroughly wet the sand. Now tamp it hard. All the tamping should have compacted the sand and gravel so that it's about an inch or two below the

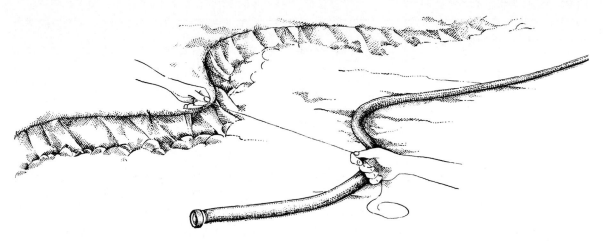

Lay out the curve of the path with a garden hose, then use string to lay out the other side of the path.

level of the surrounding soil. Bricks are from 1½ to 2 inches thick, so they'll make the path surface flush with the surrounding soil. And that's what you want.

You will need a retainer at the edge of the path to hold in the sand and to prevent erosion, and to help keep creeping weeds and grass roots from crossing into the bricked area. The easiest retainer is a line of bricks set vertically.

To lay the bricks, first set a course of bricks across one end of the path. This establishes the width. Now lay in several retaining bricks on both sides of the course you've laid. You may have to adjust the width of the path to accommodate the retaining bricks—either widening it a little, or filling in behind one of the lines of retainers. You *don't* want to have to cut bricks to make them fit.

Using the pattern you've chosen, place the bricks as close together as you can. As you put in each one, use a wooden mallet to tamp the brick level with the others. A spirit level should be your guide, both to check absolute level and to make sure the

bricks are flush with one another. If a brick sits too high, remove it and take out a little sand. If it's too low, sprinkle sand under it until it sits flush with the others when tamped. As you progress, set the vertical bricks on both sides of the path first, then lay the walkway in between them.

When you're done, dump sand on top of the bricks and sweep it around to fill the cracks between them. When the cracks are full, remove any piles of excess sand, then hose down the path gently, so as not to wash sand out of the cracks. Any loose sand on the bricks will be washed to the cracks and edges of the path. Bricks laid like this will not heave and buckle.

Steps

Gardens planted on slopes have several advantages. They drain well. They may present a favorable angle for people to see rising masses of plants and flowers. They may catch more or less sun, depending on how they slope, and you can build a garden around that. And there can be steps up through them. In the best cases, steps lead somewhere unseen—up around a corner, or down to a grotto of flowers, perhaps. Even on a small property, you can get some mystery into your steps by planting tall shrubs to hide the area where they lead. Not all steps can be mysterious, though. Sometimes they're out in the open and are used to get people from one level of the grounds to another. But in all cases, see if you can give your steps a gentle curve or sweep, to echo the curvilinear form of your gardens.

Large, flat stones set firmly into the ground to overlap one another are often used as steps in rock gardens. Railroad ties cut to size and drilled through with 1-inch holes to accept anchoring pipe also make good steps. If bricks are used behind ties or retaining rocks, they need to be set as described in the previous section on walks and paths.

Wide, shallow steps are inviting. Steep, narrow steps aren't. Steps wide enough to accommodate two people shoulder to shoulder are a minimum for a generous look and feel. A rise of 5 to 8 inches is shallow; from 8 to 10 inches is fairly steep; and over 10 inches is steep. Walk up the area where you want to put in steps. Do you need a step up with every step you take, or every other step, or every three steps? Try to place the steps to make walking natural and easy.

Preparing the Soil for Improvement

Look at the area where you want to put a perennial garden and make a note of what's growing there now. The possibilities include trees, big shrubs, a wild jungle of thorns and second-growth scrub, brambles, weeds, and grass. Let's look at these possibilities one by one.

Trees

If you want to keep the trees and put in a shade garden, dig a few test holes a foot deep in the area. Is the soil filled with tree roots? If so, it's going to be rough going for your perennials. They'll have to compete with established trees for moisture and nutrients. One answer is to chop out the roots in that area. This may harm the trees if they're main roots. Most likely it won't cause problems, though, since only a small portion of the roots of large trees will be right near the surface. You'll have to free the soil of roots to a depth of at least a foot.

Another tactic is to make raised beds of soil, retained by a low stone wall or bricks, around or among the trees. You should still remove surface roots before putting in the raised bed, or the tree's roots may grow to interfere with your perennials.

Let's say you want to remove some or all of the trees where you want the perennials. If they're small trees, you could remove them yourself with a chain saw, shovel, ax, and pick. If they're of any size and you're not an expert with the chain saw, seek help. Felling trees is extremely dangerous work. You can wait for the roots to rot away, but you'll be waiting a long time. Better get someone with a tractor or backhoe to pull the stumps for you, then backfill the hole and cover with topsoil.

Shrubs

I'm referring here to shrubby growth and young trees that spring up before the forest reappears. By hand, removing shrubs is a matter of cutting off the shrubs and young trees and digging out the roots. This is hard work, and if you're clearing a large area, consider hiring a backhoe operator to scrape off the top growth, then dig up the area to a depth of 2 to 3 feet. You'll then be able to go through it and pull out most of the loosened roots. The backhoe may also turn up some nice rocks for landscaping.

Wild Jungle of Thorns and Scrub

Cut off all top growth and dig the area a foot deep to get out as many roots as you can. A backhoe may also make sense here if it's a large area or matted with heavy roots.

Brambles

These are blackberries and raspberries that follow the weeds after bare soil is exposed. They usually propagate by underground runners, and sometimes by rooting from tips of canes that fall over and touch the ground. The soil has to be turned up a foot deep to get all the runners and roots out of the ground.

Weeds

If these are mainly broad-leaved weeds, cut everything down and turn over the soil to a depth of 1 foot. Pull out the obvious weed roots as you go. If there's a lot of grass among the weeds, try to get out as many of the grass roots as you can, as they are tenacious.

Grass

Thickly matted sod is pretty easy to work with, since most of the roots are in the top 6 inches of soil. Using a spade or edger, cut turves from the area in 4-square-foot blocks (2 feet on a side). Pry these loose by sliding the spade underneath them and take them to an area you use for composting—or decide now where you want to start a compost pile and take them there. Lay the turves on the ground upside down, so the roots are up, and start building a high stack of them. Make it as high as you can.

Then forget about the stack. In a year, it will have rotted into a pile of soft humus, with some grass alive and growing on the outside. Pull off this grass and use the decayed, crumbly turves as compost.

Grass can also be killed on the spot. By covering the area with sheets of clear polyethylene for several weeks in the June or July sun, the soil will be baked and steamed underneath to such high temperatures that all plants will die out. Doing this may also kill off nematodes, small soil-borne worms that attack plant roots. When all the grass is dead, spade up the area and turn the roots under, or remove them to the compost pile.

At this stage, you're trying to free the garden spot from roots and weeds and get the top layer of soil turned up into loose, fertile earth. When preparing an area for a garden, I generally remove any rocks or stones larger than a softball, except the very large ones, which I might leave as landscaping elements.

Improving the Soil

At a recent meeting of the national Perennial Plant Association, I asked dozens of growers and experts there this question: "What's the single most important thing people can do to insure success with perennials?"

To a man and woman, they all had the same answer, which I'll paraphrase this way:

"Tell them to prepare their soil well."

Creating beds and borders of perennials requires a lot of moving plants around. To do this easily and properly, the soil has to be rich, dark, and loose. Almost all perennials like adequately drained soil, especially in winter when standing water will kill plants. Loose, rich, deeply dug soil will help drain away that excess water. Loose soil also allows for easy, strong root growth of the plants. And when it comes time to divide them, they'll lift easily and entirely from loose soil. In hard, dense soils, the roots are cemented into the clods and break when dug, instead of lifting out easily. Loose soil allows a better flow of nutrients to the roots to make for strong plant growth, and humus in the soil keeps plant nutrients in storage until growing roots call for them. Humus also prevents droughty conditions by making the soil spongy and able to hold more water.

Loose soil also helps when weeding, for the weeds come out entirely and easily. If the gardener pulls a weed in hard, dense soil, the top of the weed is likely to come off in the hand, and the root remains to grow again.

There are two secrets to improving the soil so it becomes a perfect medium in which to grow perennials: double-digging, and the addition of actively decaying organic matter and other soil amendments.

Double-Digging

Double-digging means removing the top shovel-depth of soil and digging up and loosening the subsoil, then replacing the top layer. If it sounds like a lot of work, it is. But then, there is no substitute for soil that is loosened deeply and fertilized well.

Start at one end of the bed and dig out the top 10 to 12 inches of soil, putting it in a wheelbarrow or garden cart, or lacking that, onto a large sheet of polyethylene. With a spading fork, loosen the exposed layer of subsoil to 10 to 12 inches. If it's a clay subsoil, add some compost, rotted manure, or other organic matter to the bottom layer, along with some sand. Now move to the next section of topsoil and shovel that onto the first trench's exposed and improved subsoil, which exposes the subsoil in the second trench. Repeat the loosening and improving procedure and move to the third section, and so forth, right across the bed. At the last row, you'll end with exposed subsoil. Cover this with the topsoil you took from the first trench.

Adding Actively Decaying Organic Matter

At this stage, the subsoil will be improved, but the topsoil won't be. Lay on a thick layer of compost, or well-rotted cow, horse, or pig manure. Two inches is too little. Four inches is best. Turn this loosely into the topsoil. If your soil is clay and hard, add sand to the top layer to help loosen it. If it's sandy, the actively decaying organic matter will give it structure.

Don't dig in the soil when it's wet, or it'll turn to hard clumps when it dries. The soil should be slightly moist, however, as dry soil is hard to dig and turns to erosion-prone powder.

Once you've double-dug and fertilized the soil, don't step on the beds. Assuming you'll do this work in the fall before the spring when you will plant the bed, cover it with mulch and let the winter soften and rot it further to make the best bed possible come spring.

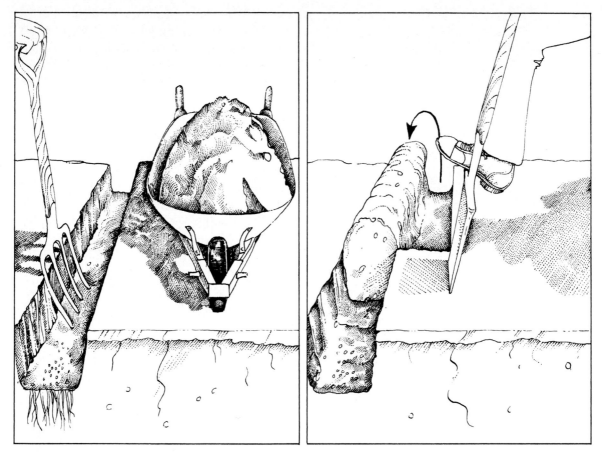

To double-dig a bed, dig a trench along one end and load the soil into a wheelbarrow. Loosen the subsoil with a spading fork. Soil from the second trench is shoveled into the first trench. Continue in this way until you reach the other end of the bed, and use the soil in the wheelbarrow to fill the last trench.

In very poor, hard-to-work soil, it may take two or three years of soil improvement before the ground is good enough for most perennials. No matter how bad your soil, it will respond to this treatment by becoming acceptably dark, fertile, friable, and crumbly at least by the third year. Most decent soils will be ready in the spring following the first fall improvement.

One reason why it's best to do soil-improvement work in the fall is that it gives the soil bacteria plenty of time to digest the added organic matter before plants go in. If an area is planted before this digestion process takes place, the soil can be short of nitrogen, which is being used to create bodies for the rapidly proliferating microorganisms as they digest the organic matter. Once digestion is slowed down or complete, the microorganisms start decaying themselves, spilling their cell contents into the soil solution. These transmogrified, dissolved nutrients then can feed plants.

If you must dig and fertilize in the spring with an eye to planting that year, wait a good six weeks after fertilizing before planting. This is doubly important if you're fertilizing with fresh cow, horse, or pig manure, since fresh manures contain nitrogen compounds which, undigested by soil microorganisms, can burn young plant roots. And make sure the soil is kept moist during those six weeks, for digestion slows down in dry soils and stops altogether if the soil is bone dry. That's why I find it best to double-dig and fertilize in the fall: The soil usually stays moist all winter.

Plant spring bulbs in the fall in newly dug and fertilized earth, since they'll lie dormant until spring and won't be bothered by any temporary shortage of nutrients as the new organic matter is digested.

I'm a bit of a fanatic about getting the soil prepared right. I triple-dig my raised beds—go down to the layer *beneath* the subsoil and loosen that. I add about 4 inches of compost a year to the top layer of my best-cared-for beds. The soil is so loose that I can literally plunge my arm straight down into the beds up to my elbow. In soil such as that, caring for perennials is easy.

By contrast, we also have perennial beds at our place that have never been properly dug and fertilized. Some of the plants that can take poor soil, such as *Achillea*, do all right there. Everything else just kind of limps along, eventually dying out. Even the weeds are stunted.

For most of us, perennials are expensive, at least until we start propagating new plants from our store-bought ones. There's no sense in planting up a bed with $100 worth of plants, only to have them crowded out by tree roots and weeds, or starved out by droughty, poor soil. There is no substitute for good soil. If you're starting with poor soil, grow some beans during the first two years. The bean plants will add nitrogen to the soil as their roots are colonized by nitrogen-fixing bacteria. Or grow sweet peas or annuals the first two years. But save the plantings of tender, often delicate perennials for the year when the soil is loose and deep. Then you can be sure of success, and you'll protect your investment in plants.

Mulches

A mulch is anything that covers the soil, but in this book we're talking specifically about organic mulches—that is, plant matter. After you've put your perennial bed or border in shape in the fall, you need to cover it with a mulch. Mulch protects the soil from erosion and compacting under driving winter rains, and it gives the soil microorganisms in the top couple of inches of soil something to feed on when the weather gets above freezing.

What can you use for mulch? With perennials, something dark and chunky, such as wood chips, bark, shredded bark, disintegrating leaves, or cocoa bean hulls, will later set off the green plants. Grass clippings are also nice-looking when they turn light brown. Hay and especially straw are too coarse-looking for my taste.

In spring mulch prevents some weed growth and also keeps the soil cooler longer—which is no particular advantage or disadvantage until you get the area planted.

Weed seeds persist in the soil for decades. There are endless numbers of them in soils that were recently weedy. They tend to be a little less troublesome in areas that were under sod. Weeds come into the garden constantly through horse and cow manure, unless it's composted to a temperature high enough to kill weed seeds.

Be prepared to cope with weeds. One of the best ways in newly turned-up soil is to cover the double-dug and fertilized bed with several thicknesses of newspaper (black ink only—colored inks contain poisonous heavy metals that should not be incorporated into the soil). Avoid newspapers over bulbs, however, as the paper can smother them. When the bed is covered with papers, apply a covering of mulch. No one will then see the newspaper. It will form a good weed barrier the coming year, and in the spring you can simply poke holes through it to plant perennials. Eventually it will decay. Most of the newspaper will be gone by the second spring.

The technique used to kill grass—covering the ground with polyethylene so the summer sun can shine on it—also works to kill weed seeds in the top inch or two of soil. And weed seeds deeper than that don't usually germinate anyway. They'll wait 3 to 4 inches under the soil until someone turns up the soil and puts them in the top 2 inches. Then they'll germinate. So, by sterilizing the top 2 inches of soil under polyethylene, and not turning the soil subsequently, you can kill off a lot of weed seeds.

Starting Small

Unless you have a staff of gardeners, put in just one bed or border the first year.

Keep it small—something you can fill with plants without busting your budget. Make it a practice garden and don't expect the world from it. I know perennial gardeners who have been trying for years to create a border that always has a spectacular association of flowers and foliage going on in it at all times, and they're still trying. Plan for a spectacular show at just one certain time—late May, or early July, for instance—and don't expect the garden to look like that during the rest of the season. It may have beautiful associations going at other times, but not a bed-encompassing spectacular.

Sources of Perennials

We're at the point where we're about to consider putting together a plan for a perennial bed. The foundation structure of evergreens, rocks, grasses, and other permanent design elements has been considered. The beds have been laid out, and the borders are in place. The paths are in, and the walls have been built. The soil has been double-dug and prepared. The only thing lacking is plants. Here are suggestions for ways of getting them.

Catalogs

We've gotten many of our perennials from mail-order firms. The chart in chapter 7 lists only plants available from the list of suppliers in the appendix. One of our guiding principles in putting the book together has been to make sure that all our perennials are available to gardeners in the United States. Too often plants are written about that are rare or difficult to find. Such plants have little practical value for the gardener, who must work with what's available. Our mail-order list is not a complete list, but it does include most large suppliers of perennials to the mail-order market. Write for their catalogs at the addresses given, and you'll be able to locate any of the plants described in the chart.

Local Nurseries

We find that it's endless fun to visit local nurseries. Most specialize in selected kinds of plants, or in unusual plants. Don't be afraid to try a cultivar that is not listed in this book, for there are many thousands of perennial cultivars on the market and more coming every year.

Friends

We've gotten some of our choicest plants from friends. Don't be shy about asking for seedlings, cuttings, or divisions. It gives the grower an excuse to divide the perennials he or she has been meaning to divide. Perennial flowers are like the loaves and fishes: The more you divide them among your friends, the more there are to divide. Around here, in the Pennsylvania Dutch country, a social convention holds that one should never say thanks for a plant given as a gift or it won't grow. It's been hard at times to resist the temptation when a friend has given us a particularly nice plant, but the times I've blurted out my thanks were the times that people chided me. I've learned to keep quiet. It's an interesting discipline.

Plant Rescue

We've "rescued" plants from abandoned buildings and from places scheduled to be torn down or bulldozed to make way for apartment complexes. One of our peonies came from an abandoned farm, as did some of our old-fashioned irises and species tulips. Marilyn has "rescued" hundreds of spring bulbs from old properties where the workmen were already busy with their 'dozers.

Perfect Strangers

Since perennial flower growers usually love to talk about their plantings, we've sometimes stopped in on perfect strangers to ask the name of a plant, or even to ask for cuttings or a root of the plant itself. We've found most people happy to share.

The Wild

We've brought several plants, such as wild ginger (Canadian snakeroot or *Asarum*), bee balm (or *Monarda*), and various ferns, into the garden from the wild. *Cimicifuga racemosa* also grows wild around here, although we've never brought any in. My personal rules about taking flowers from the wild are these:

1. Never take a rare or endangered species, unless you're rescuing it from land developers.
2. Never take all or most of a group of wildlings. If there are ten plants, I might take one or two. Collect carefully, so that the main growth of plants is not disturbed. And ask the plant first—it may say no.
3. Know something about the plant's horticultural needs. Pink lady's slipper, in addition to being a rare plant, has very special requirements for transplanting success. If you don't know what the plant's needs are, it's very possible you'll kill it. And that's equivalent to mindlessly tearing up wildflowers.

4. When taking the seeds of wild plants, disperse a few in the area. We've managed to establish a small patch of ginseng by planting its yearly crop of seeds around in our woods. When taking seeds of wildflowers, do the plant a favor by poking some seeds into the soil nearby.

Now you've got your catalogs and sources. Some perennials will be easiest grown from seed. With others, you may need to buy rooted plants. These differences will be described in the chart of perennial varieties in chapter 7, under the heading of Propagation.

The next question you will tackle is how to design a bed or border. The answer starts with an appreciation for and understanding of color.

CHAPTER 2

Understanding Color Harmonies

In this chapter, we'll discuss the nature of color and how it harmonizes. The information is intended to guide flower growers in their plant selections.

The Nature of Color

A while back, scientists decided there were four basic forces in the universe: electromagnetism; the weak force manifested when electrons are ejected from atoms; the strong force that holds the neutrons and protons in the atomic nucleus together; and gravity. Since then, they've been working to unify these forces in one theory that would explain them all in terms of one another. This they have done with electromagnetism and the weak and strong forces. They still haven't figured out how gravity relates to the others, although Einstein laid some good clues when he described gravity as the local warping of space due to the proximity of massive bodies.

Electromagnetism is thus a basic force of the universe from which all substance is produced and all qualities devolve. Its force is arrayed along a spectrum from very short wavelengths (cosmic rays) to very long wavelengths (radio waves). Included along the spectrum are such diverse phenomena as radar, heat, visible light, X-rays and gamma rays. Visible light, then, is just a small portion of the whole electromagnetic spectrum, related to and a part of everything else in the universe.

A prism breaks visible light into bands of component wavelengths. At one end we see red emerging from the infrared bands we call heat. It passes on to orange and into the glowing yellows, which shade into green, and then blue-greens. These shade into blue, which changes into violet, which is lost as the spectrum enters the ultraviolet range.

You'll notice that in nature the colors in the center of the visible spectrum—yellow-green to blue-green—are the most commonly seen. Some reds are mixed in to form browns, but pure reds and blues are usually found as accents rather than dominant colors (except, of course, for the big blue sky).

What we see as color is the portion of the spectrum of visible light that a substance reflects. The other colors are absorbed. Thus a bright red paint absorbs all the yellows, blues, and greens, and reflects only red. Similarly, a blue shirt absorbs all the reds, yellows, and greens and reflects only the blue. Earthy, natural colors, such as ochres and greens and the colors of bark and rocks, tend to absorb a little of everything and reflect a little of everything. In nature, intense pure wavelengths of any color are normally seen only in the sky, in the plumage of birds, and the coloration of animals, or in flowers.

41

Auric Colors and Their Associated States of Being

	RED	RED-VIOLET	PURPLE	BLUE-VIOLET	BLUE	BLUE-GREEN
Lighter, Purer Colors ↑	Affection		Transmutation	Spirituality	Love	
						Benevolence
		Friendship			Religiosity	
						Compassion
	Sensuality		Love of Ceremony			
					Devotion to Ideals	
Darker, Greyer Colors ↓	Physicality		Pomposity			Jealousy
	Desire	Avarice			Hatred	Deceit
			Sloth			
	Anger					

Thus each color seen in nature is actually a little portion of reality, with its special messages and concerns. A blue flower says something very different than a red flower. The color's message is wordless, general, poetic, but never literal. It speaks to the heart, where feelings reign, rather than to the mind with its penchant for substantive content.

The Meaning of Color

People through the ages have tied colors to the other senses, or to states of being. Sensitive people who see the colored auras surrounding living beings have generally agreed on the meanings of the colors they see. The chart above shows a generalized arrangement of colors with their associated states of being. Notice that the blacker the color, the more the state of being tends toward the negative. The lighter the tint, the more positive.

Thus, if a sensitive viewer saw a lot of dark, smoky red in a person's aura, he or she would usually assume that the person was angry. The orange of wisdom is often similarly interpreted as a mixture of pure red's affection with pure yellow's intellectual penetration.

Pale, delicate colors are often associated with smells, probably because they recall fragrant flowers. This effect is acknowledged by our language in the names of the following scents, each of which strongly brings a color to mind: rose, lilac, pine, lily-

	GREEN	YELLOW-GREEN	YELLOW	YELLOW-ORANGE	ORANGE
↑ Lighter, Purer Colors			Insight		Wisdom
			Intellectuality		Justice
	Charity				
		Ingenuity			
	Love of Nature				
				Ambition	
Darker, Greyer Colors ↓			Cunning	Pride	
	Malevolence		Selfishness		

of-the-valley, violet, coffee, balsam, cedar, wintergreen, chocolate, carnation, orange, and vanilla. Disagreeable odors don't carry such color associations. Consider kerosene, fish, turpentine, vinegar, and body odor. Baudelaire wrote that "perfumes, colors and sounds are interchangeable. There are perfumes fresh as the flesh of babies, sweet as oboes, and green as the prairies."

Many attempts have been made to tie the colors to notes on the musical scale. Both visible light and sound propagate in waves of varying lengths, and these can be compared. In the 1930s, A. B. Klein put together a combined scale of colors and notes so that the ratios of the colors' wavelengths matched ratios of the sounds' wavelengths.

Klein's Color-Music Scale

NOTE	COLOR	NOTE	COLOR
C	Dark Red	F#	Green
C#	Red	G	Blue-Green
D	Red-Orange	G#	Blue
D#	Orange	A	Blue-Violet
E	Yellow	A#	Violet
F	Yellow-Green	B	Dark Violet

If, for instance, we think of the first four notes of Beethoven's Fifth Symphony (da-da-da-DUM), they can be rendered as E-E-E-C on the chromatic scale. In Klein's system, the corresponding colors are Yellow-Yellow-Yellow-Dark Red. Try to visualize those colors as you hum the four notes. Three bursts of yellow followed by dark red. It works. And it's harmonious in color as well as to the ear. Dark red is a perfect color to punctuate yellow.

If you're musically literate, it might be great fun to transliterate a favorite classical melody—the Wedding March from Felix Mendelssohn's "Midsummer Night's Dream," for instance—into a series of color harmonies using this scale. If you're not musically literate, Sir Isaac Newton comes to your rescue, for he invented a color-music scale using do-re-mi. You'll see it in the table, Isaac Newton's Color Scale.

Because middle C is red, high C in this system might therefore be a pink, low C a dark red. A C-sharp or D-flat might be intermediate between red and orange, giving a red-orange. From this chart it should be possible to puzzle out simple melodies into color schemes that you can reproduce with flowers to follow secret harmonies. I can picture the "Onward Christian Soldiers" garden, marching by in shades of blood red,

Three More Color-Music Systems

Color-Music System of A. Wallace Rimington (American, about 1900)

NOTE	COLOR	NOTE	COLOR
C	Deep Red	F#	Green
C#	Crimson	G	Bluish Green
D	Orange-Crimson	G#	Blue-Green
D#	Orange	A	Indigo
E	Yellow	A#	Deep Blue
F	Yellow-Green	B	Violet

Taylor System of Color-Music Harmonies (American)

NOTE	COLOR	NOTE	COLOR
C	Red	F#	Green
C#	Red-Orange	G	Blue-Green
D	Orange	G#	Blue
D#	Yellow-Orange	A	Blue-Violet
E	Yellow	A#	Violet
F	Yellow-Green	B	Violet-Red

Color-Music System of Scriabin (Russian, 19th century)

NOTE	COLOR	NOTE	COLOR
C	Red	F#	Bright Blue
G	Rosy Orange	Db	Violet
D	Yellow	Ab	Purple
A	Green	Eb	Metallic
E	Baby Blue	Bb	Metallic
B	Moonshine	F	Dark Red

Isaac Newton's Color Scale

COLOR	CHROMATIC	NOTES
Red	C	Do
Orange	D	Re
Yellow	E	Mi
Green	F	Fa
Blue	G	Sol
Indigo	A	La
Violet	B	Ti

Color Theory

Scientists have discovered much about color and how it works that can be of great importance to the flower gardener. We're working for an aesthetic display that people will stop and ponder for its elegance and subtlety. The computative and logical side of our brains can make this task complicated. The intuitive, emotional, and artistic hemisphere can function well in this task if we let it. However, the intuitive side of our brain functions best when it is given a matrix of knowledge and information by the analytical side, and so it's important to understand some color theory in order to use that knowledge when creating an artistic garden.

Color nomenclature has yet to be codified into a simple set of definitions that everyone agrees upon. The Glossary of Color Terms simplifies the many terms to the few that a gardener needs to know.

Two Different Color Systems

Babylonian Planets and Their Associated Colors

PLANET	COLOR
Saturn	Black
Jupiter	Orange
Mars	Red
Sun	Yellow
Venus	Green
Mercury	Blue
Moon	White

Greek-Druidic Colors for Spiritual Qualities

QUALITY	COLOR
Wisdom	Green
Truth	Blue
Purity	White

---

hitting the high blues for accent. Or the "I Only Have Eyes for You" garden, gently flowing from blues to greens to violets.

It's interesting to see what colors master musicians have pegged to musical notes, and it provides ideas for harmonies rich enough to last a lifetime. The table titled Three More Color-Music Systems shows three other systems.

Color-music systems are only a small part of the reservoir of inspiration available to the home flower gardener. There are also systems that tie colors to spiritual qualities and to the planets. The table, Two Different Color Systems, shows two more color systems.

Glossary of Color Terms

Hue	The colors themselves: red, orange, yellow, green, blue, etc.
Tint	A color given by mixing white with a hue.
Shade	A color given by mixing black with a hue.
Tone	A color given by mixing varying percentages of white and black (grey) with a hue.
Value	The inherent brightness of a color. Pure yellow is inherently brighter than pure blue, for instance.

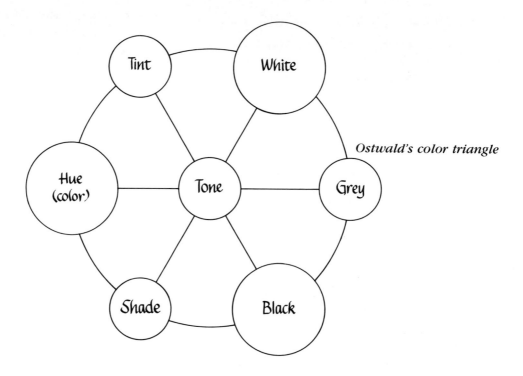

Ostwald's color triangle

Ostwald's Color Triangle

One of the simplest ways I've run across to understand what these terms are driving at is Wilhelm Ostwald's color triangle. It shows all the color associations seen by the eye. Tints are formed when pure hues are mixed with white; shades are formed from pure hues mixed with black. Tones are formed when shades are mixed with white or tints are mixed with black, or when pure hues are mixed with grey (the mixture of white and black). Pure hues are found among the garden's flowers, but rarely. We almost always work with flowers that are tones, tints, or shades.

Any pure color is a hue. Pure yellow-green is a hue; cobalt blue is a hue; crimson is a hue. Without mixing in any white or black, we can create an endless assortment of colors by mixing them in endlessly vary-ing amounts. This is best illustrated by a familiar color wheel in which the colors grade into one another in a 360-degree cir-cle, ending where they started. This is only true of pigments or colored light, however. It's not true of the spectrum that becomes visible by way of a prism or a rainbow. There, red is on one side of the spectrum and violet on the other, and they don't come full circle to meet one another. If one keeps short-ening the wavelength past blue, one passes out of the visible range into ultraviolet and eventually on toward X-rays and cosmic rays. If one goes the other direction beyond red, one leaves the visible spectrum and plunges down toward long-wave heat rays and radio waves.

There are three systems of primary colors: primary colors of pigment, primary colors of light, and primary colors of vision. Let's look at them one by one.

The Primary Colors of Pigment

When paint, ink, or other pigments are mixed together, they function according to the system shown in the illustration on page 48.

The Primary Colors of Light

Beams of colored light projected on a screen in combinations produce the system shown in the illustration on page 48.

The Primary Colors of Vision

This is the way our brains—through our eyes—mix pure colors that are close together. If, for instance, you had a garden of many small red and blue flowers planted in close proximity, and you viewed it at such a distance that the individual colors were indistinguishable, you'd see a violet appearance overall. The illustration on page 48 shows the mixing of colors to our eyes.

In the nineteenth century, the French Impressionists and especially the pointillist painters understood the primary colors of vision very well. Paintings by the pointillist Georges Seurat, seen from a distance, have areas of recognizable tones such as blue-violet or orange. When viewed close up, however, these areas are seen to be made up of thousands of individual globs or points of pure pigments. The pigments were not mixed on the palette, but were put on the canvas to be mixed by the eye of the beholder. Many of the Impressionists also used this idea, but not to the extreme degree of the pointillists.

The Impressionists thoroughly explored associative colors. They showed that the inherent colors of things in the real world—the colors they would be when seen alone under standard illumination, for instance—are changed by the effects of light and atmosphere. And they painted these effects of light and atmosphere the way no representational painters before them had ever done.

There are two kinds of light receptors in the human eye—rods and cones. Cones are the organs of daylight vision, able to distinguish bright colors. As light grows dim, cone vision fades out while rod vision is enhanced. A color of low intensity may appear to increase in brightness as the sunlight fades. Here's an example of this phenomenon: We have *Platycodon grandiflorus* (balloon flower) in our garden. In bright daylight, its color is a subdued violet. But in the evening, as the light dims, the color seems to get brighter. And in the deep dusk, the flower fairly glows with an ultramarine haze.

Yellow-green is the point of highest visibility for the cones, while blue-green is the point of highest visibility for the dark-adapted rods. You'll notice that the bluish, greyish greens of lamb's-ears or artemisia also glow in the dusk.

In full sunlight, yellow is inherently lighter than orange. Orange is inherently lighter than red. On the other hand, violet is inherently darker than green. Discords, rather than harmonies, are created when this natural order is upset; for instance, when orange is placed next to pink (a tint of red lighter than orange). The colors clash. The same thing happens when a light tint of violet is juxtaposed with a dark green; however, because these colors are inherently darker, the discord is not as jarring.

Colors also have intrinsic warmth or coolness. We know that yellow, orange, and red are warm colors, and blues, greens, and purples are cool. Yellow is warmer than

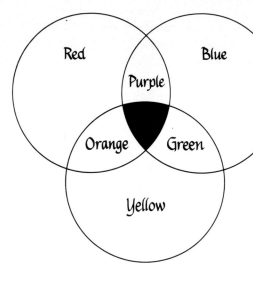

The primary colors of pigment: When paint, ink, or other pigments are mixed together, they function according to the system shown in this diagram. When all the colors combine (in center), they create black.

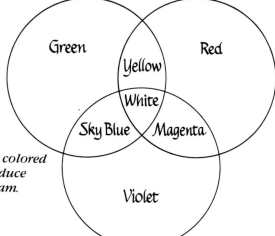

The primary colors of light: Beams of colored light, when projected on a screen, produce combinations, as shown in this diagram.

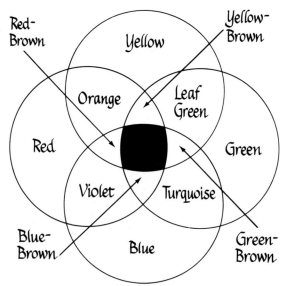

The primary colors of vision: This diagram shows the way our brains—through our eyes—mix pure colors that are added together. If, for instance, you had a garden of many small red and blue flowers in close proximity and you viewed it at such a distance that the individual colors were indistinguishable, you'd see a violet color overall.

orange. Orange is warmer than red. Green is warmer than purple. Purple is warmer than blue. A green surrounded by yellow will be the cooler color, but when surrounded by blue will be the warmer color.

There's a tendency for warm colors to appear to advance toward us, and for cool colors to recede. That's why warning signs and stoplights are yellow and red, never blue or green. The Impressionist painters knew this, for they saw these effects in nature where the colors of far-away hills and towns become cooler, greyer, and more bluish, while objects near at hand appear more intense and usually warmer in color. Thus, a clump of yellow daylilies within a planting of blue flowers will snap out in bold relief, while a clump of blue flowers in a bed of yellow ones will appear as a deep area, almost a hole of cooler color.

It's an interesting fact that optical discords and harmonies are agreed upon by almost every culture in the world, independently of one another. There's something in the human eye, evidently, that responds to a clashing pink and orange with distaste, yet accepts with pleasure a warm golden yellow as a harmonic of orange.

Related colors form harmonies. Yellows go with yellow-greens and greens on the one hand, if the color scheme is from yellow to blue. Or they go with oranges and reds if the scheme goes the other way around the color wheel. Violets and purples are made of red and blue and therefore form harmonies with them. Complementary colors are the colors across the color wheel from the given color: Yellow complements purple; orange complements blue. While these complementaries can provide an optical shock, they also provide interest and excitement in a color scheme, when used with restraint.

You can see why musical imagery is so germane to the subject of color harmonies. Four voices, singing notes in the same key, will blend into a satisfying chord. If one voice is not in the same key, it will jar discordantly. The same kind of clinker can be hit in the garden if, for instance, warm yellows and oranges are used with red-violets.

It's possible to intensify a tone, tint, or shade by surrounding it with neutral colors like beige, cream, buff, or white, or by placing it next to its complementary color. When complementary colors are juxtaposed, both colors are intensified.

Another optical effect that can appear in a flower garden was described by Michel-Eugene Chevreul, a nineteenth century physicist. He called it the Law of Successive Contrast. The law is illustrated by staring for a while at an area of any intense color. After a bit, a halo of the complementary hue will appear around the color. I think the legendary "green ray" seen just at sunset is a complementary glow from the orange sunset. This complementary glow also affects neutral colors that may surround the intense hue. A grey, therefore, will appear greenish when juxtaposed with red. The same grey will appear reddish when placed around a strong green. The same grey will be yellowish when placed around violet, and so forth.

Other common color associations are made with the seasons. Pastels signify spring; strong, pure colors connote summer; rich, deep, warm colors speak of autumn; and muted, washed-out tones are associated with winter. With the range of colors available to the home flower gardener, associations of these colors can augment these seasonal associations—such as pastels in spring—or make an interesting effect by recalling them at other times of the year—such as a bed of pastel asters and chrysanthemums in the fall.

What exactly causes flowers' colors? Biochemical compounds in the plants are responsible. Greens are produced by chlorophyll and chloroplastids. Yellow-orange is created by carotenes. Xanthophylls produce yellow or orange, and anthocyanins give us red, blue, purple, and violet.

Color Harmonies in Art

Artists through the centuries have been centrally concerned with color harmonies. Those who saw the collection of objects from Tutankhamen's tomb, which toured the United States in the late 1970s, couldn't help but be struck by the harmonious colors of many of the ancient Egyptian pieces. I particularly remember one tall, milky white alabaster vase with a collar of what looked like rose quartz inlaid around its neck—a subtle and graceful work of art, yet utilitarian, too.

Painters have led experimentation with colors in more recent times. Many early Italian masterpieces were done in just one earthy color, such as umber. Then color washes were laid over it, like a decorative afterthought. After the Renaissance, color was used more for its own sake, as an integral part of the modeled object. In the eighteenth century, Sir Joshua Reynolds, an English portraitist, claimed that an ideal color balance in a painting is two-thirds warm tones and one-third cool tones. It's said that Thomas Gainsborough, the great English landscape painter, refuted this by reversing the proportions in his *Blue Boy*.

In the nineteenth century, painters became concerned with light and its effects on color, as we've mentioned before. Paint-

ers such as Monet, van Gogh, and Gauguin were interested in using color associations to affect the emotions of the viewer—it was, after all, the age of Romanticism. This trend continued into the twentieth century, spawning German expressionism, where colors reflected the artist's feelings about the subject. Many of these canvasses have a poisonous look to them.

Through all these changes in art, the concern with color relationships has been constant. Some painters, especially in the modern era, purposefully make discordant color statements, but the task for many painters remains to seek beauty through carefully modulated juxtapositions of color.

As gardeners concerned with achieving beauty through juxtapositions of colored and textured flowers and foliage, we have a lot to learn from the masters of color harmonies. We'll use the horticultural medium to create beauty—the same kind of beauty that lives through the medium of paint. Great paintings reveal carefully controlled color harmonies that educate our eyes and allow us to see combinations that stir our sense of beauty. We can use these same color harmonies to create beautiful gardens.

Looking carefully at paintings lets us see how master colorists handled schemes of related colors. Choosing flowers for our gardens according to a color scheme is our purpose, after all. It may help to take some notes on the color schemes you see in museums. Use the notes when you look through catalogs or tour perennial gardens to find colors that match those in a favored painting. Keep foliage in mind, too. A drift of light yellow daylilies may wash out and almost disappear if the background plants are also bright and reflective. But against the deep, dark green of foliage like that of monkshood, for instance, the daylilies will glow with light and be extra visible because of the contrast. Notice how master painters skillfully use dark, contrasting areas to highlight figures, focal points, and featured objects in their compositions.

Television provides another example of the effectiveness of contrast. The first color tv tubes had phosphorescent dots placed on a light background. When engineers later changed the background to black,

the color appeared much sharper. The same sharpening effect will happen visually in the garden if light flowers appear in front of dark backgrounds.

One of the master colorists of the modern era was painter Henri Matisse. He and others in his artistic movement (the Fauves) at the turn of the century were known for their expressive use of color in interesting combinations. His *Odalisque* achieves balance in composition and color harmony,

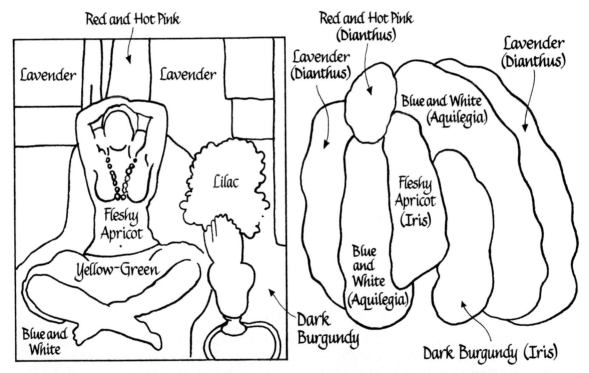

Borrowing a color scheme from Matisse: The garden design shown on the right borrows its color scheme—but not its composition—from a painting by Matisse (Odalisque, 1917). The color scheme in the painting, indicated in the sketch at left, is lavender, blue and white, fleshy apricot, red and hot pink, and dark burgundy. Other colors are used as accents. The garden, designed to bloom in May in full sun, echoes the same colors. Lavender is provided by Dianthus allwoodii cultivars. Tall bearded iris (rhizomatous Iris hybrids) provide exact shades of fleshy apricot and dark burgundy. Blue and white are given by masses of Aquilegia caerulea, the Rocky Mountain columbine. The small patch of red and hot pink is supplied by Dianthus 'Spring Beauty'.

but there's nothing timid about it. The colors are strong and vibrant, even though they may be muted tones, because of the overall color scheme. *Odalisque* is built on lavender, blue, pink and red, and dark burgundy. The illustrations on page 51 show how I used this exciting color scheme as the inspiration for a full-sun garden in May.

Ruthlessness is the right attitude about these color associations. If what appears to work on paper doesn't work in the garden, dig up the offending plants and move them elsewhere. Don't live with an association that doesn't thrill you just because it's there. Marilyn planted a drift of daylilies along one of our paths years ago. Since then, we've moved many plants around until now our summer color scheme in the area behind the daylilies tends toward the lavenders, purples, blues, whites, and red-violets. Yet our daylilies remained until we noticed how ugly their orangey flowers were with our lavender-blue-violet associations. The daylilies were fine until one year they weren't. At that point, out they went. Similarly, you might think that the light blue of *Scabiosa caucasica* would work with the golden yellow of *Rudbeckia* species (black-eyed Susans), only to find that their colors are atrocious together in the real garden. Pull up and replant the rudbeckia next to the *Platycodon grandiflorus,* whose violet is just as intense as the rudbeckia's yellow, if you want an eye-tingling sensation that works. The delicate blue of the scabiosa might be better displayed in front of a dark shrub and behind low bluish clumps of *Artemisia schmidtiana* 'Silver Mound'. You can bet that the master painters scraped off more paint than they left on, changing colors to achieve an effect that was just right. Don't be shy about moving plants, since it's the only way the garden will ever come together.

Color Harmonies in Nature

There's a place I go not far from my house, where grape hyacinths bloom shoulder-to-shoulder over two to three acres of what later becomes high-mown lawn. The spot is near the restored ruins of an eighteenth century iron furnace and mill, close by the eighteenth century farmhouse that still stands nearby. I suspect those hyacinths have spread from original clumps planted by a Pennsylvania woman back when the furnace ran hot iron into sand castings. I love the spot because the grapey blue hyacinths are seldom seen in such masses.

Nature's first lesson to the flower gardener who would work with her, then, is that flowers need to be planted in drifts or clumps large enough to make a visual difference when viewed from the farthest vantage point. Nothing's more ineffectual than a few spindly flowers checkering the border with odd colors. Of course, the gardener's pocketbook makes its demands, and one can seldom afford to buy enough of a perennial to start out with a large drift or clump. But large masses of flowers are more dramatic and satisfying, and as your plants grow and you divide them over the years, you will be able to augment the areas where color harmonies appear and move the plants that detract into a large mass elsewhere, to begin a new association with other plants. Once again, it's important to start small. That way your few perennials will at least be massed together. Expand the gardens as your plants give you divisions, cuttings, or seed.

As for color harmonies in nature, I am constantly knocked out by nature's color displays, in all seasons, at all times. Just yesterday, I was inspecting my grapes, checking to see if the summer's shoots had hardened properly into canes that will overwinter well, when I spied a caterpillar on a grape leaf. He was a symphony of color in exquisite harmony: reddish brown, white, black, and chartreuse. What an inspired color scheme!

Some of the most common color associations in nature are the most beautiful. Last spring I saw the combination of a red bud maple with its reddish glow hovering above a golden forsythia. This was more than a simple combination of a warm yellow and red—the tones were such that I wrote in my notes, "If the forsythia's yellow were a red, it would be the red of that maple."

Nature's color harmonies are always all around us. Haven't we all loved the pale pink of apple blossoms above a carpet of bluets? Or the wonderful buttery tones— from yellow to red-orange—in the tiny flowers of wild butter-and-eggs? And think of autumn's colors: the rich brocade of related golds, wines, reds, purples, and oranges. Nature's harmonies are written small: on an insect or a single blossom. They're also written large: across the sweep of a field, on a hillside, in the evening sky. Nature intensifies her colors at the end of things: The woods flame up in autumn just before the leaves fall. The colors of the day are pulled and concentrated toward its end, where they fade in the west with the dying sun.

Nature's colors are sometimes coy, sometimes wantonly voluptuous. When she's feeling subtle, she uses color in analogy. When she's feeling dramatic, she uses color in contrast. Color theorist Faber Birren wrote, "Analogy [likeness] is the first natural principle of color harmony. The petals of a red rose will appear red-orange in the highlights and purple in the shadows. Water appears green, turquoise-blue, and violet in various depths and movements." Such analogous color schemes, using only a limited palette of two primaries mixed into hundreds of tones of intermediate hues, show refined beauty.

But nature also tosses starkly contrasting colors together. She routinely turns out blue or purple flowers with yellow or orange centers. She outlines the veins in bluish green rose leaves with red. Her blue creatures often have accents of red or yellow. And however she arranges her natural hues, she'll wash them all over with an atmospheric haze or a pink sunset glow to tie them all into harmonies.

While nature often uses color riotously in the particular, in general, she is most subdued and restrained. From a hilltop, you'd think all she knew was green, "annihilating all that's made," as poet Andrew Marvell said, "to a green thought in a green shade." And so our perennial gardens will also be mostly green. This can be monotonous if all the greens are alike and the shapes similar. That's why we make sure to vary the greens from lightest yellow-green down to darkish blue-green, and to vary the leaves from wide and broad to thin and tiny. In nature, pastel tones are the next most common colors after green, especially variations on yellow and gold; off-whites, buffs, and beiges also abound; then blue-violet, red-violet, orange-reds, and purples; and finally the strong, vibrant painter's primaries of red, blue, and yellow, which are usually used to accent the more subtle overall combinations. These proportions of color are also the foundation for color in the perennial bed or border.

CHAPTER 3

Planning the Flower Garden

The first step in planning your perennial plantings is choosing a dominant color for a group or garden. Whether you're working with a group of three plants or a large garden that you want to coordinate, you should have a dominant hue in mind. What are your favorites? Plan for major masses of flowers that are a light tone or pastel variation of your chosen color. Augment that tone with related colors in darker shades and lighter tints. Use pure hues, even of your chosen color, sparingly.

If lavender is your chosen color, that falls on the red-violet side of the color wheel and relates to purple, violet, red-violet, pink, red, and blue. If orange is your chosen color, you can use anything from pure red to yellow-green, but stay out of the blue-to-red part of the spectrum, except where you purposefully want to dash the display with a clashing color. Clashing colors can be used in accents and for effect, but only with great care, and never when you want to promote quiet harmony among your dominant colors.

Color Accents

Color accents relieve the monotony of masses of related colors. Complementary (or near-complementary) colors are used as accents: yellow to accent the violets-to-purples; red to accent the blue-greens, blues, and yellow-greens; bright blue to accent areas of pale yellow-orange flowers. A shiny, bright red or yellow geum, the scarlet Maltese cross, or the brilliant red of the cardinal flower may be used to accent gardens of blues, such as perennial flax, campanula, veronica, lavender, *Iris sibirica,* or *I. kaempferi.* The dominant color should be a pastel tone of the hue you choose with accents used sparingly.

Accent plants will stand out in the border or bed and become an important part of the composition. They'll lead the eye forward from one spot of accent to another. Thus, perfectly regular spacing of the accent colors can give a contrived look to the placement of the plants. You may find it nicer to space them in a syncopated rhythm, varying the intervals between accent plants to create a more interesting pattern. Accent colors are one way of leading the viewer's eye toward a focal point in the composition, or toward a point of climactic color association. Your nicest color combination might revolve, for example, around tall, dark blue delphiniums, magenta *Phlox paniculata,* and light lilac foxglove. It may also be surrounded with pale blue and creamy yellow flowers. In this case, small patches of intense red daylilies, penstemon, or *Monarda didyma* will lead the eye through the pale colors to the featured combination.

Color Balance

Because you're starting small, you can saturate your bed or border with color, rather than having to spread a handful of plants over too wide an area. When color is found throughout, the garden will have a vital, floral enthusiasm.

Sometimes colors can be too enthusiastic, however, and so they should be balanced. For example, let's say that in July you want to grow an area of bright red bee balm (*Monarda didyma*) in a sunny spot. You would not then flank the bee balm with hot pink on one side and bright orange on the other. The bee balm is bright enough. Use soft colors and subtle shades, such as given by baby's breath, around the bee balm to hold it down and to balance it in the overall harmony of the garden. Too many concentrated hot colors together rivet the eye, forming a visual maelstrom into which our gaze is irresistibly drawn. All of us have spent an hour around a campfire or a candle, talking with friends and staring into the flames. Like the moth, we are held. The same thing happens when a pool of hot colors dominates an otherwise sensitive arrangement of plants in the garden.

Instead, we want the viewer's eye to play from place to place, enjoying the associations, eventually being gently led toward the featured association of perennials by accent colors, shrubs, rocks, or other compositional elements. Color balancing helps you achieve a picture that invites the eye to light anywhere, there to find something interesting to see, but soon enticed away to something else that's just as pretty.

Light colors also need balancing. Let's say you want to feature an area of tall, luminous, light yellow lilies. Putting a drift of intense yellow lysimachia next to the lilies would usurp their beauty. To balance their light yellow, you might use a pale, dusty shade of gold, such as *Achillea taygetea* 'Moonshine', soft green foliage, and tones of burnt orange. Related colors in subdued tones balance light hues. Accents of strong related color pull the light hue of the featured plant into a spot of intense color, as if the accent is the essence of the featured plant. For a mass of light yellow lilies 5 feet across and 3 feet wide, one small gaillardia or crayon-yellow geum would be enough accent.

Color balancing can also be used to exaggerate the depth of a bed or border. Using bright, strong colors close to the viewer and getting progressively bluer and greyer and lighter in tone as we go farther back, we can reproduce the atmospheric effects of distance seen in nature. You can see why pale blue spruces and evergreens are used so often in the back of borders.

Shade will reduce the brilliance and add blue or black to the tone of a strong hue. In an area of partial shade that is in shadow all afternoon, stronger tones can be used closer together, as the shade will tend to harmonize them.

To exaggerate a depth effect even more, emphasize the height differential between the little plants in front and the tall ones in the back. A flat or only slightly rising bed of flowers looks to a viewer at a distance as long, thin strips of color. But if the drifts are of ever-increasing heights, more of each color is seen, and the visual effect is like looking out over a valley, rather than like looking over a plain. The sense of distance and space is more palpable when looking out over a valley from a vista than when looking over flat land.

Color Strategies

We're going to consider the three color strategies—color grouping, dominant color, and spectacular effect.

The Color Grouping Strategy

The bed or border is thought of as many discrete planting areas. A group of three to five plants that will give a spring crescendo goes in front of a shrub and beside a rock. The shrub and rock separate the association from another group nearby—one that won't bloom until mid-June. This second group is separated from a third by a pale, almost neutral mass of flowers, and so on. Shrubs, rocks, paths, foliage, and neutral colors can separate groups of plants that bloom together.

Such a garden always has spots of interest, but also lots of places that are coming or going and are thus shades of green. Choosing plants for foliage that is interesting and pleasing together is of great importance in this strategy, for most of the garden will be foliage most of the time.

Color schemes that are very different and would clash if put together will look fine if separated by enough green or soft pastel tints.

Many people say that white flowers are the best choice to separate color associations, and occasionally this may work. But I find that bright whites are too strong—they dilute the subtleties of the flower harmonies nearby. White snaps out at you and bites the eye. From a distance it can overpower any other color. Like the strong primary hues, I think it's best used as an accent, not as a buffer against color clashes. Choose creams, soft greys, or pastels as buffers, but go easy on the bright whites.

Color associations that follow close upon one another can be put together without any buffering if they relate. Let's say that on the right of our border we have a color association that's dominated by blues: strong blue spikes of veronica, pastel sky blue flax, and the pinkish blue, fringed flowers of the dianthus. A nearby color association, which may overlap the blooming period of the veronica-flax-dianthus group, may be built on pink: pinkish blue hollyhocks, pink-lilac liatris, and deeper, reddish pink daylilies. Yet the two groups will work together during the time of overlapping bloom, because pink and blue themes echo in both associations.

Color associations in this strategy can start in earliest spring, and you can have something peaking every two to three weeks from then on. But the main effect is of a subdued, mostly green garden, with discrete spots that show off groups of flowers.

The Dominant Color Strategy

This strategy can be broken down into two variations. First, you can plan for a dominant color in spring, another in summer, another in fall—different dominant colors in the different seasons. Or, second, you can plan for the same dominant color from spring to fall. Let's take them one at a time.

Some of the most common perennial flowers in spring are yellow and white. For early summer, they're the rosy pinks. For midsummer, blue and yellow. For late summer, pink and purple. For autumn, blue, purple, orange, and gold. Your garden could follow this seasonal progression—that is, a dominant scheme of yellow and white in spring could pass and give way to the rosy pinks of early summer, and so on. Even though the dominant colors change seasonally, they harmonize the whole garden at their specific time of bloom. The only trouble may come when one season is passing into another, and the yellows of spring are still haunting the rosy pinks that are coming, clashing as they go. One answer is to cut off the offensive spring flowers. A better answer is to move plants around or even remove a plant if its color carries too far into the next dominant color scheme.

On the other hand, you may be a fan of lavender and wish to see it from spring to fall in a certain bed. Related colors are blues, pinkish blues, purples, violets, and pale red-violets. There are plenty of plants that can take you all through the season, varying the lavender effect. For accent, small spots of strong yellow are complementary and will relieve the numbing effect of too much lavender, as can strong red-violets and white.

A white garden is another possibility, using strong, brilliant primaries as accents. This can be quite spectacular. But unless white gardens are well accented with strong colors, they leave me unsatisfied.

A spring-to-fall garden predicated on one color avoids the awkward moments that can occur when dominant colors change from season to season. From beginning to end, everything relates or it's taken out.

Much of the dominant color garden will be green during the year, as plants grow and bloom; then either retain good-looking foliage or die back.

The Spectacular Effect Strategy

If there's a specific time of year you like best, or if there's a time when you're frequently outside and would like to see a mass of blossoms, the third strategy may be for you. It involves devoting a garden to a spectacular display at just one time of year.

For instance, you may find that you spend a lot of time outside, eating, relaxing, gardening, or playing games, in mid- to late-June. And so you plan a garden that's visible and close at hand with plants that all bloom in late June, massing them close together in drifts and pools, for an absolutely spectacular display at that time of year. There really is no room for other plants that may bloom earlier or later. When this garden peters out in July, it remains pretty much as a place of green foliage. In another part of the yard, you could plan another garden for an August display, and so on, for as many gardens as you want to devote to such displays.

Such gardens are beautiful, dramatic, and lush, but they are only so for a short time. You get in spectacle what you give up in time. Such gardens are a trade-off, but they have their place.

To sum up: Your choices are to segment your garden into separate areas that offer varying color harmonies in small groups through the year; to have a dominant color scheme that changes from season to season or one that remains from spring to fall; or to go for a massed spectacular at one time of year. All three gardens are lovely.

Planning the Garden on Paper

The most common way to plant a perennial garden is to start with a few plants and keep adding as you acquire more. When things come up helter-skelter, they can be moved in order to separate warring colors, but most often they're left where they are. This is what's called the cottage garden. It contains someone's favorite plants in no particular design. Such gardens can be wonderful for the gardener who uses them as a horticultural zoo, where he or she can visit old favorites, see them in bloom, spend a minute just communing. While cottage gardens speak of the gardener's industry in collecting plants, they don't suggest much in the way of aesthetic accomplishment.

To achieve a garden that's aesthetically accomplished right off the bat, it is necessary to plan it on paper. Get a sheet of paper with half-inch squares large enough to represent your bed or border at a scale of ½ inch on the paper to 1 foot in the garden. Transfer the dimensions of the garden to the paper and outline it. If there are any permanent elements, such as rocks, walls, evergreen shrubbery, or trees, put them in.

Obviously it helps a lot to have living experience with all the perennials you'll put into the garden. The verbal information in books is only a shadow of the real knowledge that experience imparts. So if you're experienced at all with some perennials, start your list with those. Add others you think you may want but don't know very well firsthand. Your mastery and your garden can only grow by trying new plants every year.

Here are some considerations to make when planning a garden on paper.

Planning the Color Grouping Strategy

Now's the time to decide which color strategy you're going to use. Plans will differ depending on the strategy. Since the color grouping strategy is the one most people use, we'll look closely at how we'd plan out that strategy on paper.

Plan for Color Masses

Enough plants of the same cultivar should be massed to give single-color drifts that are several feet long and at least a foot wide, or clumps from 2 to 3 feet around. Thus, a single peony or large hosta may measure 2 feet in diameter, while clumps of daisies may be only 10 inches across and you'd need several of them. Drifts should get thinner along the forward edges of the border, where the lowest-growing plants will be placed. These can be just a single line of plants extending for a couple of feet before giving way to other plants.

Follow the Contours

Remember that oblong drifts should follow the contours of the border or the curves of the bed. Interlace them so that associations of color form where they overlap.

Plan for Foliage, Too

When planning for color, plan at the same time for foliage. Make sure your group has foliage of differing types, which will keep some interest and beauty happening before and after bloom.

Accent with Spires and Mounds

Think also about tall spiked plants. Their vertical lines are best used as accents in gardens made primarily of horizontal drifts and rounded clumps, rather than dominating a few horizontal drifts. Put tall spiked plants in two or three widely separated places in the garden, where they will relieve the flatness of the drifts and echo the verticals of trees and shrubs behind them. Space them using the Golden Section (see page 18). Let me remind you that all tall plants go in the center of island beds or the back of the borders, but not all tall plants have vertical flower spikes. A group of from three to five spiked plants may be placed forward of tall back-border flowers, giving an upward thrust to the flat areas of bloom around them.

Outline the Garden

Since a color-grouped garden is thought of in discrete parts, let's add the outlines of those parts to our emerging garden plan. In the illustration below, you can see that I've chosen to break a border into twelve parts. We now have the border outlined, permanent features marked in, and parts outlined. It may look like what is shown in the illustration. Area 1 is shady and forward—a good place for spring bulbs. If Area 1 is going to be bulbs, they should be spotted elsewhere

in the garden, too, to balance the areas of color. Area 6 might be a nice place to put the taller tulips, and bulbs in Area 12 would give a spread of early color across the width of the garden and toward the viewer. Because bulb foliage gets ratty looking soon after bloom, we need to think of succession plants to mix with the bulbs: low hostas in the forward areas (1 and 12) and ferns, perhaps, in Area 6. Both of these are just emerging when the bulbs are blooming and will hide the spent foliage.

Areas 2, 8, and 10 might be chosen for associations of May-blooming plants. Areas 3, 7, and 11 would provide June bloom across the garden, especially in the back portion. In July, Areas 4, 5, and 9 would be in full bloom. See the box on A Few Great Marriages for suggestions for some beautiful perennial associations.

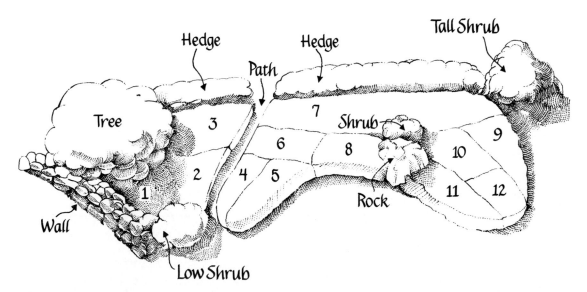

A color-grouped garden can be planned in separate parts. The garden diagramed here is 6 feet wide at the narrowest point and 12 feet wide at the widest. Its overall length is 25 feet.

A Few Great Marriages

Like human marriage, plant marriages—that is, plants grown together—cover the distance from total incompatibility to ecstatic union.

Here are a few ecstatic unions of mostly low-maintenance perennials. By low maintenance we mean that the plants can be left in place without dividing for at least four years, they need no staking or spraying, and they won't become rank or invasive under ordinary conditions. The plants in these associations like the same conditions of sun, soil, and climate. The associations are suggested by Robert Hebb of the Carey Arboretum.

Achillea taygetea 'Moonshine' with *Nepeta faassenii*

The handsome silvery grey foliage of the achillea goes well with the catmint's lavender bloom, and all are set off with the pale, sulfurous yellow of the achillea's umbel. Cut back the nepeta after it flowers.

Amsonia tabernaemontana with *Sinoglossum nervosum*

Amsonia's steel blue to grey flowers are quite unusual and the plants don't need dividing. *Sinoglossum nervosum* is a biennial ornamental borage that grows to 3 feet and carries blue flowers that marry well with amsonia.

Aruncus dioicus with *Iris sibirica*

Iris sibirica is an easy-to-grow iris that comes in various colors, from blue to red. They are spectacular surrounding a taller clump of aruncus crowned with its showy, creamy white plumes.

Asclepias tuberosa with *Platycodon grandiflorus*

The brick orange color of the asclepias (butterfly weed) and the violet-blue balloon flowers make a sensational, if violent, color combination.

Chrysanthemum maximum with *Achillea* species

Chrysanthemum maximum is the large, white Shasta daisy, usually with yellow centers, that mixes well with various achilleas, especially the yellow variations such as 'Gold Plate'.

Cimicifuga racemosa with *Filipendula rubra* 'Venusta'

This tall association is one of the very best for drawing the eye to the back of the garden and then satisfying it. The high spikes of the creamy white cimicifuga are surrounded by the deep pink feathery plumes of the Queen of the Prairie, as *Filipendula rubra* is called.

Dicentra spectabilis with *Brunnera macrophylla*

The brunnera has big, heart-shaped leaves with small, forget-me-not–type flowers of pastel true blue that make an unforgettable association with the pastel red and white hearts that drip from the flower wands of the dicentra. And when the dicentra leaves die back after bloom, they'll be covered up by the brunnera.

Remember the Late Months

But what about August, September, and the fall months—nothing for them? There are several ways of getting late bloom into a small garden like the one in the illustration on page 64. One option is to plant fall-blooming perennials among the plants grouped in an area. When the early bloomers have finished and need cutting back, the fall bloomers are just putting on their major growth. The presence of fall bloomers dilutes the massed effects of earlier color associations to some extent, as the roots of the fall bloomers take up space that otherwise would be devoted to the early color associations.

Another way to have fall flowers is to keep a separate nursery bed going and move some divided chrysanthemums and asters or other late bloomers into the areas where flowers are fading and holes are opening up.

A third way is to make sure that many of your color associations contain at least one plant that blooms for months, the way *Campanula carpatica* or *Geranium endressii* does.

A fourth way to get fall color is to plant annuals when the perennials die down. Many annuals don't really take off until August. You can also use the bare areas to plant biennials. Biennials grow leaves and roots the first year and flower the second. You'd put first-year biennials among the spots left by perennials and plan for their bloom in next year's garden. The gorgeous blue myosotis of spring and later foxgloves are usually handled this way. Both are biennials. After they bloom their second year, pull them out and plant the area with new plants or with divisions from other perennials in the garden.

One could add a fifth way—breaking the color-grouped garden into enough areas to allow for bloom in the late months. In a garden as small as the one shown in the illustration, breaking the garden into more areas would reduce the size of the drifts and give an overall spotty effect. In a larger garden, though, it could work.

Repeat Colors

To tie the whole garden together, repeat colors in each of the areas that are blooming. If, for instance, I plant an association of blue and violet myosotis, grape hyacinth, mertensia, and chionodoxa in Area 1, I might add an accent of pure red *Tulipa praestans* 'Fusilier', perhaps a small group of five. Area 6 could pick up on this red and splash it across the middle of the garden using *Bergenia cordifolia* 'Rotblum', *Anemone blanda*, and pink hyacinths. *A. blanda* has yellow centers that could be echoed in Area 12 with a large mass of daffodils, accented with more red tulips and a few of the blue flowers used in Area 1. Notice that each area has its own color scheme (blue in 1, red in 6, and yellow in 12), yet they are echoed, repeated, and tied together across the garden. This, then, gives good effects from afar and close up.

Break Any Rules You Don't Like

If you want to make an association of twelve lavender plants billowing up toward a raspberry red center display, then make it. The information in this section is designed to help you think about the way plants grow and the way they look, and it is more suggestion than command.

Choose Plant Associations

For each of the discrete areas outlined on your garden plan, make your plant choices based on height, form, color, foliage, season of bloom, suitability to your climate, soil needs, light requirements, and water needs. To help you easily take all these into ac-

(continued on page 64)

A Few More Great Marriages

We asked folks who attended a recent meeting of the Perennial Plant Association to tell us their favorite combinations. From the many suggestions we so gratefully received, we've selected these as among the most interesting and widely plantable.

White *Iberis sempervirens* with yellow, blue, and purple *Viola cornuta*, mixed with yellow *Alyssum saxatile.* This is accented by the red-coral droplets of *Heuchera sanguinea.*

—Smithtown, New York

Golden *Rudbeckia fulgida* 'Goldsturm' with the ornamental grass *Pennisetum alopecuroides.*

—Robert Lyons
Blacksburg, Virginia

Hostas with asperula for foliage contrast in the shade.

Coreopsis lanceolata with *Chrysanthemum maximum* (Shasta daisy) for a good yellow and white theme, good foliage contrast, and the ability to cover the ground after blooming.

Hemerocallis and narcissus, because their foliage is similar and the daylilies unobtrusively replace the spring bulbs' failing foliage.

Ajuga reptans and *Pachysandra terminalis* for foliage contrast using two shade-loving ground covers.

—Mike Jones
Lansing, Michigan

White Shasta daisies and yellow daylilies.

The magnificent fiddleheads of cinnamon fern open to set off astilbes.

—Walter Heist
Heistaway Gardens
Conyers, Georgia

Artemisia schmidtiana 'Silver Mound' with absolutely anything.

—Doug Greene
Simple Gifts
Athens, Ontario

White *Arabis caucasica* and blue-violet *Delphinium tricorne* with tulips.

Blue *Baptisia australis* with yellow *Lysimachia punctata.*

Rudbeckia 'Goldsturm' with red *Monarda didyma.*

—Ruth Kvaalen
West Lafayette, Indiana

Sedum spectabile 'Autumn Joy' with lavender-blue eupatorium (hardy ageratum) and purple sage to make a nice combination about October 1.

—Allentown, Pennsylvania

Red *Lobelia cardinalis* with white *Lysimachia clethroides* and yellow *Coreopsis grandiflora.*

—Silver Spring, Maryland

Hosta grandiflora with *Narcissus* species—the unfolding hosta leaves cover the leaves of the spring bulbs when they're dying back.

—Avon, Ohio

Gold *Helianthus multiflorus* 'Flore-Pleno' with light blue *Linum perenne.* Their foliage contrasts nicely, too, as helianthus is coarse and flax delicate.

—Francis Gambino
Bordine's Better Blooms
Clarkston, Michigan

For a low group of early bloomers, I like *Arabis alpina* 'Snowcap' (white) with yellow *Alyssum saxatile,* pink and white *Dianthus allwoodii* 'Alpinus', and yellow *Doronicum caucasicum.*

—Mary Odom Brown
Soergel Greenhouses
Wexford, Pennsylvania

Linum perenne with *Achillea* species. Rudbeckia's golden flowers with echinacea's unique pink.
Alyssum saxatile with *Iberis sempervirens.*

—Allen Bush
Holbrook Farm & Nursery
Fletcher, North Carolina

Low, white madonna lilies (*Lilium candidum*) with tall blue *Delphinium elatum* for a gorgeous June association.

—Lyn's Greenhouse
Horseheads, New York

Rosy lavender *Liatris spicata* and rosy pink *Echinacea purpurea.*
Pink *Geranium endressii* 'Wargrave Pink' with purple sprays of *Salvia nemorosa* 'Superba'.

—Paul's Perennials
Muskego, Wisconsin

White *Anemone sylvestris* with deep pinkish red *Dianthus deltoides* and blue *Myosotis alpestris* 'Victoria Dark Blue'.
White *Platycodon grandiflorus* 'Alba' with raspberry-rose *Liatris spicata* 'Kobold'.
Dicentra spectabilis, Brunnera macrophylla, and *Aubrieta* 'Purple Gem'.*

—Shirley Peckosh
Cedar Rapids, Iowa

For the rock garden: *Campanula carpatica* 'China Doll' has blue-violet flowers that mix well with the carmine *Potentilla* 'Miss Willmont', red *Sedum* 'Dragon's Blood', and the tiny purple flowers of *Thymus citriodorus.*

For the perennial bed or border: coral pink *Heuchera sanguinea* with yellow *Hemerocallis* 'Hyperion' and dusty blue *Echinops ritro.*

Also, the pink of *Pulmonaria saccharata* 'Mrs. Moon' with raspberry *Liatris spicata* 'Kobold' and the blue Connecticut Yankee strain of *Delphinium elatum* hybrids.

—Eugenia Wiss
Whispering Pines Nursery
Dingman's Ferry, Pennsylvania

Phlox paniculata 'Orange Perfection' with *Gypsophila* (baby's breath).
Powder blue *Linum perenne* with the hotter colors of *Papaver nudicaule* 'Champagne Bubbles'.
Raspberry *Liatris spicata* 'Kobold' with *Rudbeckia fulgida* 'Goldsturm'.

—Virginia DeArmond
Flint, Michigan

*This combination of bleeding heart and *Brunnera macrophylla*'s baby blue forget-me-nots was the most mentioned and most beloved combination by our respondents.

count, we've listed this information in the chart in chapter 7. Plant your groups in drifts or mounds that overlap and intermingle.

One Plan, One Notebook

For each garden you plan on paper, keep a separate notebook. You'll find plenty to put in it. For instance, you may find that one of the plants in an association is not the pink you wanted. You pull off a few flowers and hold them up against other flowers in the garden. You make a note of which flowers they harmonize with and which they don't and decide where to move them next spring. When next spring arrives, use your notebook to accomplish all the rearrangements and fine tunings that occurred to you last year.

The only way to avoid using a notebook is to dig up awkward plants on the spot—in full flower—and put them somewhere else. That sets plants back, and you'll wait another year for good bloom. It can also kill many of them if they aren't deeply and constantly watered and shaded until their roots take hold. But for some people, anything's better than keeping notebooks.

Planning the Dominant Color Strategy

Here's how to plan the dominant color strategy. Outline the garden's shape and its permanent features, as before, but don't draw in outlines of discrete areas. If you're planning for a succession of bloom that changes its color scheme as the seasons progress, proceed as shown in the example in the illustration opposite. The choice of bloom is yours.

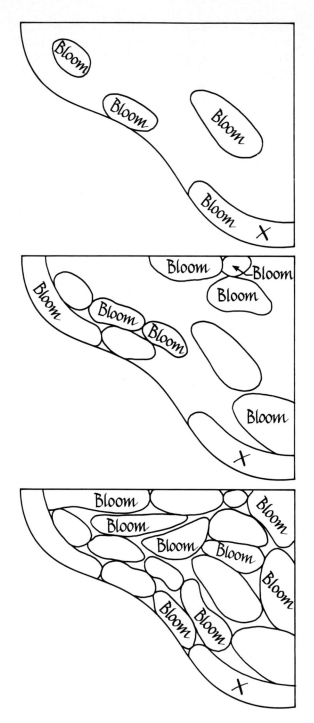

Three color themes: This garden is planned for bloom all season. In May (shown at top), the beds labeled "Bloom" will show a yellow and white theme. In June (center), pink and blue flowers will bloom. In July (bottom), the theme will be blue and yellow. Bloom can be had in later months by interplanting early spring flowers with late-blooming ones. For instance, if the drift labeled "X" is interplanted with yellow and white species tulips and Astilbe chinensis *'Pumila', the tulips will blossom yellow and white in May and the Astilbe raspberry pink in late August.*

If you want the same dominant color throughout the year, proceed just as with a changing dominant color scheme, but choose colors and accents that work with your chosen color.

Planning for the Spectacular Effect Strategy

This is a relatively simple task. The garden and its permanent features are outlined, and then plants are chosen to fill up the garden with a profusion of blossoms at one specific time of year. Drifts, mounds, and groups of spiked flowers in compositions should still be used.

These are the mechanics of creating a garden plan based on your choice of strategy and your own tastes. All our tastes, however, are informed and educated by others who have gone before and blazed trails, setting our standards. The following chapter looks at some groups of plants that master gardeners have put together.

CHAPTER 4

Color Harmonies Month by Month

How wonderful it would be to take a garden tour that begins in the earliest spring and continues through summer until hard frost, and which includes some of the nicest gardens in America. We've tried to create such a tour for you in the pages of this chapter.

We chose the photos in this chapter with these qualities in mind: that they be exquisite photographs in their own right, that they illustrate a good range of subtle and strong color associations, that they focus on the beauty of the small and compact as well as the overall look of a garden, that they reflect a range of growing conditions from coast to coast, and that they illustrate techniques of building a garden. Not all the photos meet all these conditions, but among them, all the qualities are somewhere found.

At the end of each flowering period, we've included a list of the perennials that bloom in that period, grouped by flower color. This should facilitate locating plants of the proper season and color as possibilities for your garden planning. Check sun, soil, and other requirements in the large chart in chapter 7 to see if your possibilities fit the garden conditions you plan for them.

Let's begin the garden tour where it always must begin: in late winter, when expectations of seeing the first flowers quicken the heart. Love's labor is never lost when it's applied toward perennials, for their promise is to bloom again.

March–April

The sun was warm but the wind was chill.
You know how it is with an April day
When the sun is out and the wind is still,
You're one month on in the middle of May.

—Robert Frost

Suddenly, there will be a snowdrop. "Galanthus," I say to myself, bending over to study it. Often thrusting its small lily-like leaves through melting snow, the plant opens the first flowers of spring in our area—inconspicuous little hanging bells of green and white. Soon will come the yellow winter aconites, *Eranthis hyemalis. Eranthis* is Greek for "spring flower," and in many places, it will bloom before galanthus.

All the first blossoms are bulbs. Crocus pops next, and then the Siberian squill and chionodoxa. For your earliest garden, think about mixing scads of eranthus with galanthus, chionodoxa, 'Kaufmanniana' tulips, scilla, puschkinia, crocus, and muscari.

67

Photo 1. Among the rooted plants, *Anemone pulsatilla,* or pasque flower, soon strikes a vibrant note with its deep violet or magenta blossoms with glowing yellow centers. It's said that *pulsatilla* means "strike violently," and while that may be carrying imagery too far in the case of this ferny little plant, there's nothing quiet about its color.

In the photo, the anemone shows itself against the bare earth. Its strong color is attenuated by the *Phlox subulata,* or spring garden pinks, at its feet. Soon the leaves of other perennials will appear out of the raw earth around these early bloomers.

Photo 2. While the perennials may just be starting, out in the fields and lawns the grasses are greening up. Emerging with them are the spears of the daffodil leaves. While daffodils are perfectly welcome in the perennial garden, they are most spectacular naturalized in huge masses along a bank or in unused places in the grass. Remember that you'll have to allow the leaves of daffodils and other spring bulbs to remain over the next six to eight weeks so they can manufacture enough food for next year's bloom. They therefore won't be cut before mid-June, even though their flowers will have disappeared by early May. One can't have displays of withering daffodil leaves in the garden, however. One answer is to interplant extensive daffodil beds with ferns and hostas that will cover up the messy look of the bulbs' leaves. Another is to simply allow the beds to look messy until they can be cut like grass along with the rest of the lawn.

Photo 1

Here, a gentle countryside rolls before the camera lens, the convex hills echoed with the arch of the white bridges. On the near side of the small stream, the lawn is carpeted with naturalized daffodils in yellow and white varieties. The scene is irresistible. The Mother Goose rhyme, "Daffy-Down-Dilly's come to town in her green petticoat and yellow gown," comes to mind. The leaves are yet to appear on the trees, but it hardly matters at this farm in southeastern Pennsylvania, for the attention firmly flows along the bright beds of flowers toward the declaration made by three evenly spaced conifers on the hill across the stream.

Photo 2

Photo 3. Besides ferns and hostas, which aren't grown for their flowers, peonies make a good interplant with early spring bulbs. Peonies are racing out of the ground while the daffodils are in bloom, and so don't ordinarily interfere with them.

By the time the daffodils finish blooming, the peonies will open their leaves and begin preparations for flowering in June. The bushy peonies perfectly cover up spent bulb foliage. As you can see from the photo, the coppery red tone of the emerging peonies works as a softening foil to the bright buttery yellow of the daffodil.

Photo 4. The exciting colors of spring bulbs are most welcome after the drabness of winter. After the daffodils finish, their cousins, narcissus, begin to bloom. These have the added bonus of a rich, cedary aroma.

The photo shows narcissus on the left, with pale yellow petals around rich orange centers. In the center, the yellow is repeated deep in the cups of the bright red tulips and repeated again in the petals of the tall tulip on the right. They say that good flower arranging makes cut flowers look like they are growing in a garden, but here's a garden that looks like an arrangement! The gardener created this group by planting the bulbs where she did, but the arrangement and composition—so exquisite here—are by the flowers themselves. They have arrayed themselves before their miniature waterfall, adding their laughter to its splashes.

Photo 5. The color scheme is based on themes expressed in a single flower. This hybrid tulip's name is 'Rembrandt'. We find the pale yellow of the narcissus in its tripartite pistil, the black of the tulips' cups in its stamens, and their golden yellows and reds in its petals. When stuck for good ideas for color schemes in the garden, look closely at individual flowers like 'Rembrandt' and be inspired.

Photo 3

Photo 4

Photo 5

Photo 6. Of course, many flowers strike one note, and strike it hard. Usually these are flowers that naturalize well. Among the most prolific naturalizers in the spring garden are the many species of *Muscari,* or grape hyacinth. Its small bulbs can smother acres with little purple bells. The photo was taken near an eighteenth century iron mill and an equally ancient farmhouse. I like to think that this amazing field of naturalized muscari was started by one of our progenitors a couple of hundred years ago in her small cottage garden. From then until now, the ground must not have been plowed or seriously disturbed. Then again, perhaps someone with a huge fondness for muscari sowed them just a few decades ago. But I doubt it. Although shown in this photo in

isolated grandeur, muscari is beautiful mixed with light pink flowers such as dogwoods above and pink hyacinth or *Dicentra formosa* closer to the ground.

Photo 7. Early spring is a triumph in Anita Kistler's rock garden. *Phlox subulata* makes bright mounds of pink, and *P. divaricata* makes mounds of pale blue among the structural elements of vertical cedars and rounded coniferous shrubs and broadleaved evergreens. Notice how the front of her border includes areas where the flowers spill out onto the lawn, and areas where shrubs interrupt the flowers. This is a much more interesting arrangement than a line of flowers edging the entire interface with the grass. The lighter tones of *P. subulata* are

Photo 6

Photo 7

accented with red and orange-red tulips—the spots of bright color at the center left of the picture.

Photo 8. If we journey close into this superb spring garden, we find the phlox making a rich association with the fresh green of emerging iris swords.

Photo 9. Not all early spring color schemes have to be so bold. Tucked away in Anita's rock garden, we found this combination of *Iris mellita* and *Antennaria dioica* 'Rosea', the latter also known as pussytoes. To achieve subtle color harmonies such as this, one must know these plants from personal experience, unless they're seen in the garden of a master colorist like Anita. Although Marilyn and I have never planted these, the photo makes us want to try them in our garden.

Photo 8

73

Photo 10. Springtime in the West has a special beauty all its own. Let's jet across the continent to visit Harland Hand's garden near San Francisco. Harland's house is on a hilltop, and he has created a fantasy in flowers on the land leading down the slope. At the bottom of a path are the salmon flowers of a hybrid *Aloe,* grown with the dark mahogany rosettes of *Aeonium* leaves. Many different echeverias and grasses line the steps. To the left is the bright pink of a tree rose, and at the top of the steps there's a tree fern on the left and a magnificent *Wisteria longissima* var. *alba,* full of cascading, white-panicled flowers.

Photo 11. A bold explosion of forms and a delicious combination of colors re-

sulted when Harland placed the salmony flowers of hybrid aloe in front of the iris-like spikes of dwarf *Phormium tenax* 'Variegatum', and interspersed this with deep blue strings of the jewellike flowers of *Salvia* 'Superba'.

Photo 12. A bright salmon pink *Kalanchoe blossfeldiana* hybrid dominates the center of this composition. It's mixed with mahogany *Aeonium* and set against powdery grey concrete planters with great effect. *Lithodora* 'Grace Ward' spills across the picture. Bromeliads at bottom left and rabbit's-foot fern at bottom right anchor the association. Aloes are visible at top, and a spray of cymbidium orchid leaves enters the scene at upper left.

Photo 9

Photo 10

Photo 13. Artful combinations of sedums and echeveria fill the spaces between rocks in this lovely part of Harland's garden. The grey-lavender rosettes are *Echeveria elegans,* and the leafy rosettes fringed in brownish red are *Echeveria* hybrids, including 'Afterglow'. Smaller echeverias add coppery red notes near the center. The spiny texture of the succulents is softened with white *Iberis sempervirens, Arabis* (rock cress), and *Stachys byzantina* (lamb's-ears).

Photo 11

Photo 12

Photo 13

MARCH–APRIL FLOWERS

BICOLOR *Aquilegia canadensis, Primula auricula, Viola tricolor*

BLUE *Brunnera macrophylla, Mertensia virginica, Polemonium reptans, Pulmonaria angustifolia, P. saccharata, Vinca minor*

PINK *Aethionema × warleyense, Aubrieta deltoidea, Bergenia cordifolia, Dicentra eximia, Helleborus orientalis, Lamium maculatum, Peltiphyllum peltatum, Pulmonaria saccharata, Viola odorata*

PURPLE *Anemone pulsatilla, Aubrieta deltoidea, Primula denticulata, Viola odorata*

RED *Anemone pulsatilla, Bergenia cordifolia, Primula auricula, Pulmonaria saccharata, Trillium erectum, Viola odorata*

WHITE *Allium neapolitanum, Anemone pulsatilla, Arabis procurrens, Asperula odorata, Bergenia cordifolia, Dicentra cucullaria, Helleborus niger, Lamium maculatum, Pachysandra terminalis, Primula denticulata, Pulmonaria angustifolia, P. saccharata, Sanguinaria canadensis, Trillium grandiflorum, Vinca minor, Viola odorata*

YELLOW *Alyssum saxatile, Doronicum caucasicum, Draba sibirica, Primula auricula, Pulmonaria angustifolia*

Photo 14

May

Photo 14. In 1956, the Connecticut property in photo 14 was untamed woods and raw fill around the house. Mrs. Ruth Levitan started a small vegetable garden in a clearing behind the house that year, and in subsequent years lined the path with flowers. The flower gardens grew "like Topsy," she says, and now her one-acre property produces an annual May crescendo of color.

She admittedly started with no real horticultural knowledge, but as her interest in flowers grew and her gardens took shape, knowledge came along. "Working with a piece of land is like a marriage. You *think* you're going to make him over. But you learn that what you marry is what you've got," Ruth said.

She kept the property's woodsy effect by growing many shade-loving perennials. According to Ruth, "Nature has something to say, and the gardener has something to say, and their voices should harmonize."

The photo shows the original path to

Photo 15

the vegetable garden as it looks today. Dog-woods that were growing there when the Levitans bought the property fill the sky with white blossoms. Along the right side of the path, azaleas add bright spots of pink. Blue *Myosotis sylvatica* (forget-me-nots) and *Polemonium reptans* (Jacob's ladder) edge the path, with red tulips for accent. The yellow flowers in the middle distance at left are *Alyssum saxatile*, basket of gold.

Photo 15. When approaching Ruth's flower beds closely, you see that they are groups of flowers, not just masses of a single plant. The myosotis and alyssum here form a backdrop for the falling stars of red *Aquilegia canadensis,* a wild columbine native to eastern North America.

Ruth has interplanted these borders of alyssum and myosotis so that they will be followed by lysimachia, then oriental poppies, then monkshood, and finally finish the year with chrysanthemums.

Photo 16. In one of the prettiest associations of the May garden, the trailing flower stalks of bleeding heart (*Dicentra spectabilis*) drip pink flowers over lavender

Photo 16

clusters of Jacob's ladder. Bleeding heart is sometimes called the lady in the locket, for if you turn one of the "hearts" upside down, a tiny figure emerges from the center. If you peel back the red petals that surround the figure, you may see the lady in the bathtub, as she's then sometimes called.

Photo 17. The variegated colors of pansy-like Johnny-jump-ups add bass notes to the association of myosotis and alyssum in Ruth's garden. The blues of the myosotis are concentrated and enriched to an intense royal purple, then mixed with black

and red in the petals of the Johnnies. Similarly, the gold of the alyssum is captured by the centers of these small, but potent, flowers.

Photo 18. Here's another view of May popping in the Levitan garden, facing away from the house. The color theme includes white, pink, blue, red, and yellow, and many other colors if one looks at the gardens up close. Selected wild trees give the yard its vertical elements. Broad-leaved evergreen and deciduous shrubs form the understory, *(continued on page 84)*

Photo 17

Photo 18

Photo 19

just as in the wild woods, and they bloom beautifully through June. Perennials cover the ground, mixed with some biennials. Notice how your eye is led back along the path by the soft blues and pinks, and by the red accents, following the generous grass swards. This view invites people to explore the twists and turns, where Ruth has provided floral surprises around each bend.

Photo 19. The light in the Levitan garden is soft and eastern, softened even more by the branches of the overarching trees. A harder light falls on gardens in the Rocky Mountains of Montana, and May flowers there respond with dazzling displays. In the foreground, the brightest pink is given by *Phlox*

subulata, while *Aubrieta deltoidea* gives a more rosy and subdued pink. Mounds of white *Iberis sempervirens* flank the phlox and aubrieta, while a trail of blue myosotis winds back toward a solar greenhouse.

Sam Bibler, whose garden this is, accents the low-growing flowers in the foreground with yellow daffodils and separates them from the house with primary tones, using yellow and red tulips. He finishes the background with a blaze of *Alyssum saxatile,* basket of gold.

From within the solar greenhouse, the color aspects will be quite different to the viewer, although no less joyful. It's the mark of a well-planned garden to look good from almost any angle.

Photo 20

Photo 20. Most of our familiar garden peonies bloom in June, but *Paeonia tenuifolia*—the fern-leaved peony—blooms a month earlier. Here in Elsie Yarema's garden in eastern Pennsylvania, it's used to edge a border of emerging iris and red tulips. The fern-leaved peony is a native of eastern Europe that does well in the eastern parts of the United States. A patch like Elsie's can be one of the most visually interesting areas in a May garden, and the plant's ferny foliage continues to look good throughout the summer months.

Photo 21. At Butchart Gardens in Victoria, Vancouver Island, British Columbia, the light softens again. In this perfectly composed garden and photo, we see aubrieta and *Alyssum saxatile,* basket of gold, growing from between crevices in the rock wall bordering the brick path. In the beds above the rock wall, myosotis and red and yellow tulips draw the eye immediately back to large displays of rhododendrons.

And all of this—path, wall, flowers, shrubs, ivies, and lawn—leads the eye to the dark vertical evergreen that serves as

Photo 21

the focal point of the composition. I can't say enough about the quality of the plantings at Butchart Gardens, as shown so well by this photograph. Careful study of this picture can help you achieve similar dramatic effects in your garden, although perhaps not on this scale.

Photo 22. Not all the beauty in the May garden is found in the flowers. This group of *Hosta sieboldiana* in Grace Rose's Pennsylvania garden writhes with texture and form although the palette is limited to green. You can see from the wide leaves why *H. sieboldiana* makes such a good plant to cover the ground in shady areas. Although its flowers won't appear until late in the year, there's no lack of interest in the plants themselves.

Photo 23. Simplicity is often an attribute of great associations of perennials. Tall pink tulips and short garden pinks (*Phlox subulata*) harmonize quietly and gracefully against a plain white garage wall at Grace Rose's home. The composition would not be complete without the spiky spray of daylily leaves to the left of the tulips. Thus the compositional elements are reduced to three and the color scheme to pinks and greens.

Photo 22

Photo 23

And yet this simple scene speaks clearly to the viewer of Grace's well-tuned artistry and sensitivity, as well as her horticultural talents.

Photo 24. Speaking of simplicity, although this association of three perennials in Grace's garden is only a couple of feet in breadth, it's a deft harmonization of colors and a perfect example of the color grouping strategy (see chaper 3). The light pinkish lavender of the five-petalled *Phlox divaricata* works perfectly with the deep violet of *Ajuga reptans*. These are gaily interspersed with the tiny, white, fragrant flowers of *Asperula odorata* (sweet woodruff).

Photo 24

Photo 25

Photo 26

Photo 25. Certain flowers carry color harmonies in their genes. Here *Anemone blanda*—the windflower—opens flowers that range from light violet to pink to light magenta. When color harmonies occur among flowers of the same plant, as with these windflowers in Martha Barnett's garden in southeastern Pennsylvania, it's best to surround them with greens and neutral colors so they can show off by themselves. Worked into a group of other flowers, they would lose their delicate, yet profound, impact.

Photo 26. In Martha's garden, we see a small tower of violet-flowered *Ajuga reptans* protruding through leaves of *Convallaria majalis* (lily-of-the-valley). The cheerful note of the ajuga is picked up and sounded again by the white bells of lily-of-the-valley. For an added treat, catch the scent of the white bells, which smell so sweet. Don't be tempted to put them in your mouth, however, for convallaria is poisonous. Both ajuga and lily-of-the-valley make excellent ground covers.

Photo 27

Photo 28

Photo 27. Many perennials will die out if planted directly above the roots of trees, mostly because trees take the lion's share of the soil moisture. But hostas find a real home in just such a difficult place and are often used to cover the ground beneath large trees, as Martha has done in her garden with *Hosta crispula* and Christmas fern (*Polystichum acrostichoides*). The hostas also visually tie the tree trunk to the garden, dressing it up with a green and white ruff.

Photo 28. A subdued color scheme can still be dramatic as shown by this weather-bleached conch shell holding bronze-leaved hens and chicks (*Sempervivum* species). The shells are placed against the bole of a large white birch, its varied bark textures setting off the chalky, smooth white of the shells and reddish color of the sempervivums. In the foreground, moss provides a dark green that doesn't conflict with the quiet harmonies behind it.

Photo 29. May is an exuberant time of year. As we were leaving Martha's garden, we noticed a specimen of *Cypripedium calceolus* var. *pubescens* (yellow lady's slipper) growing by her neighbor's house. A member of the orchid family, the yellow lady's slipper is a native woodland wildflower, although it's so showy that people have tended to eliminate it by picking and digging it up to bring home. Lady's slipper is not an easy plant to transplant, by any means, and it's fussy about its conditions, but where it finds a home, it's as beautiful and strange as a life form from another world.

Photo 29

MAY FLOWERS

BLUE *Ajuga genevensis, A. pyramidalis, A. reptans, Centaurea montana, Geranium himalayense, Iris cristata, I. germanica* hybrids, *Linum narbonense, L. perenne, Mazus reptans, Myosotis alpestris, M. scorpioides, M. sylvatica, Phlox divaricata, P. stolonifera, P. subulata, Polemonium caeruleum, Primula polyantha* hybrids, *Veronica prostrata, Viola cornuta*

ORANGE *Geum borisii, G. chiloense, Iris germanica* hybrids

PINK *Antennaria dioica, Armeria maritima, Cypripedium acaule, Dianthus allwoodii* hybrids, *D. deltoides, D. gratianopolitanus, D. plumarius, Dicentra formosa, D. spectabilis, Geranium sanguineum, G. sinereum, Geum rivale, Heuchera sanguinea, Heucherella alba, Incarvillea delavayi, Iris germanica* hybrids, *Phlox subulata, Primula japonica, P. polyantha* hybrids, *Saponaria ocymoides*

PURPLE *Allium aflatunense, Iris germanica* hybrids, *Primula japonica, Thalictrum aquilegifolium, Verbena rigida*

RED *Armeria maritima, Dianthus deltoides, D. gratianopolitanus, D. plumarius, Geranium sanguineum, Geum chiloense, Heuchera sanguinea, Iris germanica* hybrids, *Lychnis viscaria, Paeonia officinalis, P. tenuifolia, Phlox subulata, Primula japonica, P. polyantha* hybrids, *Viola cornuta*

WHITE *Achillea ageratifolia, Aegopodium podagraria, Anemone sylvestris, Arenaria montana, Armeria maritima, Convallaria majalis, Dianthus allwoodii* hybrids, *D. deltoides, D. plumarius, Dicentra spectabilis, Epimedium youngianum, Geranium sanguineum, Heuchera sanguinea, Iberis sempervirens, Iris germanica* hybrids, *Mazus reptans, Phlox subulata, Polemonium caeruleum, Polygonatum biflorum, Primula japonica, P. polyantha* hybrids, *Tiarella cordifolia, Viola cornuta*

YELLOW *Allium moly, Anthemis biebersteiniana, Chrysogonum virginianum, Corydalis lutea, Cypripedium calceolus, Epimedium pinnatum, Geum chiloense, Iris germanica* hybrids, *Lamiastrum galeobdolon, Potentilla verna, Primula polyantha* hybrids, *Trollius europaeus, Viola cornuta*

June

Photo 30. After dainty May come the *Hurrays*! of June. It's not hard to plan for a crescendo of color during this month—in fact, it's almost impossible to avoid one. The palette is no longer limited, except by the gardener. Some of the best-loved perennials bloom now, including these at White Flower Farm in Litchfield, Connecticut.

A misty, moisty morning in June softens the sunlight of this clever landscape.

The slope at left is bordered with several fine evergreen specimens alternating their green, gold, and blue boughs. In the foreground, the slope has been terraced with dry stone walls—laid without mortar.

Notice how the picket-fence jag of the house's roof line is repeated in the evergreens at the left and suggested again on the right by the light area that includes the street. In the left bed, Chinese peonies (*Paeonia lactiflora* hybrids) lead the eye back toward the focal point of the com-

Photo 30

position. The dark red cultivar in the foreground is 'Lowell Thomas'. Behind that is 'Nippon Gold', white with yellow centers. Farther back is the pure white 'Bowl of Cream'. The color scheme changes in the middle bed of oriental poppies (*Papaver orientale*). 'Curlilocks' is closest to the camera, followed by the pink and white variegated flowers of 'Pinnacle', with the darker 'Mahogany' behind them. In the lowest bed, several cultivars of tall bearded iris produce a gentle blue and yellow effect. The bed combines 'Debby Rairdon' (yellow), 'Sapphire Hills' (blue), 'Silver Shower' (white), and 'Golden Plunder' (yellow).

Photo 31. Someone with a good eye for subtle colors decided to put these bearded *Iris* ✕ *germanica* 'Pink Taffeta' in front of the oriental poppies in the background. The decision violated the so-called rules of color harmonics by mixing the delicate shell pink of the iris with the hard salmon-red of the poppies. But notice the "beards" of the irises: They are the same color as the poppies. Nature herself has struck the very same color harmony within one iris flower as the gardener has between the beds. And let's remember that it takes a good photographer to *see* this going on and to capture it on film for us.

Photo 32. With a white house in the background, the gardener was wise to choose a color scheme for the front border that includes a lot of white. White here is given by *Chrysanthemum leucanthemum,* the

long-lasting daisies. They are contrasted with deep violet *Iris sibirica* and accented with the light carmine-pink oriental poppies near the hedge. Tall white spires of biennial foxgloves are beginning to open in the back border. Notice the generous drifts and large clumps of flowers that are quite suited to a big border. Out of sight to the right is a large expanse of lawn, as would be expected with a border of this size.

Photo 31

Photo 32

Photo 33

Photo 33. Like an underwater scene from some heavenly ocean, the graceful flowers of *Aquilegia* 'McKana Hybrids' swim among the blossoming fronds of *Astilbe arendsii* 'Deutschland'. The lemon yellow anthers set off and tie together the violet and magenta association of the columbines. The petals of both colors of columbine eventuate in white, which then coordinates with the astilbe. Partial shade-loving plants like columbine and astilbe are usually seen against darker grounds than plants in full sun, and the colors seem more jewellike and suggestive for it.

Photo 34. Close harmony is achieved between the graceful arabesques of *Aquilegia* 'McKana Hybrids' and the magnificent lilac *Campanula lactiflora* in the background. This is a relatively tall association of plants, found in the June garden as the tall-growing plants have had enough time to reach blooming size.

Photo 35. Nearest the viewer are snowy white mounds of *Phlox arendsii* hybrids, accented with one of the bright pink *P. arendsii* cultivars. Contrasting in shape, but harmonizing softly in color, *Astilbe arend-*

Photo 34

Photo 35

sii hybrids hold their plumes aloft in the background, looking like snow-covered conifers in the pale pink dawn of a January day. If one were able to mix together the bright pink and white phlox colors, the resulting color would probably be close to the tone of the astilbes. This wonderful group of plants is rather low in maintenance, too, and will bloom together in a shady corner of the garden for many years.

Photo 36. Imagination and inspiration combine in a group of three sun-loving perennials at White Flower Farm. The overall color scheme is lilac and yellow, but the reddish flowers at lower left resolve it into a red, yellow, and blue triad. The strong lemon yellow, which will turn paler as the flowers age, is given by *Achillea taygetea* 'Moonshine'. The little lilac bells belong to a *Nepeta faassenii* hybrid, and the reddish, single, rose-like flowers with white centers are *Dianthus gratianopolitanus.* The achillea and nepeta together are wonderful, and, with the red note of the dianthus added, are superb.

Photo 37. Light magenta *Thymus serpyllum* (creeping thyme) tumbles over the stone stairs of a garden in the Rockies in June. Greenish yellow sedums and white-webbed sempervivums add to the charm. *Arenaria verna*'s mossy leaves and small white flowers cover the ground at the base of the steps. The plants in the rocks thrive where there are dry conditions, although they need a weekly soaking to look as lush as this group does.

Photo 38. A fine example of the dramatic effects of contrasting shapes while harmonizing colors is shown in this pho-

Photo 37

Photo 36

tograph. The round flower balls of *Allium giganteum* (a perennial ornamental onion) project up before a shaggy mass of *Aruncus dioicus* flowers. This is a very tall association of plants, about eye level for many gardeners, and so would be placed toward the back of the border or middle of the bed for best effect. Although the leaves of the allium aren't seen, they are typical of the onion family and also contrast well with the large-leaved, ferny foliage of the aruncus.

Photo 38

JUNE FLOWERS

BICOLOR *Gaillardia grandiflora* hybrids, *Hemerocallis* hybrids, *Lilium* hybrids, *Lupinus polyphyllus*

BLUE *Amsonia tabernaemontana, Anchusa azurea, Baptisia australis, Campanula carpatica, C. lactiflora, C. persicifolia, C. poscharskyana, C. rotundifolia, Catananche caerulea, Clematis integrifolia, Delphinium belladonna* hybrids, *D. elatum, D. grandiflorum, Erigeron speciosus, Geranium endressii, Iris kaempferi, I. sibirica, Lavandula angustifolia, Lupinus polyphyllus, Penstemon heterophyllus, Salvia haematodes, S. jurisicii, S. superba* hybrids, *Scabiosa caucasica, Tradescantia andersoniana, Veronica incana, V. latifolia, V. spicata*

ORANGE *Helianthemum nummularium, Hemerocallis fulva, H.* hybrids, *Lilium* hybrids, *Papaver orientale, Trollius ledebourii*

PINK *Astilbe arendsii, Campanula lactiflora, Chrysanthemum coccineum, Dianthus caryophyllus, Dictamnus fraxinella, Digitalis mertonensis* hybrids, *Erigeron speciosus, Filipendula palmata, F. rubra, Geranium endressii, Gypsophila paniculata, G. reptans, Helianthemum nummularium, Hemerocallis* hybrids, *Lavandula angustifolia, Lilium* hybrids, *Lupinus polyphyllus, Lychnis coronaria, Lythrum salicaria, Paeonia lactiflora* hybrids, *Papaver orientale, Penstemon barbatus, Potentilla nepalensis, Sempervivum tectorum, Thymus lanuginosus, T. serpyllum, Tradescantia andersoniana*

PURPLE *Allium giganteum, Aster frikartii, Astilbe arendsii, Campanula glomerata, Centaurea dealbata, Delphinium elatum, D. grandiflorum, Hemerocallis* hybrids, *Hesperis matronalis, Hosta venusta, Iris kaempferi, I. sibirica, Lavandula angustifolia, Lilium* hybrids, *Lupinus polyphyllus, Lythrum salicaria, Nepeta faassenii* hybrids, *Penstemon barbatus, Thymus serpyllum, Tradescantia andersoniana*

(continued)

JUNE FLOWERS—*Continued*

RED *Acanthus perringii, Achillea millefolium, Astilbe arendsii, Chrysanthemum coccineum, Dianthus caryophyllus, Helianthemum nummularium, Hemerocallis hybrids, Iris kaempferi, I. sibirica, Lilium hybrids, Lupinus polyphyllus, Lychnis chalcedonica, Paeonia lactiflora hybrids, Papaver orientale, Penstemon barbatus, P. gloxinioides hybrids, Rheum palmatum, Sedum sieboldii, Thymus serpyllum, Tradescantia andersoniana, Veronica spicata*

WHITE *Achillea millefolium, A. ptarmica, Aruncus dioicus, Astilbe arendsii, Campanula carpatica, C. glomerata, Cerastium tomentosum, Chrysanthemum coccineum, C. maximum, C. parthenium, Clematis recta, Delphinium belladonna hybrids, D. elatum, D. grandiflorum, Dianthus caryophyllus, Dictamnus fraxinella, Filipendula ulmaria, F. vulgaris, Gypsophila paniculata, G. reptans, Helianthemum nummularium, Hesperis matronalis, Iris kaempferi, I. sibirica, Lilium candidum, L. hybrids, Lupinus polyphyllus, Paeonia lactiflora hybrids, Papaver orientale, Phlox carolina, Rodgersia aesculifolia, R. tabularis, Shortia galacifolia, Thymus serpyllum, Tradescantia andersoniana, Verbascum chaixii, Veronica spicata*

YELLOW *Achillea filipendulina, A. taygetea, A. tomentosa, Anthemis tinctoria, Chrysanthemum maximum, Coreopsis auriculata, C. grandiflora, C. lanceolata, Digitalis ambigua, Helianthemum nummularium, Heliopsis scabra, Hemerocallis flava, H. hybrids, Iris pseudacorus, Lilium hybrids, Linum flavum, Lupinis polyphyllus, Lysimachia nummularia, L. punctata, Oenothera missourensis, O. tetragona, Opuntia humifusa, Thermopsis caroliniana*

July

Photo 39. A grand example of the color grouping strategy (see chapter 3) of creating a perennial bed basks in the late afternoon July sun at Sir John Thouron's Glencoe Farm near the Delaware-Pennsylvania state line.

Here we see the sweeping border of the great south lawn of this magnificent estate. Behind the border, on the right, a path twists among flowers, ornamental trees, and clumps of ornamental grasses. The border's gentle curve, resembling a stretch of beach along a sea of grass, carries the eye back to the dramatic dark ball of an evergreen, growing alone in the lawn. Notice how the border is made of many drifts, clumps, and patches, each containing many plants of the same cultivar for massed color effects.

Now that it's July, many of the early-flowering perennials have finished and will remain in declining foliage until they disappear. All through the border, clumps of August- and September-flowering plants are also all in foliage. Here and there, in pleasant and easy association, July-flowering plants

Photo 39

carry the midsummer colors. At left, edging the lawn, are the silvery leaves of *Stachys olympica,* or lamb's-ears. The purple drift in the middle is *Campanula glomerata.* The tall, unopened flower spikes at lower right are a form of ornamental mullein.

Photo 40. Familiar perennials, such as iris, phlox, campanula, and many others, have been bred over the years into dwarf forms or come in small, alpine forms that are particularly suited for rock gardens. These inviting stone steps have been made with areas of soil where some of the flagstones would ordinarily be, making it a rock garden as well as a staircase. Visitors cannot fail to be charmed, walking through a miniature garden of perennials as they climb the steps.

Photo 40

Photo 41

Photo 41. Some gardeners claim that the intense purple of *Campanula glomerata* and the equally intense magenta of the hardy geranium, or cranesbill, are hard to coordinate with other colors. In photo 41, the gardener has solved the problem of these two plants by putting them together. The campanula is in the foreground, with the cranesbill behind and to the right. The glaring colors are softened and subdued by the fancy accents of yellow-orange *Lilium hybrida* and palest pink *Oenothera rosea*.

This is a very clever treatment of colors that belong in the July garden but may be hard to fit in. It shows how a clashing color can relieve an intense dominant color.

Photo 42. Another brilliant July color, as shown in photo 42, is given by the Maltese cross, *Lychnis chalcedonica,* the vermilion, ball-shaped flower at the top of the picture. Iceland poppy, *Papaver nudicaule,* just below it, softens the searing vermilion into a yellow-orange and attenuates that to a sunny yellow in the center of its cup. The white Iceland poppy at bottom softens the yellow to a pale hint in the center of its cup and loses color altogether in its petals. Provid-

ing such artistic associations of plants for friends and neighbors to discover is the secret goal and heartfelt joy of perennial gardeners.

Photo 43. Mat-forming clusters of *Dianthus deltoides,* or maiden pinks, swarm below the taller, cooler, blue spires of *Veronica spicata* 'Nana'. While the subdued blue helps to cool down the hot pink, the association heightens the intensity of the

Photo 42

Photo 43

blue. Even though the veronica is closer to the camera than the dianthus, its blue recedes while the pink advances.

Photo 44. The hot magenta-pink of *Dianthus deltoides,* here seen in a soft band of color across the top of the photo, finds an exquisite association with the creamy petals of an annual, *Dimorphotheca sinuata,* which sends up a single, daisy-like blossom.

Although annuals are not covered in this book, they form a large group of colored plants for you to use in creating color harmonies. Because of their growing habit, annuals usually don't reach a bloom crescendo until midsummer, but the flowering then continues until frost.

Photo 45. July is the time for some spectacular single acts, as well as associations. Here the strange, mathematical, but

Photo 44

Photo 45

gorgeous flower balls of *Echinops* 'Taplow Blue' are given a place by themselves. This flower is also quite commonly seen in combinations, due to its soft, easy-to-harmonize color, its peculiar shape that lends interest to groups, and its artichoke-like foliage that contrasts well with other plants.

Photo 46. Another plant that carries plenty of color association within itself is the rose campion, *Lychnis coronaria.* No color could better harmonize with its brilliant cerise flowers than its own moss-soft,

grey-green leaves. Here it grows by itself in a corner of one of Glencoe Farm's flower beds, in a spot it obviously enjoys very much.

We use rose campion with the gentle grey-green of lamb's ears, and tumbling masses of faded-peach rock rose—a woody, trailing, flowering plant that stays evergreen under winter's snows. As this book is limited to herbaceous perennials, we've not listed the woody flowering shrubs, but they can add a great deal to any perennial garden, especially when they bloom in spring at taller heights not reached by the herbaceous flowers until summer.

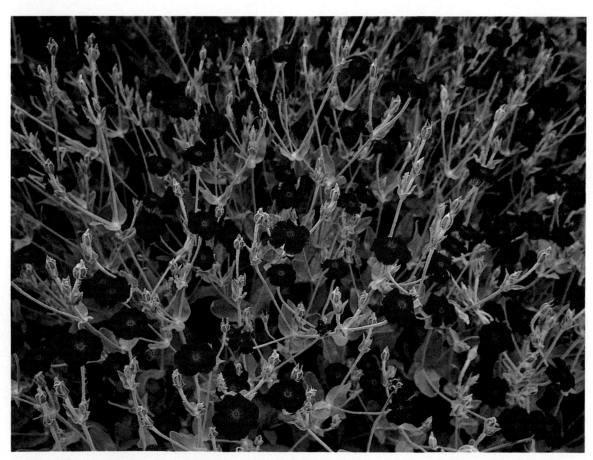

Photo 46

Photo 47. An area of tumbled rocks turns into a fantasy in color and form. A small stream flows down between the rocks and emerges in a pool at the bottom. Low-growing evergreens and prostrate woody perennials, such as Japanese maples, accentuate the diagonal at left, while combinations of annuals, perennials, sedums, ferns, and shrubs soften the tangled lines of the rocks and pull the picture together.

The scene was created by gardeners to take advantage of a natural stream that coursed down this hillside. Although the scene was created by human beings, it does not look forced or unnatural.

Photo 48. An extraordinary color arrangement appears from unexpected elements. Small and dainty *Helianthemum nummularium* sprinkles the foreground with rose and salmon blossoms. Rocks separate it from the grey-green leaves and blue spires of *Veronica spicata* 'Nana', which itself edges a harmonious blue spruce. The foreground color is pulled through the veronica-spruce passage by the tall *Lupinus* 'Russell Hybrids' in the background, tying the picture together. This photo shows the creativity of a great perennials gardener, who used only four plants to make a bold, and yet delicate, statement.

Photo 47

Photo 48

Photo 49. To show what a simple flower border can do, just imagine this yard if the grass ran all the way to the fence. Martha Barnett, instead, has anchored the back of her property with a succession of beautiful combinations from spring until fall. *Echinops* 'Taplow Blue' is here in the July border in the very foreground. Its dusty blue spheres flank the bright yellow of *Hemerocallis* 'Tawny Gold' at the front of the border, with *Heliopsis scabra* 'Summer Sun' abutting the fence. A group of *Monarda didyma* 'Adam' in scarlet follows. The tall pinkish spikes at top center are *Lythrum salicaria* 'Morden Pink'.

Photo 49

Photo 50. Lythrum salicaria 'Morden Pink' leans out from the back of this walled border at the right side of the picture. Bright yellow *Coreopsis* 'Goldfink' grows just below it, also at the very right. The light, faded yellow to the left of the lythrum is *Achillea taygetea* 'Moonshine', and just above it are the upright, pale yellow trumpets of *Lilium* 'Edith'. The July garden is mostly green, yet there's hardly a lack of color. The overall color scheme is yellow and lavender, accented with the spot of bright orange in the background provided by *Lilium* 'Pirate'.

Notice that the dry wall is a simple arrangement of three courses of blocky native stone with a profusion of flowers above and the simple, spare look of the grass below. This border would not be nearly as effective visually if the dry wall were edged with low-growing flowers at grass level, as the plants would break up the clean, containing line of the wall.

This photo of Grace Rose's border illustrates many of the principles of creating a satisfying border of perennials. The choice of plants shows a nice gradation in size from

Photo 50

Photo 51

in smaller groups. At the center of the photo, for instance, is an interesting group of blue, white, and pink plants. Let's take a closer look.

Photo 51. An appropriate red, white, and blue centerpiece theme for Grace's July border is softly suggested by the blue bells of *Campanula persicifolia* 'Telham Beauty', its sister *C. persicifolia* 'Grandiflora Alba', and *Achillea millefolium* 'Red Beauty'.

Photo 52. The cool white petals of *Platycodon grandiflorus* 'Alba' carry thin violet highlights along their center ridges. It's this violet that's dominant in other varieties of this useful and long-lasting plant.

Photo 52

the small clumps along the wall to the tall perennials in back. These are placed in front of the dense, dark background given by close plantings of evergreen trees. The border is planted in drifts and clumps of perennials that start blooming in April and don't stop until fall. And yet at a given season—here July—the plants that are blooming form a pleasing harmonization of color overall and

Photo 53

Photo 54

Photo 53. A soft, subdued combination of graceful plants includes the blushing *Lilium hybrida* 'Embarrassment' and the reddish puffs of *Filipendula rubra* 'Venusta'. Notice how the red-brown anthers of the lilies find a counterpart in the spots on the petals, and a harmonious association in the deep tones of the filipendula flower heads.

Photo 54. Achillea taygetea 'Moonshine' has colonized this spot in the border, but is getting a welcome challenge from the elongating flower spikes of *Veronica spicata.* Soon the veronica will open its blue-violet flowers to sing bass to the achillea's soprano.

Photo 55

Photo 55. Because of its soft yellow, which goes so well with so many different plants, *Achillea taygetea* 'Moonshine' has become one of the all-time perennial-garden favorites. Here it's grown with a dazzling clump of yellow *Lilium hybrida* and emphasizes, but in no way interferes with, the lilies' truthful yellow.

Photo 56. A perfect match and a close color harmony is created with this superb planting of *Hemerocallis* 'Gusto' with *Astilbe* 'Red Sentinel'. The arching spears of the daylily leaves also mix well with the ferny bushes of the astilbes. Without the blazing yellow centers and pinstripes of the hemerocallis, the dull reds and greens would be far less arresting an association.

Photo 56

Photo 57

steiger at the Rodale Research Center in Maxatawny, Pennsylvania.

Photo 59. Another variation of orange and yellow is found in this combination of orange Butterfly Weed (*Asclepias tuberosus*) with the bright yellow daisies of heliopsis. Butterfly Weed is native to eastern North America and grows well in much of the country. It's a taprooted plant, however, and doesn't transplant very easily.

Photo 58

Photo 57. Like an assortment of flavored French pastilles, a mixture of *Hemerocallis* cultivars shows a little of the range of wonderful colors available to the gardener. Although most often these colors are grouped into discrete clumps, I always find the confetti effect charming.

Notice that the gardener has violated a cardinal rule of daylily culture. The rule admonishes us to plant them so that the viewer stands to the south, since they turn their flowers to the sun. These blossoms are facing away from the path.

Photo 58. Rich oranges can keynote many July color schemes, especially when used with annuals. Here orange *Lilium hybrida* and yellow calendulas erupt in the flower border created by Eileen Wein-

Photo 59

JULY FLOWERS

BICOLOR *Aconitum napellus*

BLUE *Aconitum napellus, Adenophora confusa, Echinops ritro, Eryngium amethystinum, Gentiana asclepiadea, G. septemfida, Limonium latifolium, Perovskia atriplicifolia, Phlox paniculata, Platycodon grandiflorus, Stokesia laevis, Veronica longifolia*

ORANGE *Asclepias tuberosa, Belamcanda chinensis, Ligularia dentata, Lilium canadense, Phlox paniculata*

PINK *Althaea rosea, Echinacea purpurea, Hibiscus moscheutos, Lathyrus latifolius, Monarda didyma, Phlox paniculata, Platycodon grandiflorus, Sidalcea malviflora, Teucrium chamaedrys, Tunica saxifraga*

PURPLE *Hosta sieboldiana, H. undulata, Liatris spicata, Monarda didyma, Phlox paniculata, Thalictrum rochebrunianum*

RED *Althaea rosea, Centranthus ruber, Hibiscus moscheutos, Lilium tigrinum, Lobelia cardinalis, Monarda didyma, Phlox paniculata*

WHITE *Aconitum napellus, Althaea rosea, Anaphalis yedoensis, Cimicifuga racemosa, Echinacea purpurea, Echinops ritro, Hibiscus moscheutos, Lysimachia clethroides, Macleaya cordata, Monarda didyma, Phlox paniculata, Platycodon grandiflorus, Stokesia laevis, Valeriana officinalis, Yucca filamentosa*

YELLOW *Althaea rosea, Centaurea macrocephala, Coreopsis verticillata, Inula ensifolia, Rudbeckia fulgida, Ruta graveolens, Thalictrum speciosissimum*

August

By August, the spring gardening fever has entirely worn off. The days are hot and languid, and swimming seems a better choice than gardening. It is just at this time of year, when so many gardens are losing the battle to weeds and rank growth, that Fred and Mary Anne McGourty have planned some spectacular displays of color harmonies using mostly low-maintenance perennials on their property in Connecticut.

Fred has been seriously developing his gardens in Connecticut for about eight years. His work has inspired many others to give as much importance to the mixture of leaf textures as to flower color. His plantings don't lack on either score.

He groups lavenders, pinks, reds, and blues, keeping them separate from oranges mixed with reds and yellows. For separation, he uses silver-foliaged plants, white or blue flowers, or sometimes pale yellow and chartreuse. "I don't think there's a bad color," he said, but acknowledges that there are bad color combinations. Fred and Mary Anne have avoided any of these, as our photos show.

Photo 60

Photo 60. With the McGourty house in the background, a stunning combination of *Phlox* 'Bright Eyes' and *Echinacea* 'Bressingham' greets visitors. The cosmetic pink of the echinacea's daisy-like flower harmonizes with, but doesn't copy, the more straightforward pink of the phlox.

Photo 61

Photo 62

Photo 61. A good example of the McGourty passion for contrast in leaf texture within the bounds of color harmony is found in his arrangement of the pale blue-green sprays of blue oat grass (*Helictotrichon sempervirens*) with the green-reddish-tan colors of *Sedum spurium.* The small flowers of the sedum are strawberry red when young, making perfect accents for the color of the grass. Additionally, the graceful arcs of the grass leaves convey simplicity,

elegance, and serenity, while the busy little leaves of the sedum convey opulence and complexity.

Photo 62. There's a quiet, pretty beauty to the *Stokesia laevis* in the foreground that contrasts well with the flaring, white-edged swords of *Iris pallida* in the background. Two clumps of the iris flank a small *Artemisia stellerana* of a similar grey-green color. Harmonies, contrast, dramatizations—all are packed into an unassuming group in a few square feet of a garden.

Photo 63. Two very popular perennials congregate by a rock wall. The large, yellow-edged leaves are those of *Hosta sieboldiana* 'Frances Williams', rated as the most popular hosta of all by the American Hosta Society. Beside it are the emerging floral bouquets of *Sedum* 'Autumn Joy'. Its florets are green in August, but within a month will turn a dusky rose, then a darker reddish pink, then a reddish brown, before finally falling to the frosts. As 'Autumn Joy' changes color, it will reveal unsuspected harmonies beside the yellow and green of 'Frances Williams'. Although 'Autumn Joy' does produce flower heads, it's the combination of foliage that carries the scene elegantly through the summer months.

Photo 64. If the Queen of August were to have a bower, it would lie beneath this magnificent white hydrangea pruned into a high, spreading tree behind a drift of *Astilbe chinensis* 'Pumila'. Notice how the ferns on the right continue the form of the astilbe fronds. Along the wall in front of these are the fan-shaped leaves of *Alchemilla mollis,* or lady's mantle.

Photo 65. Blowsy stars of *Anemone hupehensis* nod above the pink spires of *Astilbe chinensis* 'Pumila'. A clump of Shasta daisies strikes a brighter note in the background. The rose-like anemone blossoms couldn't be more different than the astilbes' soft tufts, and yet their cotton-candy pinks match perfectly. As the photo shows, an August garden can glorify the lushness of late summer.

Photo 63

Photo 64

Photo 65

Photo 66. A green fountain decorates a quiet corner of the McGourty property. The planting is anchored by 8-foot-tall *Miscanthus sinensis* 'Giganteus'. The light green spray in front of it is *M. sinensis* 'Variegatus'. At left, between these two ornamental grasses, a clump of *M. sinensis* 'Zebrinus' tosses its striped leaves upward. The wall gives a horizontal, settled feeling to the composition, which without it would be all upward and outward motion. The severe horizontal of the wall is broken in turn by the carefully placed fern.

Photo 67. Foliage types in an exciting mixture are accented by the bold red of *Lobelia cardinalis* in the center. The grape-like or maple-like leaves at ten o'clock belong to *Kirengeshoma palmata*, a member of the Saxifrage family that will put forth

Photo 66

Photo 67

Photo 68

yellow blossoms in September. The extra-large leaf at twelve o'clock is *Rodgersia tabularis*. At one and two o'clock are the small leaves of *Thalictrum aquilegifolium*, named because its leaves resemble those of the columbine. The white-edged plant at three and four o'clock is *Disporum sessile* 'Variegatum', and from five to nine, we see the mottled leaves of *Pulmonaria saccharata*.

Photo 68. The almost spent, but still beautiful, flower spikes of *Cimicifuga racemosa* rise like fireworks above a storybook mixture of yellow *Heliopsis scabra* 'Gold Greenheart', *Echinops* 'Taplow Blue', and a pink *Phlox paniculata* hybrid. The scene is enjoyed by the faunlike statue whose grey surface adds another dimension to the association of colors.

Notice that the deep shade of a large evergreen was chosen as a backdrop for the tall white cimicifuga. If its spikes were set against a bright sky, much of their bold effect would be lost.

Photo 69. Sometimes bright yellow is quite enough, all by itself. This drift of *Heliopsis helianthoides* (often found as *H. scabra* 'Karat' in catalogs) creates a golden riot atop a quiet stone wall. Its bright bluish green leaves make the perfect foil for its flowers. Here the gardener is saying that

more is probably going to be less and has kept his planting isolated.

Photo 70. Wise application of gardening knowledge is evident everywhere in this photo of Fred McGourty's property. For instance, consider the use of distance. There's a well-defined foreground, which contains yellow potentilla and white Shasta daisies. The sinuous line of a glacier-worn rock sets off similarly shaped drifts of golden rudbeckia and red *Monarda didyma* in the middle of the picture. The yellow and red

Photo 69

Photo 70

theme is repeated, but intensified, in the far background, where we see a splash of sunshine-yellow *Heliopsis helianthoides* 'Incomparabilis' and a vivid red-pink given by *Phlox paniculata* 'Starfire'.

Strong and coherent diagonal, horizontal, and vertical lines make a masterful composition, using trees, shrubs, rocks, and perennials as design elements.

Photo 71. In this photo, bright yellows tie together the daisy-like *Rudbeckia fulgida* 'Pinwheel' and the hot vermilion bells of *Crocosmia pottsii.* These both gain intensity and charm from the turquoise leaves of the crocosmia beneath the flowers. The rudbeckia gives a radial movement to the association, while the crocosmia gives graceful, reverse curves. Together they resemble fireworks: the bursting skyrocket of the rudbeckia, and the crocosmia like a string of firecrackers.

Photo 71

AUGUST FLOWERS

BICOLOR *Kniphofia uvaria*

BLUE *Ceratostigma plumbaginoides, Clematis heracleifolia, Lobelia siphilitica*

ORANGE *Kniphofia uvaria*

PINK *Anemone vitifolia, Aster novae-angliae, Astilbe chinensis, A. taquetii, Chelone lyonii, Kniphofia uvaria, Physostegia virginiana, Sedum spectabile* hybrids

PURPLE *Aster novae-angliae, Eupatorium coelestinum, Hosta albomarginata, H. decorata, H. fortunei, H. lancifolia, H. ventricosa, Liatris pycnostachya, L. scariosa, Liriope muscari, L. spicata, Thalictrum delavayi*

RED *Aster novae-angliae, Helenium autumnale, Physostegia virginiana*

WHITE *Boltonia asteroides, Hosta plantaginea, Kniphofia uvaria, Liatris scariosa, Physostegia virginiana*

YELLOW *Helenium autumnale, Helianthus multiflorus* hybrids, *Kniphofia uvaria, Ligularia stenocephala, Rudbeckia laciniata, Santolina chamaecyparissus, S. virens, Solidago* hybrids

September

If you have a thriving vegetable garden on your property, the mammoth pumpkins approaching ripeness, the corn, onions, peppers, squash and beans—as well as the tomatoes and melons—will be pouring forth, stealing the show from the flower gardens. Let the show be stolen! Harvest is here, the cold weather's coming, and it's time to add a few guilt-free pounds for a little winter insulation.

Photo 72. Sic transit gloria mundi. The tendency in September is for plants to make seed fast, and the blazing drifts of August begin to burn down to brownish embers. And yet, there's no lack of beauty in the September border. Annuals are now usually in full bloom, as seen in the gold *Zinnia augustifolia* in the foreground of this scene.

Behind the zinnias, the red and yellow blooms of *Gaillardia grandiflora* are opening faster in the cooler weather, and behind them the feathery green foliage of *Coreopsis verticillata* with its lemon-yellow blossoms is even more beautiful for being thick and bushy. A small drift of blue *Lobelia siphilitica* intervenes, and behind the coreopsis is an almost-finished drift of *Rudbeckia* 'Goldsturm'. This is partially overlapped from behind by the tall *Filipendula rubra* 'Venusta', whose flowers have gone

Photo 72

to seed. These are bordered with still-green ornamental grasses, culminating in an 8-foot spray of *Miscanthus sinensis* 'Giganteus'.

Photo 73

Photo 74

Photo 73. Some perennials achieve their greatest beauty when they set seed. The upper right side of this picture is dominated by dripping sprays of *Artemisia lactiflora* going to seed in a greenish white haze. Sir John Thouron has here set a group of annual *Cosmos sulphureus* against the artemisia's spectacle.

Photo 74. The season of fruit and seed has special rewards for the gardener. Here the orange hips of *Rosa rubrifolia* dangle beneath its reddish green foliage. Below, a white cranesbill opens a single, late flower.

Photo 75. The rock garden and pool at Sir John Thouron's estate return to green in September after a summer of colorful

Photo 75

Photo 76

successions. *Sedum* 'Autumn Joy' strikes the red-brown note in the foreground. Although most of the perennials are now entirely foliage, bright flowers continue to appear here and there. Notice the evergreens once again taking over the job of leading the eye through the scene, a task which had been performed by flower colors during the spring and summer months.

Photo 76. Of course, fall has its own special, fiery climax waiting in the asters and chrysanthemums. These yellow and orange chrysanthemums were caught being rowdy in a September garden in Spokane, Washington.

SEPTEMBER FLOWERS

BICOLOR *Chrysanthemum morifolium* hybrids

BLUE *Aconitum carmichaelii, Aster novi-belgii, Salvia pitcheri*

ORANGE *Chrysanthemum morifolium* hybrids

PINK *Anemone japonica, Aster novi-belgii, Chrysanthemum morifolium* hybrids

PURPLE *Aster novi-belgii, Chrysanthemum morifolium* hybrids

RED *Aster novi-belgii, Chrysanthemum morifolium* hybrids

WHITE *Anemone japonica, Aster novi-belgii, Chrysanthemum morifolium* hybrids

YELLOW *Chrysanthemum morifolium* hybrids

October–November

Although few plants start to bloom in this final period of the gardening year, many are continuing bloom begun in earlier periods. The frosts bring their own colors now: dark browns and blacks in tissue that has died back, a darker green down among the tall, spent grasses. The crickets are big and fat in their tumbled-down lairs of summer's seedy wreckage. But above the falling plants, flowers still appear and blaze as brightly as ever. Now the sunlight takes on a steely cold glint, which accentuates the colors that turn the fall woods, fields, and gardens to flame.

Photo 77. Fluffy, lavender tufts of hardy ageratum (*Eupatorium ageratoides*) at the extreme lower left of the photo announce the wonderful masses of pink and purple chrysanthemums that flow down the border. Color-harmonized annual petunias line the front of the border, and hostas edge the chrysanthemums behind. A clump of grey-green dianthus edges the bricks at bottom

Photo 77

Photo 78

center. Despite the lateness of the year, this garden looks as fresh and flower-filled as a June border.

Photo 78. The pink stars of dwarf *Aster novi-belgii* bloom in October near the gnarled stump of an old tree. Here they're accented with pale blue perennial flax (*Linum perenne*). The flax had been blooming since May at this spot near our home in Berks County, Pennsylvania, and nature had obviously saved the best for last. Shortly after this photo was taken, there was a killing frost.

Photo 79. In October and November, the garden suddenly loses its borders, and the wide world becomes one vast garden of color associations. The flaming trees get most of the attention during this period, but

Photo 79

Photo 80

perennial gardeners—always on the look-out for fine color combinations—should keep an eye on the fields. We found this exquisite group of fringed gentians hobnobbing with the fluffy sprays of golden solidago, or gol-denrod, in a roadside field just a mile from home. Both solidago and gentian have cul-tivated species available to perennial gar-deners through catalogs.

Photo 80. Who is the gardener that put together such a lovely and simple associa-tion as these asters and goldenrod, both wild species that chanced to bloom together along the roadside by our house in October? Mere mortals can work the soil, set out their plants, and hope to realize their dreams, but this gardener dreams, and it is fully realized.

Our gardens, after all, only reproduce the profligate beauty we see in the wild around us. And then not always success-fully. But as this photo shows, we need only turn to nature to find the source of inspi-ration, to try again come spring, to keep edging toward more beauty, until finally our gardens are as beautiful as the world that encloses them.

CHAPTER 5

Featured Players in the Perennial Garden

This chapter highlights 21 genera of perennials, chosen because each of them plays a featured role in almost every garden of perennials. Each comes in widely varying forms and colors. Many of them have national societies devoted to their appreciation and horticulture. Many of them have several excellent characteristics, such as long periods of bloom, good foliage, exquisite color variations, and low maintenance. These are garden mainstays that deserve a closer look.

This chapter also focuses on four groups of perennials that include more than one genus, all finding extensive use in most fine gardens. The four plant groups are:

• Bulbs. Although bulbs come in many forms and colors and bloom during most seasons, they all need much the same kind of treatment.

• Ferns. These feathery-leaved beauties afford foliage contrast with flowering plants.

• Grasses. The use of ornamental grasses is a fast-developing trend in perennial gardening that is sure to become part of the classic approach.

• Sedums and sempervivums. Both these varied genera are succulents and are used as fillers along rock walls and by themselves for their interesting foliage, and in the case of tall sedums, their flowers.

Achillea (Yarrow)

Achillea is one of the perennials that can rescue a barren, dry area and cover it with bloom. Most of us are familiar with roadside yarrow (also called milfoil). This common species is usually a dingy white color, although I've found pink ones growing wild, too. From the dry Southwest to the poor soils of the Southeast, and all the way north, *Achillea* species abound.

There are over 200 species of this plant, most of which were originally native to Europe and Asia and came here—along with so many other European plants—when early settlers dumped the earth ballast from their ships on colonial American shores. There are also native species, such as *Achillea lanulosa.* Of this welter of species, about 20 are grown for their flowers, and of these, only a handful are important to gardeners.

There are both low-growing and tall species, and they range in color from white through pink, rose, red, lavender, bluish pink, bright yellow, pastel yellow, and various shades of muted golds.

A thousand years ago, achillea growing in England was called *gaerwe* by the Anglo-Saxons, who would have pronounced it YAHR-way. The Old English word meant "healer." Legend says that Achilles, the Greek hero of the Trojan War, used its crushed

Achillea

leaves to stanch the bleeding of his troops' wounds on the recommendation of the centaur Chiron. Yarrow is still used as an astringent.

Some people use poultices of yarrow leaves to hurry the healing of bruises. The plant's herbal aroma will persist for a while when the flower stalks and heads are dried, making a dried bouquet a double treat. Yarrow has enjoyed other medicinal uses, too, and for a time in the nineteenth century, it was listed in the U.S. Pharmacopeia as a tonic, stimulant, and emmenagogue. Although not considered poisonous, some people are allergic to yarrow, and today it's listed as a plant to avoid for medicinal purposes.

Yarrow has a long history in many countries. In England, it was woven into bridal wreaths. Young girls who wished to dream of their future lovers would put a sprig under their pillows. Necromancers in medieval England used it for divination, a practice that inspired one of its nicknames:

devil's plaything. The ancient Chinese *I Ching,* the famous oracular book, still describes how to use yarrow stalks when consulting the oracle.

Achillea is an easy plant to divide, as new growth comes readily from rhizomes taken in the spring when they are budding. Scientists have discovered that pieces of the plants' rhizomes about 1 to 1½ inches long produce more viable buds than longer rhizomes, and that growth is best when these root pieces are planted 1 to 1½ inches deep. The soil should be kept moist until the rhizome cuttings grow new feeder roots, but after the plants are established, achillea is one of the most drought-resistant perennials. In fact, it's a good plant for areas of poor or dry soil. When wild achillea is kept mowed, such as in a meadow, mats of the plant will stay green during dry spells when lawn grass turns dry and brown. Achillea planted from seed often shows interesting color variations and will flower in the second year.

Rusts and powdery mildew can sometimes show up on these plants, but can be controlled with elemental sulfur dust. Galls, caused by a nematode, *Anguina millefolii,* occasionally show up on leaves, stems, and flowers. If you see these, cut or pull the plants. The nematode larvae inside the galls disperse by wind when the galls dry out, so letting infected plants stand can spread the problem.

If you have trouble growing achillea, it's most likely because your soil is too wet. Plant it on high, dry spots.

One of yarrow's nicest features is that, after peak bloom during late spring or early summer, it will continue to produce occasional flower heads until frost, especially if summer's spent flowers are nicked off. Achillea forms solid patches in the garden and takes no special care or feeding. Just make sure it gets plenty of sun—it may stay too moist in the shade, where it's not at home. Also, the stems will be weaker and may not stay erect through the winter, where the plants are grown with insufficient sunlight.

Some of the species offered in catalogs include *Achillea ageratifolia,* named for its ageratum-like foliage. This is a good rock garden plant. Like all achilleas, it likes sunny and dry conditions, and this species has light, silvery foliage that grows less than a foot tall.

Achillea filipendulina is a taller plant, rising to 3 feet above its lacy, feathery foliage. Its golden or mustard-colored flowers are superb in dried arrangements.

Achillea millefolium is the wild yarrow most of us are familiar with. It stands about 2 feet high and comes in rose, bright red, and white cultivars.

Achillea ptarmica produces very double white flowers. Its leaves aren't typical of the yarrows, being dark green and smooth.

One of our favorites is *Achillea taygetea* 'Moonshine'. This cultivar grows 1½ to 2 feet tall and looks neat and tidy in the garden. Its flowers are a light yellow that becomes even more beautiful when it dries to a pale dusty yellow. *A. tomentosa* is a short plant, with a mat-forming habit and a height of only 6 inches. Its leaves are broad and woolly. This species also makes an excellent rock garden specimen, where its greyish green leaves set off the richer, darker, more succulent leaves of other rock garden or alpine plants.

Aquilegia (Columbine)

Among nature's marvels is the form of a columbine flower. To the ancient Romans, the flower looked like a covey of birds scattering upward, and so they named it after *columbae,* the Latin word for doves. The etymology of the plant's botanical Latin name is less certain, although *aquila* is Latin for eagle, whose talons the spurs may resemble, and *aquilegus* means water-drawing, which the plant certainly does with its long roots.

The spurs that make the flowers so graceful and attractive are reservoirs of nectar for long-tongued pollinators, such as bumblebees, hawkmoths, and hummingbirds. In fact, native populations of aquilegia in the United States show spur differentiation that some scientists believe developed to fit the tongue length of their primary pollinator.

The two most common native species are *Aquilegia canadensis*—small plants with

Three varieties of hybrid Aquilegia

short-spurred red and yellow flowers—and *A. caerulea*—the Rocky Mountain columbine, with long spurs and blue and white flowers. *A. canadensis* is found throughout the United States, while *A. caerulea* grows wild from the Rockies to the Sierra Nevadas in California, and south to Mexico in the highlands. In certain places, these species' boundaries overlap, and hybrids are sometimes found. Despite complete fertility between species, mass hybridization in the wild isn't found. The species keep their integrity, some think, because *A. canadensis* is pollinated by hummingbirds that don't visit *A. caerulea,* and *A. caerulea* by moths and bumblebees that don't visit the short-spurred *A. canadensis.*

The popular 'McKana Hybrids' offered widely in seed catalogs were created by interbreeding *Aquilegia caerulea, A. longissima, A. chrysantha, A. canadensis,* and *A. vulgaris* in almost infinite permutations. These hybrids have long spurs and large flowers on tall stalks.

Because *Aquilegia caerulea* evolved in the area extending from the southern Rockies down to the arid mountains of northern Mexico, it can live in sandy, poor soil, although it will grow best for the gardener in good garden soil with adequate moisture. You could try planting the native Rocky Mountain columbine in a part of the garden with problem soil, however, to see if you can take advantage of the plant's high-country heritage. *A. canadensis,* because it evolved in the North American woodlands, likes a richer, moist, humusy soil. The hybrids of these two native species—the kind most often found in gardens—like any good, well-drained garden soil. Although columbines grow in full sun, they really prefer the dappled shade that recalls their forest and mountain homes.

Occasionally aphid populations will build up on certain plants, but syrphid fly larvae eat aphids, while the adults have been seen to jam themselves down into the long flower spurs to reach the nectar. These beneficial insects should be encouraged in the garden, so unless the aphids are destroying the plants, I'd let them alone and hope they attract syrphid flies, ladybird beetles, and other aphid predators. If the aphid herds are being managed by ants, however, you may want to wash the aphids off the plants with a strong jet of water from a hose, as the ants will vigilantly protect their herds from predators.

Leaf miners can be a problem with columbine. They form squiggly lines of eaten-away tissue on the leaves. We find that miners prefer the spinach, chard, and beet leaves in the vegetable garden and only nibble at our columbines. Regular handpicking and destruction of affected leaves will help reduce miner populations.

Columbines are very free about setting seed. The wild species come true to type only if there are no other columbines around for them to hybridize with. Because most of us can't resist having several kinds of these magnificent flowers, most home-grown seed makes hybrids with uninteresting colors. If you're planting McKana or other commercial hybrids, their gorgeous colors are almost sure to degenerate as the plants share pollen and mongrelize. To keep your plants true to type, it's worth the trouble to buy fresh commercial seed every two or three years and replant. Do it that often because individual columbine plants only last three years, then die out.

Aquilegia seed germinates best when it gets sixteen hours of darkness at 65°F followed by eight hours of light at 85°F. Under these ideal conditions, most seed will germinate in fifteen to twenty days. Under the typically cooler conditions in a cold frame or in germinating beds outside in the spring, it will take three to four weeks for the seeds to sprout. Plants grown from spring-sown seed won't ordinarily bloom until their second year. Fall-sown seed, where the plants can overwinter in a cool greenhouse, will blossom the next spring.

Aquilegia is one of the few perennials of which you can hardly have enough. The plants flower in May or June, depending on your latitude, last for a few weeks, and then are gone. They're not plants to use for mass color effects because their flowers are rather sparse. We think of them as we do hummingbirds and beautifully marked insects—welcome wherever they alight in the garden. In combination, it's hard to beat columbines, astilbes, and perennial flax. Columbines are also beautiful when grown in regal isolation against dark backgrounds. You'll discover that it's hard to miss with them, no matter where they grow.

Artemisia (Wormwood)

The old man, also called southernwood, is an artemisia (*Artemisia abrotanum*). So's the old woman, dusty miller, (*A. stellerana*). So is tarragon, the herb used to flavor vinegar; and wormwood, the herb once used to make absinthe. Several kinds of western sagebrush are artemisias, and that gives the gardener a clue to where to plant their garden relatives: Artemisias favor dry, poor soils. It's their native habitat, whether on the high plains of North America or along the shores of the Mediterranean.

Most artemisias have greyish or silvery green foliage, which, in the garden, makes solid masses of muted, neutral color against which to play the bolder and deeper hues of perennial flowers. Whenever two areas of color need separating, think of artemisias. Wherever blue, lavender, purple, pink, or red flowers need an unusual and subtle partner, think of artemisias. And in problem spots with very dry or poor soil, you can halt erosion and add beauty with artemisias.

Our favorite association of plants last year came in October with a dark, oxblood scabiosa, a bluish pink phlox, dark burgundy and deep lavender chrysanthemums, a dark blue salvia, and *Artemisia ludoviciana* 'Silver King', with its small, silver leaves growing out of tall stems.

Equally good in that association—and maybe better—would have been *Artemisia schmidtiana* 'Silver Mound'. It's the same grey-green as 'Silver King', but its much finer, silvery foliage makes an interesting mound less than a foot tall.

'Silver King' and 'Silver Mound' are two essential foliage plants for the perennial garden. Both are herbaceous, dying back each winter, unlike many other artemisias that are shrubby.

Another important garden artemisia is *Artemisia lactiflora,* the white mugwort. Its leaves are green above, silvery underneath, and not the featured part of the plant. The creamy white flowers show in August and September and are useful for separating flowers of contrasting colors.

Artemisia abrotanum, the old man or southernwood, is grown for its foliage, which is light grey-green, feathery fine, smooth, and silky. The plant is best used next to a path, despite its 5-foot height, so that people can touch it. Its appearance invites stroking. Visitors to the garden will get a whiff of a fresh, camphor-like scent if they yield to the temptation to touch the plant.

Artemisia arborescens is one of the prettiest artemisias, but it's only hardy to Zone 7, being a native of the poor, rocky soils along the Mediterranean coast. Northerners need not feel left out, though, for all the other ornamental artemisias already mentioned here are hardy to Zone 4 at least. In addition, there's a species, *A. frigida,* that's found from Alaska to Texas and across Siberia. This plant grows only a foot or so high and resembles 'Silver Mound', although it's coarser. There's even an alpine version, *A. glacialis,* which grows from 2 to 6 inches tall and has the silvery, feathery-silky leaves typical of the genus.

'Silver King' is useful as a medium-height plant for the middle of the bed, and white mugwort can help in the back border. *Artemisia stellerana,* the old woman or dusty miller, is more whitish than silvery, with leaves like felt. It, too, is of medium height. The low-growing varieties like 'Silver Mound' and *A. frigida* can be used to bring neutral and muted tones to the front of the border, the sides of pathways, and the rock garden.

Artemisias like poor soil, but they grow just fine in average garden soil. Good drainage is a must—they won't grow where their feet stay wet. If the soil is too rich, the plants will grow long, weak, and spindly, and in the low-growing types like 'Silver Mound', the tufts will separate and fall over, ruining the pretty moundlike effect.

Artemisias are among the easiest plants in the garden to propagate. Most grow from underground rhizomes and have terrific rooting power, even when the soil may not have quite as much water as it should. Cuttings of *Artemisia abrotanum* can be stuck in almost any soil in the spring, watered in, and will strike twice as much root as even fast-rooting willows. They usually even survive being moved in full leaf if given a good watering. These are tough, all-purpose plants whose foliage looks good and goes with most flowers (except yellow and orange ones) in all seasons. More than this a gardener can't ask. Finally, because of the volatile, aromatic oils in most of them, pests are seldom a problem.

Aster

Aster means "star" in Greek; presumably this genus was so named because of its rayed flowers. But asters are also star-quality perennials both inside and outside the garden. The most beautiful display of asters that we saw last fall was alongside the road to our Aunt Bun's—a patch of wildlings put on a show there to mock the efforts of our local gardeners.

There are over 600 species of wild asters, most of them in North America. There are three types that usually bring welcome color to the September and October flower garden, leading up to the explosion of the chrysanthemums. The most common is *Aster novi-belgii,* native to the East Coast of the United States, also called the New York aster. In its wild state this species prefers to grow in coastal marshes. Most of the commercially available kinds of *A. novi-belgii* are really hybrids of this species developed into horticultural varieties, and they prefer average, well-drained soil. The same is true of *A. novae-angliae,* the New England aster. In the wild it inhabits moist places from New England west to the Rockies. In its horticultural incarnations, it prefers well-drained soil on the dry side. A third species,

Three types of Aster *blossoms.*

A. frikartii, is a slightly smaller type that opens its gold and lavender flowers in June and keeps them coming until the other asters open in September.

All of these species are commonly referred to in Britain as Michaelmas daisies. In North America, they're usually just called asters. Many of the aster types available at nurseries are crosses of all kinds of parents, bred to produce mounds of flowers, rather than to bloom on the end of wiry stems like *A. novi-belgii, A. novae-angliae,* and *A. frikartii.* We think these horticultural varieties can be gaudy and prefer the old-fashioned elegance of the pure forms.

If you want to make sure that your asters stay erect—for the taller ones have a tendency to flop over—place a slim green stake within clumps of three to five plants in June or July and tie the plants loosely with inconspicuous ties. This will hold them upright later, when the stems are elongated and the flowers are opening. Staking isn't necessary unless your grouping of associated plants requires the asters to stay in their place and not bend over their partners. It may be far less work for you to plan associations in which toppling asters would look fine, such as with taller monkshood (*Aconitum* species), rather than with a plant like the shorter *Anemone hupehensis.*

Asters also need to be divided at least every three years, preferably every two years, and every year if you want to keep them at their most glorious. When you see the aster foliage about 1 to 2 inches high in the spring, spade out the whole clump. Clumps are normally divided into pieces with from three to five shoots and replanted in groups of three in a triangle with 18-inch sides. This will make a fine mass of flowers. You can also divide clumps into pieces with single shoots and make a group of three to five of these pieces planted about 3 inches apart each way. These will grow together into a new solid clump, which will still be good next year. The year after that, it will need dividing again.

When your asters have finished blooming, cut off the flower heads before the seed matures and drops. The seeds rarely, if ever, produce flowers that are up to the colors of the parents. Eventually your garden will become clogged with inferior types if the plants are allowed to self-seed. Work with root divisions in the spring to keep new plants true to type.

Soil that's too rich in phosphorus and potassium has been implicated in the development of wilt disease in asters, and soil too rich in nitrogen may produce weak tissue, which is more easily colonized by dusty-looking fungi that can ruin the appearance of your asters. Deep soil of average fertility is fine for most asters. Water them during very dry spells, however, as their marshy heritage doesn't favor droughty conditions. When you water, try not to wet the foliage, as asters are susceptible to leaf fungi.

Don't pinch back *Aster frikartii* types after the second week in May, if at all. *A. novi-belgii* will produce more branches and hence more flowers if pinched a couple of times before midsummer. Pinching will also encourage flowering in *A. novae-angliae,* but don't pinch this species if you live where the frost-free season is less than 120 days, or they may not have time to regrow flowering points and open blossoms before frost.

While asters are excellent in the bed or border, they are also great for waste places and for naturalizing along the sunny edge of a wood. There they can grow and tumble to their hearts' content, while from a distance they are turning the meadow to a sea of dusty blue.

Astilbe

Astilbe is one of our personal favorites. The toothed, dark green foliage of the plants gives them their name, for *astilbe* is Greek for "without luster." Astilbe foliage looks

Astilbe

grow in partial shade, these plumes hover above the deep background, glowing in soft colors.

The most commonly seen species is *Astilbe arendsii,* cultivars of which can fill the garden with vertical accents from early June well into July. When the *A. arendsii* finishes, *A. chinensis* 'Pumila', a short, ground-covering form, bursts forth in a soft pinkish lavender. This cultivar can be planted with *A. taquetii* 'Superba', a rosy purple spire that reaches up to 4 feet high. 'Superba' flowers along with *A. chinensis* 'Pumila' in August and September.

Descriptions like these don't capture much of the beauty of astilbe. It is beautiful in form and careful in execution. There's nothing rank about it. If you don't want to multiply plants, it needs no division for many years. Its requirements are partial shade and rich, humusy, moist soil, so it's a natural selection for perennial beds under airy trees and along gardens that border woods.

Astilbes are heavy users of soil nutrients and can deplete their soil in several years, then lose the fullness of bloom that's so admirable. If you see this happening, divide the plants, enrich the soil in the astilbe bed with compost, and replant the pieces about 12 to 18 inches apart in the improved soil. It's a good idea to mulch astilbe after the soil warms up in spring. The mulch helps keep the soil moist.

We can never bring ourselves to cut the gorgeous plumes, but they do make beautiful additions to dried arrangements. Cut them just after their flowers open and hang them in a cool, dark place upside down for several weeks until dry. Store them away from light until you're ready to enjoy an echo of summer in the middle of winter.

People who work closely with astilbe

like a neat, compact rose bush, or a small *Aruncus dioicus.* It forms good-looking drifts or clumps when about five astilbes are planted together and contrasts well with broad-leaved, untoothed hostas for a superior foliage combination through the whole growing season.

But the major glory of the plant is its soft, feathery plumes of pink, raspberry, red, or rosy purple florets. Because its leaves are green to dull bronze and the plant likes to

---

Rabbit-Resistant Perennials

In some areas, rabbits can present a real problem to the gardener. If rabbits nibble off your prize perennials, try growing more plants from the following genera.

Achillea	*Convallaria*	*Narcissus*
Aconitum	*Corydalis*	*Nepeta*
Anaphalis	*Digitalis*	*Paeonia*
Anemone	*Doronicum*	*Papaver*
Aquilegia	*Epimedium*	*Polygonatum*
Artemisia	*Filipendula*	*Polygonum*
Aster	*Gentiana*	*Salvia*
Astilbe	*Geranium*	*Sedum*
Baptisia	*Helleborus*	*Stachys*
Bergenia	*Hemerocallis*	*Trillium*
Campanula	*Hosta*	*Trollius*
Cimicifuga	*Iris*	*Yucca*
Colchicum	*Kniphofia*	

---

cultivation claim that the plant's taxonomy is in a bit of a mess and needs sorting out. But none of that makes the plant any less valuable or beautiful. Astilbes come in creamy white, and in tones from shell pink to carmine red. They look exquisite when planted with Japanese iris and hosta and when flecked here and there with the cool colors of dangling columbine flowers. Ferns and astilbes are a nice duo that allows the astilbe's striking plumes to show off all by themselves.

Few pests bother this perennial. It's reliably hardy to Zone 4. Drought may burn the edges of its leaves, but won't kill the plant unless the water shortage is very severe. And it needs division only every five years. It's a carefree, superb plant in every shady garden.

Campanula (Bellflower)

The many cultivated species of campanula are so different in form that they can be thought of as separate plants. Tall-growing, and perhaps the prettiest of all, is *Campanula persicifolia.* This plant grows a basal rosette of leaves, shaped like peach leaves in spring, and sends up stems sprinkled with small blue or white cups in June. Bloom often continues until August. *C. persicifolia* 'Telham Beauty' is a tetraploid—a large version—with 3-inch, light blue flowers. The cups, or bells as some would have them, are dainty and elegant.

The most common campanula in the perennial garden is *Campanula glomerata.* This plant feels rough and scratchy to the touch. Instead of graceful, nodding bells, its funnel-shaped flowers of intense violet-blue or purple stick out from the tops of the 18-inch stems and occur in smaller numbers around the leaf axils. *C. glomerata* 'Joan Elliott' is a very common cultivar, one which we have in our border along a slate path. Amid all the pastel and refined blues and pinks, the sprightly, angular-looking and deeply colored glomeratas add an unsettling edge of drama. This species may not always be easy to group with other flowers. You could increase its dramatic effect with a striking yellow, or soften it with lavenders, but you won't make it sing sweetly. There's a little gravel in its voice, so to speak. However, a white cultivar, 'Alba', will harmonize with many other flowers.

One of our favorite perennials is *Campanula carpatica*. It makes little mounds of heart-shaped or oval leaves in the spring. In June, depending on the cultivar, it opens pale lavender, white, violet-blue, or pale blue cups about 1½ inches across on stems held a few inches above the trailing mounds of leaves. Our carpaticas keep up this quiet but exquisite show until September. Sitting on a large rock in our late August garden last year, I appreciated the *C. carpatica* 'Blue Chips' more than any other plant I saw. They echoed midsummer as the world hushed in anticipation of the autumn. The cricket chorus seemed to be singing about the carpaticas; Marilyn saw how I loved them and divided them on the spot, planting little clumps in other places for me. I can't wait until next year.

Campanula poscharskyana is a small (12 inches), vigorous-growing form of campanula that sprays out silvery blue, star-shaped flowers in June and keeps going until frost. It's often recommended for the rock garden, but it certainly shouldn't be ignored along the edge of the bed or border. It can also be used as a ground cover under light-shade ornamental trees, such as dogwood or clethra, or to border a walk or wall. The foliage of *C. poscharskyana* is grey-green

Three Campanula *species:* C. glomerata *(top right),* C. persicifolia *(left), and* C. carpatica *(bottom right).*

and compact, and it's altogether a hardy, superior species.

Campanula rotundifolia is also known as bluebells of Scotland or, sometimes, harebell. The flowers are dainty, little, lavender-blue bells dripping from 6-inch stems that tend to trail along over the rounded basal leaves. This plant might go unnoticed by a casual visitor to the garden, but someone reading the garden for beauty would surely stop and appreciate it. One problem with this campanula is that it doesn't always like the gardener to choose its spot. It will die out if not perfectly suited, but its seeds will find that little nook it likes so well, and you'll find it settling in where it will. Let it.

Campanulas are flush with bloom and luscious leaves during the hot and moist part of the summer, and so are often hit by slugs. If you find your *Campanula carpatica* chewed to shreds, check for these invaders. Handpick any you see. Diatomaceous earth spread around the base of the plants will keep slugs at bay.

As do most garden perennials, campanulas need a relatively moist soil with average fertility. It helps to divide them every few years to keep them in place, for most species tend toward rampancy. One in particular, *Campanula rapunculoides,* is too rampant for the garden, although it may work in a flowering cover for a back meadow.

If, after experience with campanulas, you find them very appealing, check a variety of seed catalogs for other types. There are many in cultivation, and hundreds that are uncultivated, and they come in tall, medium, and miniature sizes.

Chrysanthemum

No other flower in the perennial garden has such a rich and varied history as the various species of chrysanthemum. Showy fall mums are familiar to everyone, and their origin lies two thousand years ago in China, where they were first cultivated. But plants that until 1984 were also included in this genus are roadside daisies, sometimes called ox-eye daisies (formerly *Chrysanthemum leucanthemum,* now classified as *Leucanthemum vulgare*); feverfew—the little doily-edged, soft yellow, buttony flowers that look so beautifully old-fashioned; Shasta daisies, created from other species by Luther Burbank; and painted daisies, or pyrethrum, which give beautiful rich pinks and reds to the summer garden.

Hardy mums, which are *Chrysanthemum morifolium* hybrids for the most part, are grown in fancy shapes, miniature sizes, all colors except blue, and every variation and permutation you can think of. From all these classes of mums, several have been judged best for the outdoor garden. The others require either greenhouse growing or special treatment. The garden classes are: button mums, cushion mums, decorative types, pompons, and single types. Garden chrysanthemums have been reclassified by botanists into the genus *Dendrathema,* but catalogs for the most part still list them as *Chrysanthemum* species.

Button mums are low-growing with small, ball-like flowers. Their compact size eliminates the need most chrysanthemums have for staking.

Cushion mums are an expanded version of the button types. The plants grow a little taller, and the blossoms are round and puffy. They cover the plants with color, if not too crowded. These mums can go for two years before they need division, and they don't require tip pinching, the way many other mums do.

Decorative types grow on longer stems

Five of the many types of Chrysanthemum: *from left, daisy, cushion, pompon, single, and decorative.*

and with a more open habit than the cushion types. Their flowers are big—up to 4 inches across. Heavy rains can knock them to the ground, so staking is needed. For more profuse bloom and a more compact habit, growers are encouraged to pinch decorative mums. These will need division every year.

Pompon types are about the same height as the decorative types. These mums have round, ball-like flowers about 1½ inches in diameter that appear in clusters on the ends of their long stems. The foliage is open and airy. As with the decorative types, pompon mums need staking, pinching, and yearly division.

Single types are usually about 2 feet tall, or somewhat less, open and airy, and carry single flowers that look like beautifully colored daisies. They bloom in the fall, picking up where the pyrethrum leaves off.

Pinching is worth the effort for those mums that need it. Otherwise, stems get single and long, and flowers are sparse. When the plants reach about 6 inches tall in the spring, pinch out the top 2 inches. This will encourage branching. When the branches and new top grow to 6 inches long, pinch all of them back 2 inches, to encourage further branching. A third pinching can be done if there's time left before the second week of July. No pinching should be done after mid-July, or embryonic flower buds may be pinched off. This treatment will produce the most blooms and the thriftiest plants.

Staking is usually necessary with the

decorative, pompon, and single mums. Twiggy branches shoved securely into the soil in the chrysanthemum beds make ideal props. Thin bamboo will give you supports to which you can loosely tie the elongating stems in summer.

Chrysanthemums that need division every year simply fatigue after one season of bloom, although they will bravely come back and produce some sparse flowers for several years. Each spring, however, they produce light-colored, fresh, fleshy roots around the center woody parts. From these roots, little tufts of emerging leaves arise. The gardener needs to lift the plant, take off root pieces with one leaf assemblage emerging, and plant these about 18 inches apart in an already-prepared bed. Each of them will make a full-sized plant by fall. The old woody part from the previous year should be discarded. It's work, but it's necessary for good growth.

The pyrethrums and feverfews prefer average to poor soil, but all other chrysanthemums like a rich, humusy soil with plenty of nutrients, not too heavy on the nitrogen, please. This kind of soil is easily achieved with yearly additions of compost. None of the chrysanthemums like wet feet, so make sure your beds are in areas that stay well drained, especially in winter. All the species prefer full sun. All make excellent cut flowers.

Be sure to try feverfew in your garden. It self-sows readily, has a quaint, friendly, yellow and white appearance that gives an almost neutral effect, and is wonderful with intense blues. We find feverfew fills in between plant associations as if it knew that was its job.

Hardy mums are the sort of flower that can be manipulated. There are extremely ornamental versions of chrysanthemums, but they need special handling, to which they

Perennials That Can Be Invasive

Given the proper conditions, the following genera tend to spread and take over an area well beyond the borders given to them by the gardener. Forewarned is forearmed.

Achillea	Euphorbia
Aegopodium	Hemerocallis
Anchusa	Lysimachia
Artemisia	Macleaya
Campanula	Monarda
Catananche	Nepeta
Centaurea	Physostegia
Chrysanthemum	Rudbeckia
Echinops	Tradescantia
Eupatorium	Verbascum

respond miraculously. Pompon types, for instance, can be grown as a horticultural curiosity in a greenhouse into "thousand bloom" bouquets. For one year, the plants are pinched back every month, until there are 50 branches, each ending with several buds, making a hemispherical mound 6 to 10 feet across. When the plant blooms, it blooms all at once, and the flowers are fussed over to achieve a regular spacing. The result is a large mound of flowers in a spectacular arrangement—all on a single, many-branched stem.

Gardeners from Zone 3 north will have to protect their mums over the winter. The best way is to cut back the stems to about 4 inches after bloom and before the soil freezes. Lift the plants and place them in a cold frame to overwinter. The plants can also be deeply mulched. In warmer regions, mums should be cut back to 4 inches after

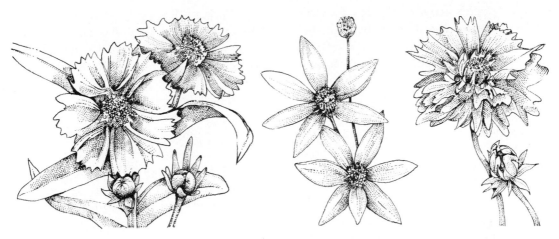

Three kinds of Coreopsis: *from left,* C. grandiflora, C. verticillata, *and a double-flowered* Coreopsis *'Sunray'.*

frosts arrive and the plants are going dormant. Mulch them when the ground starts to freeze. In cold areas where there are strong prevailing winds, mulch helps protect the plants from the scouring effect of frigid winds on the exposed plants.

Coreopsis

The name *Coreopsis* comes from the Greek words meaning "resembles a bug" and refers to the plant's seeds—hence one of our common names for it, tickseed. But don't let the name put you off, because coreopsis is one of the longest blooming perennials in the garden.

The prettiest species is probably *Coreopsis verticillata.* Its leaves are finely divided into silky threads, presenting a feathery drift of green when several specimens are planted 12 inches apart each way. The stems are crowned with 1- to 2-inch flowers with yellow rays and yellow centers. The cultivar 'Moonbeam' grows only 15 inches tall, while other cultivars can reach 3 feet. *C. verticillata* will start blooming in late

June or July and continue until frost, so it will remain through successions of other blooms as a strong yellow. It can be used in one succession as an accent or in a later one as part of a dominant yellow grouping.

Coreopsis auriculata 'Nana' grows only 6 inches tall and puts up short stems with 1½-inch orangey flowers with toothed petals. This dwarf form is excellent for the front of a border or a rock garden, but it doesn't bloom much past August. Other cultivars of *C. auriculata* grow to 1½ feet tall.

There seems to be a lot of confusion among suppliers of plants between *Coreopsis grandiflora* and *C. lanceolata.* We've found cultivars of one listed under the other species' name. In an effort to sort out the confusion, we checked with several expert sources and believe that we've placed the cultivars in their proper places in the chart in chapter 7. This is important to know, because *C. grandiflora* is a short-lived type—about two years—that usually comes back from self-sown seed, while *C. lanceolata* is a true perennial that needs dividing only every three years or so.

Both species grow to about 2 feet tall. *Coreopsis grandiflora* usually finishes blooming in August, while *C. lanceolata* will keep blooming until frost. Both have similar daisy-like flowers with jagged-edged petals. One way to tell the species apart is to notice how the leaves grow. *C. lanceolata*'s leaves are generally found only at the base of the plant, not on the tall flower stalks, while *C. grandiflora* has leaves along the stalks.

Unless you're after lots of baby coreopsis plants, cut off the flower heads as soon as they fade. A rich soil isn't necessary, but adequate nutrients and water give the best results. Avoid planting coreopsis in a very dry location.

Coreopsis is disease-prone, especially to rots and fungus, and to virus. Mostly these appear in years when the climatic conditions aren't to the plant's liking. If you find that disease is a persistent problem, try mixing finished compost in the soil, or moving the plants to a sunnier spot. Aphids and cucumber beetles can be pests. Aphids are easily washed off the leaves (both top and especially the undersides) with a garden hose. Cucumber beetles are another matter. A few cucumbers or other cucurbits nearby may act as a trap crop for these pests if the infestation is harming the coreopsis.

Delphinium

Delphiniums demand extra effort, but they're worth it. The seed and plant catalogs use words like "regal," "majestic," "spectacular," and "glorious" to describe the tall, blue spires of the *Delphinium elatum* hybrids, but such adjectives don't adequately describe the flower's strong emotional appeal.

Perhaps it's because they show tones of heavenly, translucent blues that delphiniums affect us so much. Or because their soaring spires function in the garden like church steeples in the town—silent reminders to keep our perspective and values straight. Or because delphiniums are the crowning glory of the garden. Whatever the reason, these flowers move us.

They're finicky things, though, and just as likely to move us to work. Natives of high, cool, moist areas, delphiniums can't take scorching summers and droughty soils. They need lots of nutrients to build their quick towers in early summer, and so delphiniums' beds should be dug very deeply, and the loosened soil mixed with lots of compost and enough wood ashes, limestone, or bone meal to sweeten it. They won't tolerate wet feet at all, and even plants grown in well-drained soils can contract crown rots in humid, hot weather. Mulching helps keep their roots moist and cool, and it helps to place them on a north slope.

These plants definitely need to be staked. The lower-growing Chinese delphinium may need only a few twigs stuck in the soil—if anything at all—to help it stay erect, but the taller types need slender stakes to lean on. Make sure your delphiniums have enough growing room. When crowded, they're prone to mites, fungi, and rots, so give them air at their bases.

Most of us can expect about half of our *Delphinium elatum* plants to die out over the first fall and winter. Of the ones that are left the second year, only a few will make it to three years, and maybe one or two hardy individuals will persist to four. The *D. elatum* hybrids aren't reliably perennial except in areas of cool, moist summers, like New England or the Northwest Coast. If you live in an area suited to the culture of

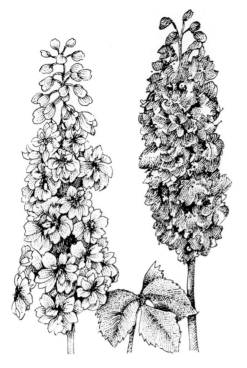

Delphinium

D. elatum, you're lucky, and you'll find these delphiniums right at home in your garden.

Delphinium belladonna is a lower-growing, more reliably perennial form that's closer to the original wild species. It's not quite as showy as the Pacific Coast strains of *D. elatum,* but it's better than most anything else in the garden.

An even smaller form, *Delphinium grandiflorum,* also called the Chinese or Siberian delphinium, has low foliage and a much looser and shorter spike of flowers. It's a pretty plant, but not the spectacle its relatives are. It has the virtues of being truly perennial and not usually needing stakes.

A mixture of sulfur dust and rotenone powder dusted on the leaves, top and bottom, every two weeks from May through early July will prevent disease and insect attack in hot, humid areas, where you know

delphiniums have these problems. In your garden, see how the plants fare before instituting controls.

Delphiniums have a cut-and-come-again habit. After their first bloom, cut off the flower stalks near their base. Water the plants if it's dry. In a couple of weeks, dig in some rich compost under the big outer leaves and water the plants well. Or water them with fish emulsion solution until each plant has had a thorough drink. When new flower shoots emerge, pinch back all but three. Cut these off also when the bloom is spent.

Other than orange, delphiniums go well with most colors. Pale yellows, light pinks, and hazy blue pastels all harmonize with the delphiniums. Because of their intense mass of blue, a scarlet-red accent, such as a single Maltese cross (*Lychnis chalcedonica*), would intensify them even more.

Some gardeners like their delphiniums against a light background, but I prefer to see them against a dark pool of woodsy shadow. In areas with hot summers, they're best planted where they get shade in the afternoon anyway.

Many perennial gardens are built around the use of June and August second-growth delphinium blossoms. They dominate the local landscape, and you'd be wise to leave a path to them, or visitors will trample their way forward to get a better look. The otherworldly blues demand a close approach, especially when they seem to be blue and violet at once. Then we notice in the center of the delphinium blossoms the little corollas that are called "bees." Bee colors often contrast with the flower color, such as violet-purple florets with bright yellow bees.

Many gardeners treat delphiniums as annuals, buying new started plants each year and forgetting about trying to carry them over the winter. For the *Delphinium ela-*

tum types, it will be less costly and more realistic to expect to treat them as biennials and remake the bed every other year.

I am always overwhelmed by delphiniums' beauty. They do take work, but it's worth it for their exquisite finishing touch in the back of the border or middle of the bed.

Perennial Genera That Can Be Air-Dried

Blooms can be cut on long stems and the leaves removed, then hung upside down in a warm, dark, dry, and airy place, such as an attic with good ventilation. The warmth and ventilation speed drying, and the darkness helps the flowers retain their color. They are dry when the stems are brittle and snap when bent.

Acanthus	Eryngium
Achillea	Galax
Aconitum	Gypsophila
Anaphalis	Heuchera
Asclepias	Lavandula
Astilbe	Limonium
Catananche	Physalis
Delphinium	Rudbeckia
Echinops	Solidago

Dianthus (Pinks)

Gardeners have been growing carnations and other forms of dianthus for hundreds of years. Somewhere in this welter of hybrids are the true species, but we're not likely to run across them. Still, dianthus types can be placed under the species they most closely resemble.

The common name, pinks, is sometimes used to refer to the low-growing, matted mounds of intense pink, lavender, red, or white *Dianthus deltoides,* more properly called maiden pinks. Don't confuse these with the early spring pinks, *Phlox subulata,* found in many a suburban lawn or rock garden.

Catalogs and growers tend to use "pinks" to refer to other types, such as *Dianthus gratianopolitanus,* the sweet little cheddar pinks that float like tiny balloons on straight stems above grassy mats of foliage. Pinks is also applied to *D. allwoodii,* hybrids of *D. caryophyllus,* the carnation, and *D. plumarius,* the cottage pinks. The latter are usually single flowered, have fringed petals, and carry an intenser shade of their petal color in a ring around the centers.

Some growers say that *Dianthus caryophyllus,* the tall carnations that bloom so fragrantly and profusely above their straggly foliage, are only hardy to Zone 8, but we've seen them growing in Zone 6, in places where they aren't exposed to winter winds and are given a little mulch. There are so many cultivars of mixed parentage that hardiness varies plant by plant.

One would think that the common name of pinks refers to the color of the flowers, but other theories have been advanced. One is that the name refers to the pinked edges of the petals—they are deeply toothed, as if cut by pinking shears. Another interpretation of the name is found in the phrase "in the pink," meaning healthy or wealthy.

All dianthus like average, slightly alkaline, well-drained soil. You can achieve these conditions in ordinary garden soil by adding ground limestone, wood ashes, or

Two Dianthus *species: the carnation,* D. caryophyllus *(foreground) and garden pinks.*

bone meal. Mixing wood ashes with compost (one #10 can of wood ashes per bushel of compost) and digging this around the plant in very early spring will keep the plants strong. Dianthus can be divided, but most types seem to resent it, so many growers find it easier to take stem cuttings of the vegetative (not flower) shoots in midsummer and to root them in soil that's kept moist and shaded, where they "take" readily. The very low types should be divided into little shoots, with roots attached, and planted 6 to 8 inches apart to form new beds.

Most dianthus, except *Dianthus deltoides,* respond well to cutting back after bloom, which stimulates them to put forth new flowers. The *D. allwoodii* hybrids, es-

pecially, will send up more bloom if carefully attended to this way.

Most dianthus are sweetly clove-scented, especially the *D. allwoodii* hybrids. No better nosegay flower can be found.

Like delphinium, dianthus needs light and air to prevent disease, so make sure the plants aren't crowded in by dense neighbors. Slugs will also feast on these plants. A dusting of diatomaceous earth or wood ashes around the base of the plants may help. Some wet years are just bound to be sluggy, however, and you may have to suffer some damage. Gardeners in the northwest coastal area will be familiar with slug problems, for the cool and wet environment there favors these slimy garden-wreckers.

Dianthus does best where conditions approximate those of England—such as Long Island. Very hot summers discourage them. But in the South or hot parts of the West and Midwest, a little shade, humusy and moist soil, and mulching in summer should all help to keep these very worthwhile plants going for you.

Geranium (Cranesbill)

When most people think of geraniums, they think of the bright red, pink, or white balls and wide tomato-green leaves of the common potted geranium, whose botanical name is *Pelargonium*. In the same family as pelargonium is the genus *Geranium*— the cranesbills or hardy geraniums—with which we're concerned here.

These are advantageous plants in the front of the border or placed where they can be often admired, for when nothing else may be blooming, the cranesbills will be sure to have a few flowers to offer.

Geranium, *or cranesbill*

We prefer the blue and softer lavender shades of cranesbill to the loud magenta varieties. Although the deep green leaves somehow subtract from the blue varieties' visibility, the magenta types of *Geranium sanguineum* give too hard a color for us.

The cranesbills are dainty plants, but most of them grow in such dense masses that they appear very solid. Their leaves are usually deeply cleft, so that deep shadow can be seen through them, which darkens the overall effect. The flowers appear over the surface of the mound of foliage, and these often have veins of a richer tone of the petal color. Their first full blooming usually happens in June, but they continue to open lesser numbers of blossoms through the season. By the end of September, in most regions, they finally stop blooming.

Geranium cinereum is a compact, small species that stands only 8 to 10 inches tall. Its grey-green leaves harmonize well with the dainty pink flowers of many of its cultivars.

'Wargrave Pink' and 'Johnson's Blue' are two clear-colored cultivars of *Geranium endressii,* a type that begins to bloom in June and continues until fall. Both varieties grow about 1 1/2 feet tall in mounds. Another species, *G. himalayense,* grows 15 inches tall and carries intense violet-blue flowers. This interesting plant combines well with white and light blue perennials of medium height, and with tall delphiniums.

Geranium sanguineum is known as bloody cranesbill, and I'm never sure whether that appellation is an attempt to describe the flower color or an epithet hurled at the plant by gardeners with a taste for more subtle tones. It grows a foot tall and its colors are bright. Because bloody cranesbill keeps producing some bloom through the summer, gardeners can use it to provide splashes of bright color in areas that have either peaked early or won't blossom until late, such as in chrysanthemum beds.

While cranesbills prefer full sun, they'll tolerate light shade, although the profusion of bloom may be lessened. About every fourth year, the plants will get crowded and stalky and will need division. This is easiest on the plant in the spring, although it can also be done in September, which gives divisions a chance to set their roots before the hard freezes come in late autumn. All cranesbills are easily divided by slicing up the large mat of an old plant into pieces 6 to 8 inches across and replanting them a foot apart.

Hemerocallis (Daylily)

It was Robert E. Lee who said that daylilies would be the sign of a neglected garden in the future. Well, the future has arrived, and he was half right.

If by daylilies we mean the common orange ones with yellow throats whose blossoms last one day and which grow in profusion along the roadsides, then he was right. But today there are cultivated daylilies in thousands of subtle, bold, and variegated colors in all kinds of forms. From these the gardener can construct a bed that gracefully changes color through its blowsy masses of flowers, and proves Robert E. Lee to have been very wrong.

Daylilies are the heart of the perennial garden, usually blooming at the peak of the sun's intensity when the world is awash in color and foliage. They're carefree and gorgeous and edible right down to their fleshy roots.

The genetic lines of the hemerocallis have been sieved and resieved through the breeding work so many times that it's less instructive to talk about species than about form and function. A knowledgeable analysis of daylily types was given by Robert Sinclair of West Chester, Pennsylvania, at a recent meeting of the Perennial Plant Association. The following is based on his talk.

Hemerocallis fulva is our native, naturalized daylily. There is a fragrant species, the yellow *H. flava,* and a light yellow, spidery hybrid cultivar called 'Kindly Light', which associates well with Shasta daisies.

In size, daylily blooms are categorized as miniatures (flowers less than 3 inches across), small (from 3 to 4½ inches), and large (over 4½ inches). Flower shapes are

Hemcrocallis *cultivars*

categorized as plain, pinched, rounded, and ornamental, and these may or may not have ruffles on the edges. Some flowers are single, others are double.

Some daylilies have a diurnal habit, opening in the morning and closing in the afternoon, which inspired their common name. After this one-day bloom, they shrivel away. Daylily breeders have been trying to create a variety that drops its spent blooms, as many fanciers think the dangling shriveled corpses of blooms past are not attractive. So far no luck.

Other kinds of daylilies have a nocturnal habit, opening in the afternoon and closing in the morning. Still others are called extenders—these stay open for more than sixteen hours.

In color, daylilies come in every shade, tone, and tint possible, except pure white and true blue. That's why daylilies are accented so nicely by the soft blue, ball-like flower heads of echinops, which blooms at the same time.

There are three foliage types. Dormant foliage types die back in the winter and don't perform well in Zones 8 to 10. For those warm areas of the far South or Southwest, there are evergreen daylilies that won't tolerate alternate freezes and thaws. And there are semievergreen kinds that partially die back in the winter. These can be grown in Zones 5 to 8.

In height, daylilies range from miniatures that grow only 11 inches tall to giant kinds that reach heights of 8 feet.

Flowers begin their day by greeting the sun in the southeast and follow it around to the southwest in the afternoon. Your daylilies will look best if you plant beds so that the flowers face the paths where visitors will be standing. This means planting along the north side of the path, rather than on the southern edge.

When making a border of daylilies, don't just mix the colors together; instead, create drifts or masses of the same color. Next to one of these masses, plant another drift of a slightly different, but related, tone, continuing to vary tones to make the entire border a pleasing, gentle sweep of color harmony.

Hemerocallis grows well in large planters if the soil is kept fertile and moist. The long leaves will arch over the edges of the pots, and the flowers will stand proudly above. Plant groups of three roots, each of the same color. Three such groups in related tones make a nice association.

There are some notable hybrid daylily cultivars. 'Stella d'Oro' is a miniature (18-inch-tall) yellow daylily that blooms from May until October. In addition to these considerable virtues, it is an extender.

Another long-season variety, 'Pardon Me', produces red blooms from July to October. 'Dance Ballerina Dance', a peach type, will not increase and naturalize, as most daylilies do, so this cultivar may be a good choice for a small spot that you want to keep in check.

In fact, generally speaking, the red-blossomed types don't seem to increase as fast as other colors.

Another interesting cultivar is 'Bitsey', a gold-colored, dormant-foliage type that blooms in the spring.

Scientists have made bud counts to see which cultivars produce the most flowers. This contest was won by 'Golden Chimes'.

Because they come in so many types and colors, daylilies can be a garden staple from late May until frost, in any color that you need, not only the yellows, golds, and light yellows, but also the reds, pinks, and violets.

Most daylilies will outlive the people who plant them, slowly increasing without being invasive. The plants grow from fingerlike, fleshy tubers. Try peeling and slicing a few of these into your salad sometime.

Half-grown, dried daylily buds are sold in oriental food shops to be used in hot and sour soup. You can dry them yourself.

Daylily tubers find nourishment and water even when grown over roots of trees and shrubs. If you want to hasten the increase of a planting, you can easily divide the clumps of tubers in spring or in mid-September. Daylilies are among the easiest flowers to grow, adapting to a wide variety of soils and environmental conditions. In the North they like full sun, but in Zone 8 and warmer, the full sun burns out the color in the flowers and shrivels them quickly. In southern areas daylilies are best planted in partial shade.

Too rich a soil will have the plants pushing leaves at the expense of flowers, and yet they like a humusy soil that drains well and holds some moisture. Leaf mold or peat moss—not rich compost—dug into the bed before planting should supply what daylilies need in an average soil. When you plant them, set the tubers 18 inches apart. Most hemerocallis is hardy to Zone 3.

For the best appearance, remove the stalks after they have finished blooming. The leaves will look good until frost. The plants never need division until they outgrow their spot—maybe in six to ten years, depending on their vigor.

Many mail-order houses sell hemerocallis, but the companies listed below specialize in the plant and have wide collections from which you can select varieties for your chosen color scheme and season of bloom.

Big Tree Daylily Garden
    777 General Hutchinson Parkway
    Longwood, FL 32750

Busse Gardens
    635 East 7th Street
    Rt. 2, Box 13
    Cokato, MN 55321

Houston Daylily Gardens
    Box 7008
    The Woodlands, TX 77380

Iris Lane Gardens
    1649 South Iris Lane
    Escondido, CA 92026

Iron Gate Gardens
    Rt. 3, Box 250
    Kings Mountain, NC 28086

Klehm Nursery
    2 East Algonquin Road
    Arlington Heights, IL 60005

Meadowlake Gardens
    Rt. 2, Box 99-A
    Yemassee, SC 29945

Stateler's Flower Farm
    Box 27
    Loughman, FL 33858

Tranquil Lake Nursery
    45 River Street
    Rehoboth, MS 02769

Gilbert C. Wild
    Sarcoxie, MO 64862

Wimberly Way Gardens
    7024 NW 18th Avenue
    Gainesville, FL 32605

Hosta

Hostas are indispensable plants in the shady parts of the perennial garden. They are grown for their leaves, which add real

Flower stalks arise in August on hostas, left, while one of the genus's many kinds of leaves is shown at right.

interest to the foliage component of any garden, but they also produce stalks which, around August, sprout long trumpet-shaped blossoms that face outward or down. Some gardeners who like to keep their hostas as foliage plants snip off these stalks when they appear. But hostas offer a floral bonus, which can include a gorgeous fragrance in some varieties.

In full sun hostas tend to lose color and vigor. They grow best in light shade, but will tolerate deeper to full shade. They prefer a humusy, well-drained soil, liberally im-

proved with leaf mold. In other words, hostas like the conditions found in the woods. This makes them perfect for visually anchoring the bases of trees and flowering shrubs to the ground, especially to a perennial bed.

Because so many of the nicest perennials have long, slender leaves, hostas provide a foliage contrast that's unequaled by any other genus of garden plants. They are low-maintenance plants, too, which don't need to be divided unless you want more hostas. Then they divide easily into sections that transplant well if kept moist and shady, especially if this is done in the spring when their tight whorls of leaves are beginning to emerge.

Cultivars of *Hosta sieboldiana* have unusual blue-green leaves, sometimes variegated, sometimes crinkled into a seersucker effect, sometimes ribbed. Other white- or yellow-edged types have wavy-edged leaves that add movement and panache to the low border.

Through the lively months of May, June, and July, hostas add shape, texture, and composition to any group of flowering perennials. Then in August, when most gardens are beginning to lessen in bloom, the hostas spray their area with misty white and lavender trumpets held above their beautiful leaves. They're perfectly hardy and almost trouble-free

The "almost" refers to slugs, which just love most kinds of hostas. Hostas like it where it's shady and moist—and so do slugs. Slugs are soft-bodied creatures, however, and can often be kept off plants by spreading sharp sand, diatomaceous earth, or slug repellent at the base of the plants.

Hostas have a decorative effect for landscaping, too. They are ideal plants for edging walkways and paths into the garden. Large kinds can hide the compost pile or the failing foliage of a spring bulb bed. A large rock takes on grace and beauty when a mass of hostas crowd into it. All hostas appear lovely from above, so consider them for the area below a deck.

Botanists are working now to standardize the rather jumbled nomenclature of this genus, but the following species are among those most commonly found in catalogs.

Hosta venusta is one of the smallest, with tiny green leaves making little mounds only a few inches tall. It's especially effective with shade-loving alpines and other miniatures, and for edging the bed or border.

We love our *Hosta plantaginea*, the August lily whose big white trumpets invite the nose to come in close. Just make sure there's no bee in there before sampling the scent. The leaves of this species are rather gross, so it's better grown for its fragrant flowers than its foliage. A line of *H. plantaginea* along a walkway near the house will perfume the air on still August nights.

Blue-green species include *Hosta tokudama* and *H. sieboldiana*. Of the latter, the cultivar 'Elegans' is a large variety with solid blue-green leaves up to a foot across, and 'Frances Williams' has seersucker leaves edged with a light gold that deepens as the summer progresses. 'Frances Williams' is, the American Hosta Society reports, the most popular variety in the United States.

Hosta albomarginata reaches about a foot in height, its 4- to 6-inch leaves decorated with white margins. Similar to it is *H. decorata*, which grows a little taller, to about 18 inches, and whose leaves are somewhat blunter and darker green than those of *H. albomarginata*. This hosta also has white leaf margins, with a fine trail of this white edge following the leaf stalk to the ground.

Another gold-edged hosta is *Hosta fortunei* 'Aurea-Marginata'. It has large, dark green leaves. 'Aurea-Marginata', unlike some of the other cultivars in this species whose gold edges bleach white over a season, keeps its gold to the end.

One of our favorite species is *Hosta lancifolia*. Its narrow, glossy leaves array themselves in tiers, which cascade toward the ground, and are lovely when given space to show off. A hosta that probably benefits in appearance from being placed with a

Fragrant Perennial Flowers

The following flowers have distinct fragrances. Because not all species within a genus are fragrant, they are listed by species name. When all or most species within a genus are fragrant, the genus name is followed by spp., the abbreviation meaning "several species."

Achillea millefolium	*Filipendula ulmaria*	*Narcissus* spp.
Allium spp.	*Hemerocallis flava*	*Nepeta* × *faassenii*
Asperula odorata or *Galium odoratum*	*Hesperis matronalis*	*Paeonia* spp.
		Phlox spp.
Centranthus ruber	*Hosta plantaginea*	
Clematis heracleifolia	*Hyacinthus* spp.	*Primula* spp.
Clematis recta	*Iris* spp.	*Saponaria officinalis*
Convallaria majalis	*Lavandula* spp.	*Sedum* × *spectabile*
Crocus spp.	*Lilium* spp.	*Valeriana officinalis*
Dianthus spp.	*Lupinus polyphyllus*	*Viola cornuta*
Dictamnus albus or *D. fraxinella*	*Monarda didyma*	*Viola odorata*
Filipendula rubra	*Muscari* spp.	

crowd of its clones is *H. undulata.* Its broad, 8-inch oval leaves reverse the usual variegation by sporting white centers with green margins. In addition, the leaves undulate and twist as they grow, making a flurry of movement in a group that adds dash to otherwise serene combinations of perennials.

Clumps of *Hosta undulata* can be interspersed with clumps of *H. ventricosa,* whose heart-shaped leaves will add quiet pools of green to the undulata's writhing shape.

This short discussion can only begin to get at the richness of this genus. Besides variations of green and blue in the leaves, and white, yellow, or green on the margins, hosta leaves are described as shiny, smooth, cupped, curly, crinkled, waxy, ribbed, veined, twisted, frosty, or mottled. These leaves make shapes described as erect, flat, or rounded. This variety of shapes, colors, textures, and massed forms gives the gardener a rich bag of compositional elements to draw from. Hosta is truly one of those plants of which it can be said, you can never have enough.

Iris (Flag)

Some people think that the "lilies of the fields" referred to in the Bible are irises. Not only did several species grow wild in the Middle East in biblical times, but the flowers were cultivated, too. The very name iris was supposedly given to the flower by Dioscorides because of its resemblance to

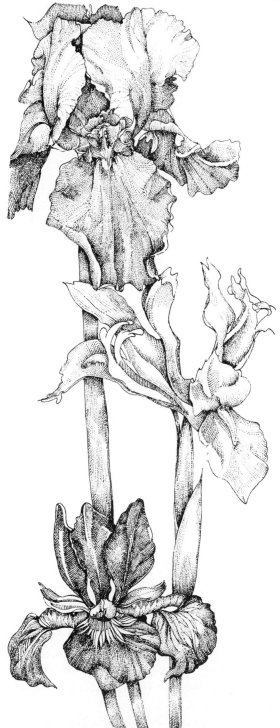

Three types of Iris: *bearded (top), Dutch (center), and Siberian (bottom).*

the "rainbow" of heaven, which suggests that not only was it cultivated, but already there were flowers in many hues and tones.

Today there are over 300 known species and who-can-count-how-many cultivars. For example, one iris catalog here before me as I write lists 20 cultivars of tall bearded iris with names that begin with the letters *SA* from 'Saber Dance' to 'Saucy Sue'.

With so many irises to choose from, how does a new gardener begin to sort them out and decide which to grow? In this section we've selected what we think are the best of the most commonly offered species or hybrids. These include *Iris cristata,* the crested iris; *I. germanica,* the parent of so many thousands of bearded German iris hybrids; *I. kaempferi,* the graceful Japanese iris; *I. pseudacorus,* for wet places; and *I. sibirica,* one of the most trouble-free species.

The parts of the iris flower have been given names: the three outer flower petals that usually hang downward are called "falls," while the three inner, more upright petals are called the "standards." The beard referred to by the name bearded iris is the furze of hairy filaments that emerge from the throat, the part of the falls closest to the center of the flower. These beards can often contrast strikingly with the rest of the flower.

There's some dispute over whether the iris or lily is the model for the fleur-de-lis of French heraldry. Fanciers of both plants claim the distinction for their own, but I'm inclined to go with the iris because of a story concerning Clovis, a king of the early Franks, whose army had been pressed up against a broad river by invading Goths. Clovis noticed that yellow irises were growing in the water quite a ways out from shore, and he deduced that the river was fordable.

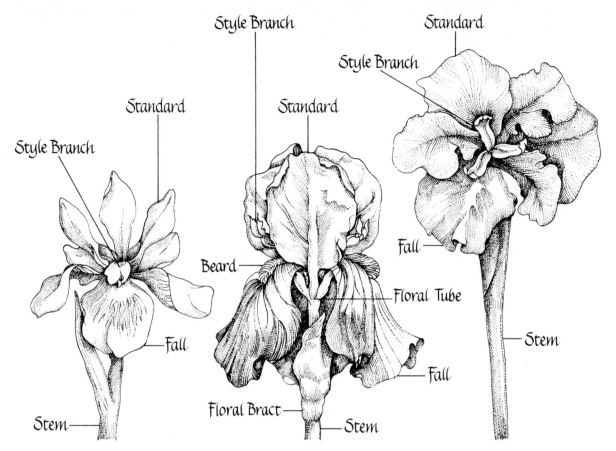

Style Branch

Standard

Style Branch

Standard

Style Branch

Standard

Beard

Fall

Floral Tube

Fall

Stem

Fall

Stem

Floral Bract

Stem

The parts of an iris flower, shown for Siberian iris (left), bearded iris (center), and Japanese iris (right).

His troops escaped the Goths, and the iris flower—probably the yellow, water-loving *Iris pseudacorus*—gained a place on French banners. Let us look at these species one by one.

Iris cristata, the crested iris—so named because the falls have a central ridge or crest—is a native of the southeastern United States. Although there are miniature forms of the taller irises, this species is truly dwarf and is considered the best of the small irises. Short, lancelike leaves produce a central flower early, in May in most parts of the country. The flowers are white, purple, or

blue, or combinations thereof, and are surprisingly large, full-sized blooms, despite the short stature of the vegetative parts, which only reach 3 to 4 inches tall. The crested iris is native to the woodlands and, as you might expect, prefers a light shade with a humusy, acid soil. It also tolerates full sun. You'll notice that the rhizomes of the plant creep along the ground. This is their habit, and they shouldn't be covered with soil or mulch or they'll rot. Keeping the *I. cristata* bed weed-free is essential if you want the plant to naturalize in an area. This is a great plant to put with some of the shade-loving, smaller hostas, Jacob's ladder, woodruff, or forget-me-nots.

Iris germanica is our catchall category for the many hybrids that are called tall bearded irises and that have *I. germanica* as a parent. These are the familiar irises, tall and showy, so frequently seen in cottage gardens. You'll notice that most of them have a slight fragrance suited to their color. *I. germanica* hybrids grow from fleshy roots that produce offsets, each with a cluster of fanned, lancelike leaves. It's best to divide these about six weeks after flowering, despite the many recommendations to divide them immediately after flowering. The delay gives the new offsets a chance to strike decent-sized roots. Dig up the old plants every three years and wash off the soil. Cut back the leaves by two-thirds and trim the long feeder roots by one-third. With a sharp knife, cut divisions from the parent plant, discarding the tuberous old roots and saving the offsets, each with a set of leaves and some good, strong roots. If any are moldy or rotted, discard them. To prevent further mold attacks, dip the roots and tuber of each division in a 50-50 solution of household chlorine bleach and water, dust with powdered sulfur, and plant so that the leaves and their growing point are just above the soil surface. Water them in well. Some will bloom the following year, and all will bloom in subsequent years if they like the spot.

Iris kaempferi is native to Japan and China. It is the iris we see in old Japanese prints, extremely beautiful and graceful in appearance. The blooms are beardless and of many colors, although you'll see a lot of reddish purple in this species. They are the largest-flowered of the irises. In its native habitat, Japanese iris likes wet or moist spots. It carries some of that preference to the garden, where it needs full sun and a moist soil. Improving the soil with humusy materials, especially leaf mold, will give good results. *I. kaempferi* doesn't have the fleshy rhizomes of *I. germanica*, but rather lots of smaller roots and growing points and buds. These can be easily divided in spring to quickly enlarge a stand.

Iris pseudacorus is a bog or waterside plant with, ordinarily, yellow flowers. They are exquisite in any wet place on your property, as long as they get full sun. If they like the spot where you put them, they'll naturalize, turning an unpleasant swamp into a place of rare beauty. In the garden, *I. pseudacorus* needs constant moisture—that is, watering whenever the soil dries out below $1/2$ inch from the surface. In areas with dependable spring rains, this iris does well.

Iris sibirica is a form that is fast winning great favor with gardeners, and no wonder. It's easy to care for and resistant to many of the pests and diseases that can attack the German irises. Sibiricas grow 2 to 3 feet tall in dense clumps with lots of thin-leaved foliage. The flowers appear on hollow stems in colors that often feature a rich, deep blue streaked with yellow. When the leaves fall, they self-mulch the ground around the plants, saving the gardener some work. The plants will grow in any good soil. They are best divided six weeks after blooming, by pulling the clumps apart into as many divisions as you want. The secret to transplanting Siberian iris is to keep them well-watered for the first two weeks after transplanting. That will allow their newly formed roots to strike into the earth, and the plants should be fine on their own after that.

The iris borer is sometimes a problem and can be kept in check by good sanitation. This pest bores into the fleshy rhizomes of the German types. Kill any you find there.

The damage may be compounded because the wounds often become infected with rot. Spread pyrethrum dust around the base of the plants in spring to kill the hatching larvae that emerge and seek out the roots.

To explore what's available in irises, you'll need to get catalogs from one or more of the following dealers, who have extensive lists of cultivars.

Bay View Gardens
    1201 Bay Street
    Santa Cruz, CA 95060

Cooley's Gardens
    P.O. Box 126
    Silverton, OR 97381

Hildenbrandt's Iris Garden
    Star Route, Box 4
    Lexington, NE 68850

Iris Test Gardens
    1010 Highland Park Drive
    College Place, WA 99324

Mission Bell Gardens
    2778 West 5600 South
    Roy, UT 84067

Schreiner's Gardens
    3625 Quinably Road
    Salem, OR 97303

Lilium (Lily)

Wonderfully fragrant, gloriously beautiful, easy to grow, and easy to propagate, lilies will be a featured flower in any garden in which they're planted. Like iris, they've been hybridized to the point where every color except true blue is available. Flower shapes range from pendent (downward hanging) types to upright chalice forms.

Except for the species *Lilium canadense,* which is at home in wet, boggy soil, all lilies like a slightly acid, humusy loam that's not too rich in nitrogen. Average garden soil improved with leaf mold or peat moss is perfect. As the saying goes, lilies like "their head in the sun and their feet in the shade." In other words, they prefer sunny locations, but need shade from the blistering afternoon sun.

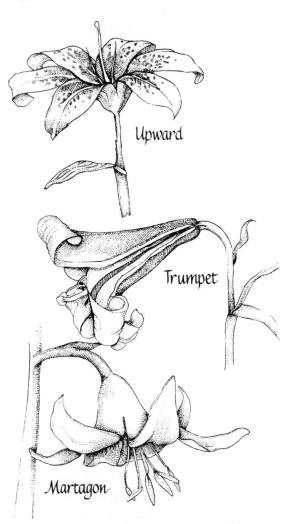

Three types of Lilium *flowers: upward-facing (top), trumpet (center), and Martagon (bottom).*

While lilies don't grow well where surface roots of large trees soak up available water and nutrients, they don't mind sharing space with some of the lighter-feeding shrubs. Many gardeners plant them to grow up through the outer branches of azaleas, which eliminates the need for the staking of taller varieties and covers the lilies' base with shade from the azaleas. The lilies also provide great interest where otherwise the post-bloom azaleas would look boring.

There are four ways to propagate lilies. Small bulbils appear in the leaf axils of many species. These can be planted and will produce a plant that is genetically identical to the parent. The flowers also make seed, which can cheaply and quickly increase stocks—and the seeds don't carry viruses that can infect many types. Lilies grown from seed will be mixtures of parent plants. In addition, many lilies produce bulblets around the stem just under the soil surface. These can be separated from the stem and will produce plants like the parents. Finally, the bulbs that you've planted will grow and can be broken into scales that also produce new plants identical to the parents, much as a garlic bulb can be separated into cloves that will each grow a new garlic plant.

The types that produce no stem bulblets are usually planted in autumn about twice as deep as the bulb is wide. Varieties producing stem bulblets are usually planted in the spring and set to a depth about three times their diameters. Planting instructions will come with your shipment of lily bulbs. Just make sure you plant them where drainage is good. Lilies will not tolerate wet feet, except for the bog species mentioned. Buy American-grown bulbs. Cheap bulbs in bulk may carry a virus or be small and unhealthy.

Because of extensive hybridization over the years, the classification of lilies is pos-

Perennial Genera That Attract Hummingbirds

Many of these flowers have elongated nectaries that most likely coevolved with hummingbirds and moths with long tongues.

Aquilegia	*Nepeta*
Delphinium	*Penstemon*
Dianthus	*Phlox*
Hemerocallis	*Salvia*
Heuchera	*Saponaria*
Iris	*Scabiosa*
Lilium	*Verbena*
Lupinus	*Yucca*
Monarda	

itively baroque. Botanists and the American Lily Society have made a good attempt to straighten things out and have developed nine official lily divisions.

Division I includes the June-flowering Asiatic hybrids, the first lilies to bloom each year. Divide bunched bulbs every few years.

Division II lilies are called Martagon hybrids, after the name of one of their parents. They make stem bulblets and carry pendent flowers with recurved tips.

Division III through Division V includes several kinds of lilies that are not generally commercially available, although they may occasionally be found.

Division VI includes the Aurelian hybrids, also known as trumpet hybrids. They resemble the Asiatic hybrids, except that their flowers are larger—up to 10 inches across—and they bloom later in summer.

Division VII lilies are the August-flowering, oriental hybrids. The flowers, which can reach a foot across in the largest cultivars, are marvelously fragrant and come in trumpet, bowl, flat, or recurved forms.

Division VIII is a special category for hybrids not classified in any other division, and examples are not ordinarily commercially available.

Bulblets below Ground

Bulbils in Leaf Axils

Scales

Three ways to propagate lilies (clockwise from top right): from bulblets that form underground, as for Lilium longiflorum; *from scales; and from bulbils that grow in leaf axils.*

Division IX includes all true wild species and their cultivars.

Lily bulbs don't have the covering that protects bulbs, such as daffodils, tulips, and crocus, from drying out, so beware of shriveled lily bulbs that are sold three-for-a-dollar in a bin at the hardware store. The bulbs should be big, juicy, and turgid. If you can't immediately plant an order of bulbs that comes in the mail, wrap them in a sheet of paper toweling, then place them in a plastic bag, twist-tied shut, and store in the refrigerator until you can plant them.

Lilies look best in groups of three, I think, although a whole bed twinkling with their various colors makes a playful appearance. Try them in combination with perennials like blue lobelia, gypsophila, and *Campanula lactiflora.*

As with most bulbous plants, lilies store food reserves for next year's bloom in their bulbs. Thus it's important to retain as many leaves as possible on the stems when taking cut flowers. After flowering, let the green stems turn yellow and then brown before cutting them down. It's probably a good idea to remove the seed heads after the blossoms drop, to prevent the plants from spending their energy ripening seeds.

Lilies need a cold, dormant period, so growers in Zones 9 and 10 can handle them like annuals, taking them up after the foliage dies and putting them in the refrigerator for six to eight weeks, wrapped as described above.

Planting bulblets may give you flowers the following year, but expect to wait for a while when propagating from scales off the base bulb or from leaf axil bulbils. You will find, if you've never grown lilies, that the wait is worth it. Whatever we grow flowers for, whether it's the floral display, scent, or to cover a spot of ground, lilies often do it the best.

Two sources specializing in lilies are:

Blackthorne Gardens
    48 Quincy Street
    Holbrook, MA 02343

Rex Bulb Farms
    P.O. Box 774
    Port Townsend, WA 98368

Paeonia (Peony)

It was one of those hot, muggy, late June days when Marilyn brought home a trunk full of Chinese peonies that she'd rescued from a yard about to be bulldozed for a housing project. These beauties had to be planted immediately. The heat was oppressive, but I dug a trench 2 feet wide and 1 foot deep on top of a knoll, where an emerging garden of perennials and shrubs was taking form.

The peonies had finished blooming but were in full foliage, so we didn't divide them. They went into the trench as they had been dug out of the doomed yard, set at the same depth as they'd been growing before. Soil, enriched with compost and a handful of wood ashes, was firmed around the roots of each plant, and soon afterward, a thunderstorm drenched everything. Our peonies hardly faltered, and next season we were rewarded with a garden backdrop of gorgeous double pink peonies.

While peonies are best dug and divided in spring or late August, they can be moved in early summer, if watered well, into fresh soil. To divide, first dig up the root ball and shake off the soil. Divide the ball so that each piece of root has at least three eyes.

The eyes are the reddish growing buds that emerge from the tops of the roots and which you'll find in early spring and fall.

The Chinese peonies (*Paeonia lactiflora* hybrids) are usually about 3 feet tall and carry huge globular flowers that will topple over in a rain and turn to mush if they lie on the ground. These plants need staking. Wire hoops on supports work well.

Other kinds of peonies grow only to about 2 feet and don't usually need staking. Among these are the pretty, deep red blooms of *Paeonia officinalis*—the Memorial Day peony—and the deep crimson cups of *P. tenuifolia*—the fern-leaved peony. Both *P. officinalis* and *P. tenuifolia* have lovely ferny foliage that persists through the summer as an interesting leaf texture in the border or bed. Foliage of the Chinese types also persists through the summer, giving a dark green background to associations of other, later-blooming perennials.

Figure that Chinese peonies will grow to a width of about 4 feet across from divisions planted about 18 inches apart in the row. The ferny types will take up about 3 feet when fully grown; that is, when they've been in place about three years. Peonies are hardy and dependable perennials and will undoubtedly outlast the people who planted them. For the biggest and best blooms, though, the plants can be dug and divided and replanted into fresh, fertile soil every ten years. Yearly maintenance is as simple as a shovelful of compost shaken down over each clump in the spring, with perhaps some wood ashes dusted on every few years.

Peonies are subject to attack by Botrytis rot. You may notice that buds turn brown and rot before opening, and even leaves can be affected. You can try spraying them with fungicides like lime-sulfur to prevent the

Paeonia *(Peony)*

Botrytis. Ants frequently visit the peony buds before they open, but don't worry about them. They're only after a sweet exudate and won't harm the plant. In fact, some gardeners say that it's the ants' tiny strokes that encourage the blossoms to open.

Some tried and true associations with peonies include early bulbs, such as daffodils, planted near the emerging foliage. When the bulbs have finished flowering, their foliage, which must be retained for six to eight weeks, will be covered over by the peonies. Ferns also make an excellent interplant with peonies and are nice behind them in the border. Planted close to the peonies, ferns can help stake them, too. Iris makes another fine foil for peonies. Few associations are lusher-looking than Chinese peonies and tall bearded Iris.

Most of the Chinese peonies are fragrant, with a light, sweet smell. They make fine cut flowers to perfume the air in the house. Especially fragrant are *Paeonia lactiflora* 'Bowl of Cream', 'Mrs. Franklin D. Roosevelt', and 'Sarah Bernhardt'. When taking cut flowers, leave at least three leaves on each stem so that the plant can use the stem to make food for next year's bloom.

While Chinese peonies stay in the area where you put them, *Paeonia officinalis* and *P. tenuifolia* will produce creeping underground stolons that slowly enlarge the area covered.

The Chinese types come in single- and double-flowered forms, and in some varieties the yellow stamens in the center have elongated to form a striking contrast with the petal colors.

There are thousands of named varieties of Chinese peonies, less of the other kinds. But they are all staples of the May and June garden, starting with fern-leaved peonies and progressing through Memorial Day peonies to the large Chinese varieties. No early summer perennial garden should be without them.

Papaver (Poppy)

First, the bad news. Oriental poppies (*Papaver orientale*) are hard to get rid of once they get their roots going. Their typical flaming oranges are not subtle. And their thistley-looking foliage dies away by July. Now for the good news: There are white, pink, crimson, and salmon varieties with easy-to-harmonize colors. The flowers are large and gorgeous, sometimes up to a foot across. And their foliage is back again by September to overwinter and produce dependable bloom in succeeding years.

Bud Peacock gave us our first oriental poppies—probably the orange 'Harvest Moon'. When our garden was primarily yellows and oranges through much of the year, they fit right in. But we've moved toward pink and blue in the past few years, and now the poppies stick out like a sore thumb. Our old patch is kept in place by nearby digging and a lot of pinching, and now it adds just an accent to set off surrounding colors.

We placed specimens of 'Big Jim', a deep carmine poppy, beneath our grapevines, and there they've stayed ever since, unable to colonize the surrounding grapes' territory or the grass that borders the arbor. At about the time the grapes are blooming with their tiny, inconspicuous flowers, 'Big Jim' adds its deep red accent to the lush, new, yellow-green grape foliage unfolding around it.

And we've placed salmon-pink 'Helen Elizabeth' with our Siberian iris to our great delight. There is also a white cultivar, 'White King', that we'd like to acquire.

Besides being dependable, these poppies are trouble-free. They like poor to average soil that tends toward dryness and so

Papaver *(Poppy)*

are great for filling an area of shallow top-soil. The plant's overwintering basal rosette grows quite large and formidable looking; it's hairy and bristly, but doesn't puncture the skin as thistles do.

Poppies will do all the filling-in you want, so division isn't usually needed to enlarge an area of them. To start a new area, divide them in August, when dormant, and take 4-inch pieces of the growing roots. Replant the root pieces as deep as they grew—about 3 inches—and water them in. By fall, new leaves will appear. The plants should flower the next year.

Poppy flowers are spectacular. The petals appear to be made of crepe paper or thin tissue, and the top of the center pod and sometimes the base of the petals are a dark black or maroon, which contrasts well with the intense petal color. Blossoms are from 6 to 12 inches across and fall soon after opening, but constantly emerging flower buds on long, sprawly, hairy stalks keep them coming for three to four weeks. When I'm around poppies at bloom time, I've taken to cutting back the spent stalks below leaf level, so that the clump doesn't become a forest of pods on stalks with only a few blooms.

If too many flowers of too intense a color start to open, they can be cut for magnificent indoor or porch displays, but they do need a little special handling. Take the cuttings of nodding buds just showing color in the evening when it's almost dark. Sear the stem ends with a lighter or match until the bottom 2 or 3 inches are burned. Immediately put them into a pail of warm (100°F) water, deep enough to immerse the stems to within an inch or so of the flower bud. Set them on the porch overnight and arrange them in a vase with water the next morning. The flowers will open and keep their petals for about four days.

The dark green foliage of poppy plants is not pretty after the bloom has finished. It declines slowly until about the third week in July, when the mostly desiccated remains can be easily removed by hand. Gertrude Jekyll solved the problem of poppy foliage by planting baby's breath (*Gypsophila elegans*) nearby and encouraging it to grow over the poppy leaves. Phlox and other later-bloomers will also help hide the foliage.

Like peonies, poppies don't do well in Zone 10, but they can be grown in Zone 9 in areas where the nights are cool, as around the San Francisco area.

Phlox

When midsummer hits full stride, the big, bright, bold flower heads of *Phlox paniculata* appear. Cultivars run from blazing pink to light blue (with white, of course), giving the gardener a range of colors for associations.

Because of its airy, empty balls of flaring petals, *Phlox paniculata* presents its best appearance when seen in masses from a distance. It's a choice selection for stating a main color theme or for drifting among other colors to harmonize them. And its bright cultivars can be used as accents with plants of complementary colors. When used in large drifts, phlox associates well with lighter-colored plants like artemisias.

Phlox paniculata's colors range from the blue-to-pink side of the spectrum to the orange-to-red side. Keep these sides apart. A little orange phlox, such as 'Orange Perfection', can be seen from a long way off—and will react from a distance with nearby

Three Phlox *species:* P. panicula *(top),* P. divaricata *(center), and* P. subulata *(bottom).*

dew, keep the individual plants about 2 feet apart, so that air can circulate freely among the leaves. We find that phlox in areas of poorer soil seems to be more prone to mildew, so make sure it has a rich, humusy, and well-drained soil. The mildew doesn't destroy the plants, but it does discolor the leaves. If it shows up on our phlox, we tend to let it alone. But many gardeners spray with a wettable elemental sulfur powder. If you spray, keep the powder away from the flowers and buds, as it can discolor them. As a final step against mildew, each clump of phlox can be reduced to four or five stems to promote good air circulation.

Phlox can be divided in the spring or in early September. It will need this treatment about every three years or so, depending on how thickly it's grown. When the centers of the plants get old, dig up the plant and shake the soil from the roots. Immediately cut sections from the outer, growing part that carries from three to five buds. Plant these root cuttings promptly in a new bed, or replant in the old spot and water them in well. Set them as deep as they grew before. Discard the old centers. When dividing plants like this, check the roots for signs of damage by soil organisms, such as knots or decaying spots on the roots. If you see such damage, use well-rotted compost to fill the planting hole, and put the divisions in that. When dividing in spring, do it as soon as the plant sends up enough leaves to be recognized. September may be an easier time to propagate, for you can tag the plants by color.

This perennial is a fairly prolific seed sower, and the seedlings usually produce uninspiring flower colors. You can prevent self-sowing by removing the flower heads as soon as they're spent.

lavenders, even when separated by a neutral color. Many gardeners reserve the orange and vermilion colors for their own spot.

If you've never grown phlox, you probably don't know that it has a secret treat: a lovely fragrance that is unique to this flower.

Phlox is notoriously subject to mildew in warm, humid conditions. To prevent mil-

Since phlox withstands the scorching heat of July, remaining in bloom for a month and presenting a large, substantial presence in the bed, it is a main player in most perennial gardens. In your planning, reserve some choice spots for it in the July garden.

While most people think of *Phlox paniculata* when they hear the name, there are several other very useful kinds of phlox.

Phlox carolina 'Miss Lingard' is a white phlox that looks a lot like *P. paniculata,* but it blooms about three or four weeks earlier. It's more resistant to mildew than the later species. 'Miss Lingard' has been a staple in perennial gardens for many years and undoubtedly will continue its role as the first and featured phlox.

Phlox divaricata is a lovely species that grows only 15 inches tall, compared to 3 feet for *P. paniculata* and *P. carolina.* It blooms in May and June, sending up loose clusters of lavender-blue flowers.

Another May and June bloomer is *Phlox subulata,* or moss pinks. This plant is the bright carpet of springtime color that people often grow along the edges of their lawns and call "pinks" (not to be confused with dianthus, which is also called pinks). *P. stolonifera* is a similar, low-growing species that spreads from underground stolons. It produces clusters of clear blue flowers, rather than the mat effect of *P. subulata* and is a jewel of the spring garden. While other phloxes like full sun or bright shade, *P. stolonifera* tolerates a partially shady spot, where its use as a ground cover is common. Both *P. subulata* and *P. stolonifera* grow about 6 inches high.

Phlox carolina is handled like *P. paniculata,* but *P. divaricata* and *P. subulata* should be divided in spring after flowering. *P. stolonifera* can be divided in spring or fall.

Perennials Frequented by Butterflies

These flowers are visited by butterflies during the day:

Allium spp.	Hesperis matronalis
Asclepias tuberosa	Lavandula spp.
Aster novi-belgii	Lychnis spp.
Centaurea cyanus	Lythrum salicaria
Dianthus spp.	Nepeta × faassenii
Echinacea purpurea	Phlox paniculata
Echinops ritro	Sedum × spectabile
Erigeron speciosus	Solidago spp.
Eryngium amethystinum	Viola odorata
Helenium autumnale	

These flowers are visited by moths at night:

Echinops ritro	Oenothera spp.
Hesperis matronalis	Saponaria officinalis
Lathyrus odoratus	Viola cornuta

These phloxes are all easy to grow and, with the exception of mildew on *P. paniculata,* are relatively trouble-free. Their colors are rich and bold. They're all worth including in your plans.

Primula (Primrose)

"Being led down the primrose path" isn't so bad, given the enormous range of color and types of these wonderful, low-growing spring bloomers. There are over 500 kinds of primroses, but we'll concentrate on the few that are most widely, and most easily, grown.

Primulas are not low-maintenance perennials, and sometimes they refuse to be perennial, acting like biennials in the warmer climates. They need to be divided when the leaves of the emerging plants are too close together, usually every other year, but often every year in soil they like. The primroses described in this section should be dug out and divided immediately after flowering. If they tend to die out on you after flowering, sow some seed in a nursery bed, or in the primroses' spot in the garden each year. Most primroses grow easily from seed.

English gardens are identified with primroses, and that gives American gardeners a clue to their cultivation. Primulas like cool, moist summers, and some varieties require relatively mild winters: conditions found in England. Fortunately, the most commonly grown kind, *Primula polyantha* (sometimes called simply polyanthus), is hardy to Zone 3, along with the fragrant *P. auricula.* Other commonly grown types are hardy to Zone 4 or 5, depending on your elevation. This genus likes a moist, even wet, soil that's slightly acid—garden soil enriched with compost or well-rotted manure will do. The plants like shade, so find them a spot, perhaps bordering a shady part of the path or lawn, where you can water them easily during dry spells.

Most primulas have tongue-shaped, leathery-looking leaves that tend to have a crinkle in them. Sometimes these leaves are evergreen.

One of the first primulas to bloom in spring is *Primula denticulata* var. *cachemiriana,* or the Kashmir primrose. It sends up an 8-inch flower stalk in April or May and covers it with blossoms of various colors, most commonly white or purple with yellow centers. Its flower petals are charmingly toothed. Another early bloomer is *P. juliana* hybrids. Juliana primroses are profuse bloomers and can be found in colors ranging from yellow through red to purple, as well as white.

Tufts of large florets with yellow centers held about 10 inches above greenish yellow leaves characterize *Primula polyantha.* Blue, gold, pink, red, and white cultivars are available for this winter-hardy type.

Primula officinalis is the wild cowslip, typically yellow or cream, although also found in red and purple cultivated varieties. Wild cowslips are common in the temperate regions.

Two Primula *species:* P. polyantha *(left) and* P. denticulata *(right).*

Then there are the candelabra primulas—so-called because their flowers are borne in tiered whorls up the flower stalk. The most common type is *Primula japonica,* which is not hardy much farther north than the middle of Zone 5.

There is one species that claims to be the true primrose. It's popularly known as English primrose, and its Latin name is *Primula acaulis.* Often found as a light yellow flower, it, too, has been bred into a range of hues from red to purple. There are even some light orange types. Its fragrance is sweet and it's hardy to Zone 4.

Most of the primroses named here are available in both single- and double-flowered forms.

One of the chief glories of the primrose is its exquisite colors, especially the creams, ivories, greys, and pale yellows, and the deep, rich, chocolate-red and chestnut-purple colors set off with yellow centers. The plants deserve a spot in the garden where they can show off these intramural color associations. Primroses are wonderful perennials to edge a bed or border because their size is right—seldom over a foot high—and their colors provide a little jingle at the base of larger masses of pure color given by bulbs and other spring flowers.

Veronica

Veronica is named after St. Veronica, who wiped the face of Christ as he carried his cross, then discovered the imprint of his face on her kerchief. And, yes, there's something heavenly about veronicas with their colors and floral fingers pointing upward.

Veronicas are wonderfully useful plants in the perennial garden. They feature tall, graceful spires that open their small blossoms from the bottom up. They come in a variety of sizes, from *Veronica prostrata* with its tiny flower spires, to large species with 2-foot candelabras of white, red, pink, blue, violet, and purple.

Most veronicas bloom in June and July, although the low-growing, mat-forming kinds often bloom in May, and the commonly seen *Veronica longifolia* 'Subsessilis' blooms well into August.

Veronicas are sun-lovers, and they need a good, well-drained garden soil with adequate moisture to look their best. About every three or four years, dig up and divide the plants to keep them young and fresh and to increase the size of the plantings. Cuttings can also be rooted in summer to more quickly increase the number of a favorite kind.

The hard-to-find true blues are given by *Veronica latifolia* 'Crater Lake Blue'— a very deep shade of blue and one of the best of the taller types. A dark royal or navy blue is produced by *V. spicata* 'Blue Peter' and 'Blue Charm'.

If you're thinking of mixing veronicas of different colors, consider *Veronica spicata* 'Red Fox' with one of the blue types. For a white addition to the association, there's *V. spicata* 'Icicle'.

We love the low veronicas, and our rock garden contains *Veronica prostrata* 'Heavenly Blue', which in May gives us 5-inch, deep blue flowers above mat-forming, glossy leaves. *V. alpina* 'Alba' is a white carpet of small spikes when it blooms in June, reaching from 6 to 9 inches.

A light blue species is *Veronica incana,* or woolly speedwell. This plant has silvery leaves with light blue flowers in June and July.

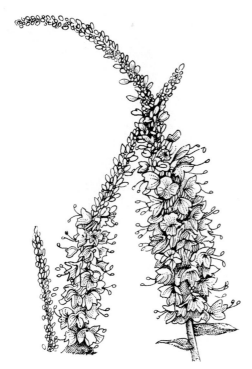

Veronica

Veronicas grow well in Zones 4 to 8. They are problematical in the warmer zones and don't do well in the southern part of Florida. You'll find them trouble-free plants, with no real insect or disease problems.

Because of their true blues, exciting pinks, vertical shape, persistent foliage, and general good nature in the garden, veronicas rank among our favorite perennials.

Viola

Both violets and pansies belong to this genus, along with over a hundred other species and types. Each spring the world abounds with violets—in our woods they grow large and purple, or small and white with a sweet perfume.

Closer to home, violets pop up every-where, both the violet-colored ones and the white and blue confederate violets (what are confederate violets doing in those colors?). Our cultivated spring violets are *Viola odorata,* so named in honor of their fragrance.

Viola odorata makes small mounds of heart-shaped leaves each spring, a few of which make it into our annual batch of homemade, seven-herb spring tonic. The typical violet flowers of garden varieties come in purple, red, pink, and white. Mixed along a border, they make a cheery sight in early spring.

One can divide violets after spring bloom, but they are most often propagated from the offset plants that arise near a parent. And they are easily grown from seed—so easily that the wild forms are a weed in the vegetable garden.

Viola tricolor—the Johnny-jump-up—also self-sows readily, and it's always welcome. This flower gets its nickname from its habit of suddenly appearing in a corner of the garden where it hasn't been planted, obviously from seed carried there by some creature or by the breeze. But *V. tricolor* doesn't take over the way dandelions do. It modestly jumps up here and there, usually just where you'd have planted it if you'd have thought of it. One of the prettiest chance associations in our garden last spring was the burgundy, yellow, and white little pansies of the Johnny-jump-ups in front of bright pink *Phlox subulata.*

Just a few plants of *Viola tricolor* will soon spread enough seed to make them a common, if unplanned, sight. They are, in essence, perennial wild pansies with a taste for nicely done gardens. The biennial form of this species, *V. tricolor* var. *hortensis,* which is not considered in this book, is the

Three species of Viola: *sweet violet (left), viola (center), and Johnny-jump-up (right).*

large, multicolored pansies familiar to everyone.

If you are a pansy lover and want more and varied colors and larger flowers than Johnnies can offer, consider the perennial *Viola cornuta,* or tufted pansy. Its flowers are pansy shaped, but usually a solid color, such as the apricot 'Chantreyland', the rich red 'Arkwright Ruby', and the simple blue 'Jersey Gem'. The heart-shaped leaves show the plant's relationship to violets, but its pansy character comes through in its long blooming season. Flowers will continue blooming until September if the plants are picked over to remove spent blooms.

Although Johnnies like sun as well as partial shade, both *Viola cornuta* and *V. odorata* prefer partial shade. Because of its woodland heritage, *V. odorata* likes rich, humusy soil that stays moist. Both *V. tricolor* and *V. cornuta* will thrive in average garden soil. Start *V. cornuta* and *V. tricolor* seed right in the garden and keep their spot moist.

Bulbs

Bulbs are among the most fascinating garden plants. The checkered fritillary (*Fritillaria meleagris*), for instance, has mauve and buff checks on its dangling petals. Leucojum has dots of light green on its hanging petal tips. *Allium giganteum,* the big ornamental onion, opens a huge lilac ball of florets. Lilies come in every color of the rainbow and some colors that aren't in the rainbow. Bulbs will start before the frost is entirely out of the ground and continue all summer, the sequence of bloom being carried forward by a couple dozen common genera.

Our first perennial plantings were spring bulbs. We set out some crocuses, snowdrops, scillas, and glories of the snow. After twelve years, they are still where we put them. They return faithfully each year with ever-increasing bloom as their bulbs replicate underground. That first year we also

These plants are sometimes found at nurseries as year-old plants and will bloom the year they're planted. They are also occasionally found as started seedlings, which are set out for bloom the following season. Most often, gardeners start them from seed in a nursery bed in the summer, then transplant them to the flower beds in the fall for bloom the following spring. After biennials bloom, they die back, and so they are usually pulled after blooming and replaced with divisions of perennials, such as chrysanthemums. Many will self-sow and so will continue to bloom annually in areas where they were originally planted.

Althaea rosea: Hollyhocks (will persist beyond the second year, but give the best bloom when treated as biennial)

Campanula medium: Canterbury Bells

Dianthus barbatus: Sweet William

Digitalis purpurea: Foxglove

Lunaria annua: Honesty, or Money Plant

Myosotis sylvatica: Forget-Me-Not

Papaver nudicaule: Iceland Poppies

Salvia sclarea var. turkestaniana: Vatican Sage

Verbascum olympicum: Ornamental Mullein

Viola × wittrockiana: Pansy

planted some *Tulipa praestans* 'Fusilier', which have long since died out, and several groups of puschkinia, which have grown spindly.

We've never fed these bulbs or dug them up to give them more room. Our experience shows most of them to be perennial, insect-free, carefree plants that make each spring something to really look forward to. Over the years, we have added many others, from the tiny yellow eranthis that blooms through the snow, to the large imperial fritillaria. Our clumps of daffodils increased to the point where digging and separating into improved soil was necessary to keep the bloom count high.

Bulb soil is good garden soil, improved with some compost and perhaps a handful of bone meal in the area covered by a handful of small bulbs. A light scattering of wood ashes in good loam, plus compost, is also a good recipe for improving bulb soil. Plant bulbs with the roots or root eyes down and the pointed tip (if the bulb has one) up. Most bulbs are like common onions, and if you can tell the top of an onion from the bottom, you'll have no problem with bulbs. Planting depth varies with the kind of bulb, and depths are given in the chart, Perennial Flowering Bulbs. You can also remember this general rule: Plant bulbs about three times as deep as they are wide. A bulb that measures 1 inch or smaller goes about 3 inches deep; one 3 to 4 inches in diameter goes about a foot deep. Exact depth is not critical.

We plant spring bulbs in late September through October here in Pennsylvania, when the soil is cooling. This preserves the bulbs' dormancy through winter. Planting too early risks having them break dormancy and push up foliage, which weakens them.

It's important to dig deeper than the bulbs will be planted in order to get improved soil and better drainage into the bottom zone, where the roots will seek nour-

Assorted bulbs (left to right): scilla, daffodil, muscari, tulip, anemone, fritillaria, and crocus.

ishment. The drainage is all important, for bulbs that sit in water will die.

So will bulbs whose top growth gets consistently cut off before the leaves can make enough sugar to pack the bulb with power for next season's growth. The best rule is to let the leaves die back naturally and don't mess with them. Before cleaning them up or cutting them, wait at least six to eight weeks after bloom, when the leaves are partially brown. By that time, most bulb foliage will be brown anyway. When you plant bulbs in the perennial bed or border, plan to group them with plants that will cover up browning bulb foliage, such as ferns, hostas, and lower ground covers like the dead nettles (*Lamium*), pachysandra, ajuga, asarum, sweet woodruff (*Asperula*), and Jacob's ladder (*Polemonium*).

Some gardeners use special beds for spring bulbs. I've never understood why. We like them everywhere, and all our perennial beds have some. They start the year with bright bursts of color, cheer things up, and get the world ready for the show to follow. They *are* the opening act in the perennial garden.

Some gardeners plant bulbs in rows, sometimes as edging for flower beds. This looks too cutesy-pie for my taste, and I like to see them used exactly like other perennial flowers—in drifts and clumps, although perhaps in smaller drifts and clumps than with rooted perennials.

Small drifts are required for the small bulbs like crocus, chionodoxa, scilla, and muscari. A drift of 25 of these little bulbs will occupy just a square foot or so of earth. They look best planted in masses, because otherwise their diminutive flowers get lost in the landscape.

Some of the larger woodsy bulbs like *Leucojum aestivum,* narcissus, and species tulips can be naturalized, which in this sense means that they can be made to look natural, as if they were growing wild. Some people toss the bulbs into an area and bury them where they fall. This could certainly result in a casually pretty arrangement, but it might also result in an awkward appearance. When I plant things to look natural, I usually ask myself where I'd like to be if I were a galanthus, for instance. Then a moment's still perception of the ground reveals the right spot. Yet another method is to plant the bulbs as you think they'd grow in the wild: in clumps here and there with a few loners. Many bulbs, like narcissus, also naturalize in the sense that they naturally grow to fill areas and take over spots, both from offsets of the parent bulb and from seed.

Colors can be grouped in the perennial garden with bulbs just as with other plants: to suit your taste, but with an eye for harmony and subtlety. Many of the spring bulbs have intense colors, however, so don't worry too much about subtlety. We are all so happy for the return of spring, as evidenced by the appearance of our bulbous friends, that their bright color associations are most welcome.

If you have poor soil, you may want to top-dress your bulbs in late winter with well-rotted manure. And it's a good idea to remove spent blooms from bulbs, where feasible, to force the plant to put its resources into bulb growth rather than seed production, and to prevent the setting of unwanted seed.

Almost all bulbs like full sun, but many will tolerate partial shade. A few actually prefer partial shade: *Leucojum* species, *Anemone blanda,* eranthis, colchicum, and erythronium.

Some "bulbs" are not true bulbs at all, but tubers, corms, or fat rhizomes. In the chart, Perennial Flowering Bulbs, we've endeavored to include the true bulbs and roots that act, and are usually grouped, as bulbs. We've kept to the bulbs and bulblike rooted plants that are found in the major mail-order catalogs.

Ferns

We're accustomed to seeing ferns in the moist woods, and that's the same environment they prefer in the garden. The ideal spot for ferns would be under deciduous trees giving a light shade, in humusy and acid soil (although some of the small ferns for rock gardens like a neutral soil) that's constantly moist but always drained. Of this set of ideal conditions, the most im-
(continued on page 176)

Perennial Flowering Bulbs

BOTANICAL NAME (COMMON NAME)	ZONE	SEASON OF BLOOM	HEIGHT (IN INCHES)	COLOR	DEPTH × SPACING (IN INCHES)
Allium aflatunense	4–8	May–June	36	Lilac	6 × 10
Allium giganteum (Giant Onion)	4–9	June–July	48	Lilac	8 × 12
Allium moly (Lily Leek)	4–9	May–June	15	Yellow	3 × 3
Allium neapolitanum (Naples Allium)	6–9	April–May	18	White	3 × 3
Allium schoenoprasum (Chives)	4–9	June	12	Magenta	4 × 8
Allium tuberosum (Chinese Chives)	4–9	July	18	White	4 × 8
Anemone blanda (Windflower)	4–8	April–May	6	Blue, Pink, White	3 × 3
Brodiaea spp. (Grass-Nut)	4–9	May–June	12	Purple	3 × 4
Camassia spp. (Camass)	3–8	May–June	24	Blue, Purple, White	8 × 12
Chionodoxa spp. (Glory-of-the-Snow)	4–8	April	6	Blue, White	3 × 3
Colchicum autumnale (Meadow Saffron)	4–9	September	12	Pink, Lilac	3 × 12
Crocosmia × crocosmiiflora (Montebretia)	6–9	June–July	24–36	Red, Yellow, Orange	2 × 12
Crocus hybrids	3–8	April	5	Blue, Yellow, White, Purple	3 × 3
Crocus spp. (Early Crocus)	3–8	March	5	Purple	3 × 3
Crocus speciosus (Autumn Crocus)	6–9	September–October	6	Lavender	4 × 4
Cyclamen spp. (Hardy Cyclamen)	5–9	September–October	5	Red, Pink, White	2 × 8
Eranthis hyemalis (Winter Aconite)	4–9	March–April	4	Yellow	2 × 3
Eremurus hybrids (Foxtail Lily)	5–9	June–August	48	Pink, Orange, Yellow, White	6 × 24
Erythronium spp. (Trout Lily or Dog-Toothed Violet	4–9	April–May	8	Yellow, White	5 × 4

BOTANICAL NAME (COMMON NAME)	ZONE	SEASON OF BLOOM	HEIGHT (IN INCHES)	COLOR	DEPTH × SPACING (IN INCHES)
Fritillaria imperialis (Crown Imperial)	5–8	April–May	24	Red, Yellow	6 × 9
Fritillaria meleagris (Checkered Fritillary)	3–8	April–May	9	Mauve, White	3 × 4
Galanthus spp. (Snowdrop)	3–8	March	4	White	3 × 3
Galtonia candicans (Summer Hyacinth)	5–9	July–August	48	White	6 × 12
Hyacinthus orientalis (Hyacinth)	4–9	April	12	Various	6 × 6
Iris reticulata (Bulbous Iris)	4–9	March–April	6	Blue, Lavender	6 × 4
Leucojum aestivum (Snowflake)	3–8	April–May	15	White	5 × 6
Lycoris squamigera (Hardy Amaryllis)	5–8	August	24–36	Pink	5 × 5
Muscari botryoides (Grape Hyacinth)	3–8	April–May	6	Blue, Purple	3 × 3
Narcissus spp. (Daffodils, Jonquils, and Narcissus)	4–8	April–May	12–18	Yellow, White, Orange	6 × 10
Ornithogalum nutans (Nodding Star-of-Bethlehem)	4–9	May–June	15	White	4 × 4
Ornithogalum umbellatum (Star-of-Bethlehem)	3–9	May–June	9	White	4 × 4
Puschkinia scilloides	4–8	April	6	Blue, White	3 × 3
Scilla hispanica (Spanish Squill)	4–8	May–June	18	Blue, Pink, White	5 × 4
Scilla siberica (Siberian Squill)	4–8	April	5	Blue, White	3 × 3
Tulipa hybrids (Hybrid Tulips)	4–8	April–May	12–24	Pink, Red, Orange, Yellow, White, Lilac	6 × 6
Tulipa species (Species Tulips)	2–9	April–May	4–20	Red, Yellow, White, Lilac	5 × 6

portant is moisture, for if ferns dry out, they turn a ghastly brown.

Ferns are one of the most useful plants in the perennial garden. Their foliage is always distinct and beautiful and mixes well in associations where foliage contrast is a consideration (that should be most associations). Taller-growing ferns make a handsome, dark green backdrop for lower plants growing in front, separating them from taller flowering shrubs behind. Ferns also emerge and fluff out their feathery fronds just in time to cover the wreckage of spring flower displays. Ferns have no flowers—although a few put out fruiting structures—but their foliage is always beautiful by itself in a shady corner of the garden.

When preparing the soil for ferns, mix in some low-nitrogen, humus-building amendments, such as peat moss or rotted leaves. The underground rhizomes of most ferns divide easily, but it's best to try to reproduce in the new location the conditions where the ferns grew before. In spring, the deciduous leaves of some ferns lie sprawled around the emerging fiddleheads that announce the new growing season like party favors unfurling upward. The old leaves can be tidied up and used as mulch in the fern bed—the use nature intended—or used elsewhere or in the compost pile. If you remove fern leaves, replace them with some kind of mulch more to your liking: Peat moss or bark chips are two good possibilities.

In case you have forgotten your high school biology, fern fronds have a midrib to which the major leaf divisions—called pinnae—are attached. Many times the pinnae are divided into pinnules. Ferns reproduce in a fascinating way. Spore cases called sporangia grow either in patterns on the undersides of the pinnae or on special spore-producing structures. When spores are released, they fall to the ground and produce a flat little structure called a prothallus, which is smaller than a penny. The prothallus produces eggs and sperm. Fertilized eggs then grow into new ferns. It's primitive, but has served ferns well for their 345 million years on the planet.

Just as ferns set off bunches of cut flowers in indoor arrangements, so too do they set off flowers in the garden. Plants like dicentra, mertensia, astilbe, aquilegia, narcissus, iberis, and many other spring bloomers can be planted with ferns, which help to hide them later.

All ferns listed here are hardy from Zone 3 south. In Zones 9 and 10, ferns can be hard to grow because the hot, dry summers are just too far removed from their preferred habitat. There are ferns native to the South, however, that Gulf Coast and Florida gardeners may find at nurseries.

• *Adiantum pedatum.* The American maidenhair fern is arguably the prettiest fern around, and one of the earliest, leafing out in light green fronds a foot and a half tall to grace the spring flowers.

• *Athyrium filix-femina.* The lady fern will persist in full sun in the North, although like its fellow ferns it prefers light shade. The yellow-green fronds grow up to 3 feet tall, while its roots creep underground to fill in areas.

• *Athyrium goeringianum.* Japanese painted fern is the plant that gives maidenhairs a challenge for prettiest fern. The light leaves of this fern toss and tumble on the ground, making a rather bold pattern.

• *Dennstaedtia punctilobula.* Hay-

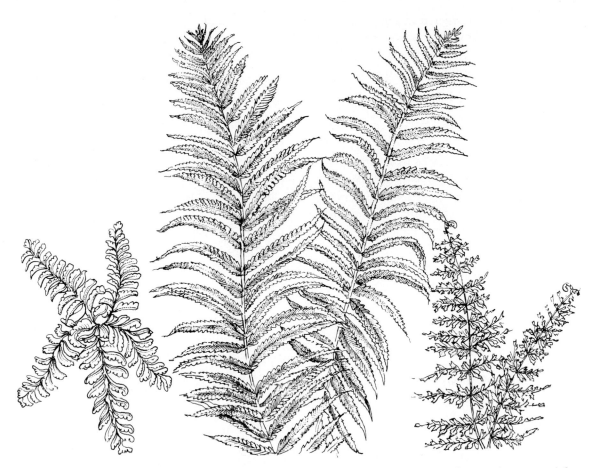

Three ferns: Adiantum pedatum, *or maidenhair fern (left);* Matteuccia struthiopteris, *or ostrich fern (center); and* Dennstaedtia punctilobula, *or hay-scented fern (right).*

scented ferns are often used as ground cover in woodsy areas of light shade. They are finely cut and dainty looking.

• *Matteuccia struthiopteris.* The ostrich fern gets its name from the fronds that resemble ostrich feathers. It likes a rich soil and tolerates full sun in the North. The fronds reach 5 feet tall. Ostrich fern is a marvelous accent plant.

• *Osmunda cinnamomea.* The cinnamon fern is a native American that likes a rich soil and light shade. Constant moisture, even bogginess, is its demand. The name comes from the cinnamon-colored down on the pinnae. This fern grows to 4 to 5 feet and gives a noble, striking appearance.

• *Osmunda regalis.* The royal fern produces spore structures that rise from the center of the circle of 6-foot fronds, forming a vaselike shape. It grows naturally in swampy places, but will tolerate drained soils if they are kept moist and mulched.

• *Polypodium virginianum.* The common polypody likes to grow in mats over rocks and stumps and makes a decorative addition to shaded portions of the rock garden. It never gets much above 10 inches in height. Plant the rhizomes at ground level and mulch them, then don't disturb them.

• *Polystichum acrostichoides.* The Christmas fern grows slowly from the crown and reaches 2 feet in height. It's an evergreen fern whose fronds are used for Christmas decorations. It looks quite like a Boston fern.

Grasses

"Break out of the English border idea," urges James A. van Sweden, a Washington, D.C., landscape designer who uses grasses in his designs to do just that. "Put perennials in new and unusual places. Get them out of the garden. Forget lawn and foundation plantings and rethink your property."

Van Sweden, for instance, designed a garden of ornamental grasses at a building of the Federal Reserve in Washington. Although common wisdom says that too many grasses used together lose importance, stop in at the Martin Building next time you're in the capital and see what van Sweden has wrought: an exquisite garden in which the repeated curved lines of the grasses dance over the horizontal quietude of the earth.

This garden is beautiful both in sum-

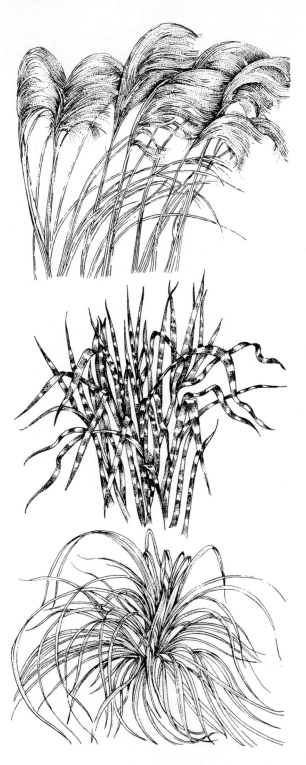

Three ornamental grasses: Miscanthus sinensis *'Gracillimus' (top),* Miscanthus sinensis *'Zebrinus' (center), and* Carex morrowii *(bottom).*

mer and in winter, for many grasses keep a bare-bones composition going even after their tops and plumes have turned brown from the frost. Many plumes, moreover, look best in late fall or early winter, when they've dried and fluffed out.

A large fountain of plume grass, *Erianthus hostii,* grows beside our long driveway, about 100 feet from the house, and screens the view of the receding driveway. This stand of tall grass throws out dozens of cotton-candy plumes in early fall and carries them until December, when winds disperse the fluff, leaving the not-unattractive skeletons of the plumes. Though it's the dead of winter, the grass still performs its functions: helping to maintain the property's composition, making a transition from driveway to lawns and gardens, and blocking the long view to promote a feeling of closeness and compartmentalized beauty.

Large masses of ornamental grasses reduce the size of mown lawn and usually need little maintenance. Most of the ornamental grasses are perennial, although there are some popular annuals. Many of the perennial kinds mulch themselves with their own long, slender leaves that form mats around the plants and keep down weeds. When you mass grasses in the garden, you need only mulch them until the grasses achieve maturity, usually by the third year.

From then on, with grasses being what they are, watch out for any that seem to be invasive. Have a set boundary in mind for your ornamental grasses, and, if they spill out of their place, ruthlessly carve them from the turf. I did this with our plume grass one year and threw the dug roots and broken tops in a heap behind the filberts. Need I say that today we have a lovely mixture of filbert bushes and plume grass?

Grasses come in forms large enough to anchor the landscape and separate areas of perennial color associations, and small enough to add foliage interest to flowering plant groups. Among the more beautiful combinations, for instance, is the lovely blue oat grass, *Helictotrichon sempervirens,* with broad-leaved perennials in blue, such as *Brunnera macrophylla,* or soft yellow, like *Alchemilla mollis.*

Grasses can be messy after snow and rain flatten their dried leaves, which blow around come spring. One answer is to cut off the leaves after frost, but in northern areas, this could lead to freezing damage. Besides, the leaves in winter are one of the best things about ornamental grasses. So, have a good rake handy and use the lawn mower to chop up any dried leaf blades that blow onto the lawn.

Grasses have fibrous or rhizomatous roots that divide easily. I simply push my shovel through the mats of grass and take clumps of the size I want, plant them as deep as they grew, water them well until they are established, and that's it. Division is best done in the spring before or during the time the leaf blades are emerging. Grasses, except the rushes and water grasses, like good, well-drained soils. Usually they like a limy soil, less often an acidic one. Most grasses prefer full sun. Those that tolerate shade are indicated on the chart, Perennial Ornamental Grasses.

Insects rarely attack grasses, but eat and let eat is the rule for the ornamental grower. As Jim van Sweden says, "You don't look perfect. Why should all the plants in your garden look perfect?"

The perennial ornamental grasses listed in the chart were selected by Richard Simon of Monkton, Maryland.

Perennial Ornamental Grasses

BOTANICAL NAME (COMMON NAME)	SEASON OF BLOOM	HEIGHT (IN FEET)	FLOWERS LAST UNTIL:	FOLIAGE LASTS UNTIL:	REMARKS
Arundo donax (Giant Reed Grass)	September	14	Early Winter	Early Winter	Flowers dry well.
Calamagrostis acutiflora (Feather Reed Grass)	June	4	Late Winter	Late Winter	Flowers dry well. Excellent mid size grass.
Carex conica 'Variegata' (Variegated Sedge)	—	½	—	Year-round	Used in masses as a ground cover.
Carex grayi (Star Sedge)	July	1½	Early Winter	Early Winter	Tolerates light shade; flowers dry well.
Carex morrowii 'Aurea Variegata' (Variegated Japanese Sedge)	—	½–1	—	Late Winter	Used in masses as ground cover; yellow variegations. 'Variegata' has white variegations.
Carex musking-umensis (Palm Sedge)	July	2	Early Winter	Early Winter	Unusual texture; flowers dry well.
Carex pendula (Weeping Sedge)	—	2	—	Early Winter	Tolerates partial shade.
Deschampsia caespitosa (Hair Grass)	July	1½	Early Fall	Late Winter	A drought-tolerant grass.
Erianthus hostii (Plume Grass)	August	14	Late Fall	Midwinter	Flowers dry well.
Festuca ovina var. glauca (Blue Fescue)	June	¾	Midsummer	Late Winter	Steel blue foliage in tufts.
Helictotrichon sempervirens (Blue Oat Grass)	—	2	—	Early Winter	Dusky blue foliage in tufted sprays.
Miscanthus sinensis (Eulalia Grass)	September	8	Early Winter	Late Winter	Good as a backdrop for smaller flowers.

BOTANICAL NAME (COMMON NAME)	SEASON OF BLOOM	HEIGHT (IN FEET)	FLOWERS LAST UNTIL:	FOLIAGE LASTS UNTIL:	REMARKS
Miscanthus sinensis 'Giganteus' (Giant Miscanthus)	September	15	Early Winter	Late Winter	Huge and bold; flowers dry well.
Miscanthus sinensis 'Gracillimus' (Maiden Grass)	September	7	Early Winter	Late Winter	Fine-textured grass; flowers dry well.
Miscanthus sinensis 'Variegatus' (Variegated Miscanthus)	September	6	Early Winter	Late Winter	Decorative variegations; flowers dry well.
Miscanthus sinensis 'Zebrinus'	September	6	Early Winter	Late Winter	Zebra-striped variegations; plant at poolside; flowers dry well.
Molinia altissima (Purple Moor Grass)	August	4–6	Late Winter	Late Winter	Impressive blooms that dry well.
Panicum virgatum (Switch Grass)	August	3–5	Early Winter	Late Winter	Flowers dry well.
Pennisetum alopecuroides	August	2–3	Early Fall	Late Winter	Works well in masses.
Phalaris arundinacea 'Picta' (Ribbon Grass)	—	1½	—	Early Winter	Very hardy.
Sorgastrum nutans (Indian Grass)	September	5	Early Winter	Early Winter	Naturalizes; flowers dry well.
Spartina pectinata 'Aureo-Marginata' (Prairie Cord Grass)	September	4	Early Winter	Early Winter	Spreads in dry and wet areas; flowers dry well.
Spodiopogon sibericus (Spodiopogon)	August	4–5	Late Fall	Late Fall	A superior grass with reddish leaves.
Uniola latifolia (Northern Sea Oats)	September	3	Late Winter	Late Winter	Tolerates partial shade; flowers dry well.

NOTE: These ornamental grasses are hardy to Zone 5, except for *Arundo donax*, which is hardy only to Zone 7.

Sedums and Sempervivums

These two succulents—plants with fleshy, sometimes evergreen leaves—find lots of uses in any garden. The tall sedums are used like late perennial flowers and the low sedums and sempervivums for ground covers in hot, dry areas. All will grow in sun or light shade.

Sedum spectabile 'Autumn Joy' is one of the most-raved-about perennials grown today. There's an entry on this plant in the chart in chapter 7, describing its easy-to-grow habits. Along with other sedums, commonly called stonecrops, it is attractive to butterflies and some moths. 'Autumn Joy' has a regular, mathematical form, as do many of the sedums, and puts up flower heads that show greenish yellow buds before opening pink flowers. The pink slowly changes to a dark mahogany by frost, giving very unusual color combinations with nearby plants. This year we discovered the value of 'Autumn Joy' in association with light purple hardy ageratum and purple sage. 'Autumn Joy' is actually a hybrid of *S. spectabile.* Cultivars are found in pink, red, and white forms.

Assorted sedums and sempervivums, clockwise from left: Sedum spectabile *'Autumn Joy', two species of* Sempervivum, *and* Sedum spathulifolium.

More even than their flowers, sedums please with their pretty growth patterns. *Sedum spectabile* is one of the tall species (it grows to 2 feet), along with similarly tall *S. aizoon, S. alboroseum, S. maximum, S. rosea,* and *S. telephium.* There are many shorter species, however, that dress up and soften the edges of rocks and walls. All these prefer average to poor soil and withstand drought. No insects bother them. They're not invasive, but they will usually spread slowly to fill areas. They are truly effortless to grow.

One of our favorite small sedums is *Sedum spurium* 'Green Mantle', which has dusty-soft, bluish green leaves that are globular and fleshy and hang prettily over walls and rocks.

Other small sedums, ranging from a couple of inches to about 6 inches in height, and having rosette forms, include the deciduous, clump-forming *Sedum ewersii, S. kamtschaticum, S. oreganum,* and *S. spathulifolium.* These plants are evergreen, the latter two making carpets of ground cover. Most of these have a somewhat dusty appearance, and you will sometimes find their leaf edges blushing with reddish color. The creamy soft colors are one of the best features of sedums, along with their neat, regular appearance.

Sedums are easily divided by simply slicing apart the root mass in the spring. They will also grow from stem cuttings rooted in wet perlite or sandy loam, then transferred to the garden. Sedums are generally hardy to Zone 3.

Sempervivums grow in low, flat rosettes that seem to live without water and retain their leaves all year, hence the Latin name meaning "always living." Their roots are short and quickly soak up available moisture, which is then stored in the thick, fleshy leaves for periods of drought. A dry wall holds our rock garden, and in its crannies two types of sempervivums live happily.

The most common kind is *Sempervivum tectorum,* better known as hens and chicks, or houseleeks. The parent rosette sends out many tiny "chicks," or smaller plants on stalky stems that protrude from its base. Propagation is simple: Pull off these small plants and bury their stalks in poor, dry soil. You can water them in, but they'll be happy to wait for a rain in the well-watered parts of the country.

An interesting variation is *Sempervivum arachnoideum,* called cobweb hens and chicks. White, cobwebby filaments connect its leaf tips; it looks as if a very thorough spider had set her web across its face.

Sempervivums are hardy to Zone 5 or 6 and need some mulch in the colder parts of Zone 5 and north.

CHAPTER 6

Maintaining a Perennial Garden

Maintaining perennials so they look good year after year means attending to soil improvement, watering when necessary, keeping weeds down, dividing the plants on schedule and starting new plants, and mulching tender crowns over winter. Let's look at these elements one by one.

The Value of Compost

Compost is partially decayed organic matter. It is the perfect fertilizer and soil conditioner in one. Most perennial plants like average, well-drained soil. An average soil is one that is loose and friable, but not too rich. Digging 4 inches of compost into the soil every three years will maintain most soils in average shape without loading on too much nutrition.

If plants call for richer soil, as do astilbes and delphiniums, adding compost every year in liberal amounts will keep it rich. Compost can't burn plants with high levels of nitrogen the way commercial N-P-K fertilizers can, even when plants are placed into pure compost. Nitrogen compounds stimulate plants to put out a great deal of stem and foliage growth. Potassium and phosphorus—the other two major soil nutrients—make the stems strong and the leaves tough, and encourage root formation

and flower development. High-nitrogen fertilizers stimulate most perennials past their ability to strengthen and toughen the foliage and stems, causing them to be weak and prone to fall over. Stem and foliage growth are produced at the expense of flowers and fruit—as all gardeners know who've overfertilized their tomatoes and ended up with huge leafy plants, but no tomatoes. Since flowers are the fruiting parts of perennials, overfeeding plants with nitrogen is counterproductive. The few that like rich soil, like delphiniums, are often the kind that put out a lot of growth quickly and need the tissue-building stimulus of nitrogen.

Leaves, lawn clippings, weeds, and even vegetable scraps from the kitchen are all organic matter, so all can go into the compost pile, recycling their nutrients to feed your favorite flowers. Compost will turn even clay soils into fluffy, easy-to-work, water-retentive loam. It contains all the nutrients that plants need and relinquishes them to the plants as they're needed. Compost, by virtue of the microorganisms in it, helps prevent plant disease organisms from gaining a foothold in the soil. It is wonderful, marvelous stuff that gives life to your garden.

Compost can be the end product of a pile of rotting organic matter that heats up to 140°F or more. It can also be the end product of the slow, cool decomposition of

184

plant matter, such as leaf mold.

Hot-rot compost contains lots of nitrogen and will satisfy the heavy-feeding perennials that need rich soil. (These special soil needs are identified in the chart in chapter 7.) We also use it for vegetables. It's great stuff, with maximum grow power—more grow power than most of your perennials will need.

Cold-rot compost is suited for the bulk of the flowers that need average soil. Cold-rot compost can be dug into the garden yearly, because it provides a smaller dose of nitrogen than hot-rot compost.

A hot-rot pile that has been exposed to a summer's rains will be leached of some of its soluble nitrogen compounds and could be applied around perennials after they enter dormancy in the fall. The compost would lose more nitrogen as it overwintered around the plants and be only moderately fertile in the spring, when new growth will call for the compounds. When any plant gets just barely what it needs, it looks "thrifty," nicely compact, which is just what we want in a flowering ornamental plant.

Making Hot-Rot Compost

A compost pile gets hot because high-nitrogen materials like fresh horse or cow manure are mixed in with the plant matter. Here's how it works: The microorganisms in decaying plant matter use nitrogen to make body tissue. When they have all the nitrogen they want—as when manure is mixed with plant matter—their populations explode until a teaspoonful of working compost will have billions of microorganisms in it. So furious is their reproductive capacity when given lots of nitrogen, that

the pile of plant matter starts to heat up. The temperature keeps rising—130°F, 140°F—until eventually only thermophilic (heat-loving) microorganisms are left. Free of competition and in a hot, nitrogen-rich environment with plenty of plant matter to tear apart, they quickly colonize the pile with quadrillions of themselves and churn through the bulk of the decomposition in a month. Then the fermentation process slows and the heat drops. At that point, the compost is full of nitrogen in the form of proteins, soluble compounds, and other by-products of microorganism metabolism.

Ingredients for hot-rot compost include manure, plant matter like cut hay or weeds, and possibly other amendments for special purposes. Most flowers need generous amounts of potassium and phosphorus—wood ashes contain lots of potassium, and bone meal is rich in phosphorus. I'd include bone meal in all composts for perennial flowers. For plants that like the soil slightly alkaline, you could add ground limestone or wood ashes, but these are better added later, dusting them on the soil before digging compost into it. Compost made from manure and plant matter, with some bone meal added, will naturally finish at a pH of about 6.5.

Choose a shady spot for composting, one that's near the garden and within range of the garden hose, for you have to water a compost pile. It's not necessary to scratch up the ground where you'll build the pile. I build mine right on top of whatever's growing there. If the weeds or grass are tall, however, I cut them down with a scythe.

I build my compost heaps in a square with 6-foot sides, but the pile can be round or rectangular. I don't use wire or boards to make a bin, either, although some people do. Since hot-rot piles need turning, sides would just be a nuisance. I start with about 8 inches of plant material and spread a couple of inches of manure on it. Horse and cow manure are good; pig manure is excellent. Chicken manure is very high in nitrogen and will make a very rich compost—better for vegetables than flowers. The manure of any herbivorous animal is fine, but don't use the manure of carnivores, such as dogs or cats, since it may carry intestinal parasites harmful to humans.

After spreading the manure, I dust on some bone meal. A 10-pound bag of bone meal would be enough for the whole pile. Then on goes another 8 inches of plant matter, another 2 inches of manure, and another dusting of bone meal. At this point, moisten the pile thoroughly with the hose, but don't drown it. Then continue to build the pile layer by layer, making the upper layers a little smaller so the pile has slightly sloping sides. Moisten the pile after each two layers. When it reaches 4 to 5 feet high, cover it with hay or with a sheet of black plastic.

After a week, take your pitchfork and shovel and turn the pile. Turn the top layers onto the ground next to the pile and rebuild it in the same shape. This gets air to the pile. If it has dried out at all, moisten it, but don't get it sopping wet. Cover again. You'll notice the heat beginning to build at this point.

This first turning is essential to mix the materials and get air to the exploding populations of thermophilic bacteria. Whether you turn the pile again depends on how much ambition you have. If you do, the compost will finish faster. Three weekly turnings will have it done in a month. If you don't turn it again, it will be three months before it's finished.

For gardeners who'd like to avoid trucking manure around, an excellent compost for perennials can be made from a 50-50 mix of leaves and grass clippings. You start by saving bags of leaves in the fall. I'd shoot for a dozen bags. In the spring, when grass bags start to appear along the sidewalks, get about a dozen full of fresh green clippings. Spring is when many lawns are treated with broad-leaf plant herbicides,

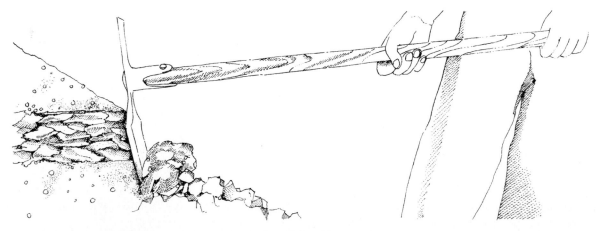

Use a mattock to break up a large compost pile.

however, so make sure that the clippings are from untreated lawns.

Build the pile with alternate 6-inch layers of leaves and grass clippings, moistening and dusting with bone meal as you go. Build the pile 6 feet wide and about 4 feet high, letting the length be determined by the amount of material you have. Let it sit for a week. Then turn it with a mattock and shovel. Stand before the front of the pile and swing the mattock so that it slices down through the layers, taking off 4- to 6-inch slices.

Rebuild the pile in a spot adjacent to the material sliced off by the mattock. Moisten if necessary as you rebuild. Because grass clippings are about as rich in nitrogen as cow manure, this type of pile will heat up perfectly well. From this point on, handle just as with the pile made with manure. It will be ready to use in about the same amount of time.

Making Cold-Rot Compost

This method is simplicity itself. Make a round enclosure about 6 to 8 feet in diameter, from chicken wire and stakes, poles, or what-have-you. Throw in all the grass clippings, leaves, pulled weeds, cut hay, or other plant matter you have available. No turning is necessary to make cold-rot compost. You need nothing but patience. After a year or two, the material on the bottom of the heap will become dark, rich, crumbly mold. Use this compost around your flowers and dig it in. It has rotted slowly and is

Compost bins can be made from all kinds of materials, including (top to bottom) chicken wire reinforced with wood, hardware cloth, snow fencing, and cinder blocks.

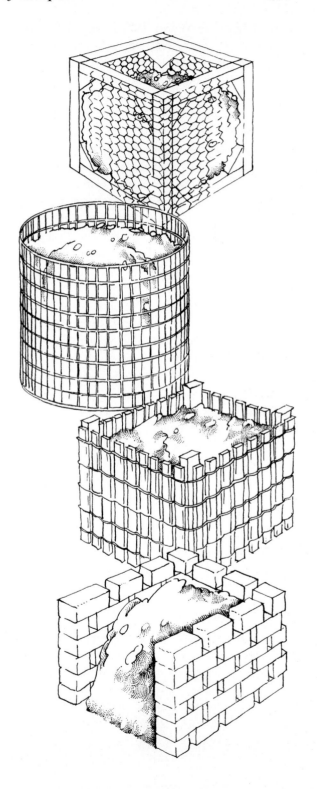

not rich in nitrogen, but it has plenty of nutrients tucked away in its humus particles, ready to feed perennials that like an average soil. Keep adding plant matter year by year to the top of the pile and taking it out of the bottom.

If some of the material is not completely decayed, either toss it back on the top of the heap or use it as a mulch. This method produces compost slowly, but if your bin is big enough and your garden small enough, it could be adequate. Most likely it won't be, though, for the first law of composting is that there is never enough compost. It just demands to be used liberally.

In the flower garden, it's probably a good idea to keep a few areas of relatively low fertility, where compost is seldom used, for those plants, such as irises, that actively *like* a poor soil.

With compost, maintaining adequate soil fertility isn't a problem. The richer the soil must be for a plant, the more compost you use. The poorer the soil must be, the less you use.

Finally, compost will maintain a good soil structure, keeping it light and loose. This will really help, you'll find, when it comes time to dig up plants in order to divide or move them.

Watering

There are sprinkler and irrigation systems for dry regions that can make the desert bloom. If that's where you live, go for the soaker-hose type of watering system. This keeps water off the plants' leaves and directs it right to the roots. A soaker hose can be laid through a bed or border so that it winds around through the plants, giving each one a drink.

In many regions, watering will mean only an overhead sprinkling with the hose during dry spells.

Whenever you water, water thoroughly. A sprinkling that doesn't penetrate more than a half-inch of soil will only encourage plants to keep their drinking roots near the surface and make them less able to survive droughts than if their roots had to strike deep for water. The conventional wisdom is that most plants need 1 inch of water a week. Some perennials need far less, although if the soil is well-drained, they won't mind that much water. Before I water my perennials, I dig a little hole in the soil. If it's dry only in the top inch, I don't water. Once the soil is dry to a depth of 1½ inches, and especially when it's dry down 2 inches, water.

Try to water your plants in the morning, so the leaves can dry off during the day. Watering in the evening and letting the plants sit wet overnight encourages fungi and molds to colonize the foliage.

It's especially important to water in the first half of the growing season, when most plants are doing most of their growing. Water is the chief limiting factor of plant growth, although sunlight and fertile soil are equally essential. We all want tough plants that can survive in local climatic conditions, but drought will ruin almost any perennial garden, because the plants in question are herbaceous and usually fitted for climates with adequate moisture. Watering is an extremely important chore to perform in order to protect your garden and your investment.

Weeding

Weeding is one of those garden chores we like to keep to a minimum, and the best way to do that is by mulching. I've described mulching before: It's covering the ground with something that will smother weeds and slow the evaporation of moisture. We find that grass clippings are marvelous as mulch. When they dry out, they look neat and take on an unobtrusive buff color. They pack down on the soil and provide good "smotherage." Two other good-looking mulches are leaf mold and bark chips. Sawdust dries to a relatively bright color and takes contrast away from the garden, I think. As I have mentioned before, a layer of newspapers, laid on the soil underneath the mulch, will not be seen but will do a mighty job of keeping weeds down. Another way to lessen weeding chores is to make sure no weeds set seed.

Spring weeding is probably the most important. You need to be able to distinguish between emerging perennials and emerging weeds. When you're just beginning in gardening, that may be difficult. My rule was never to pull anything that might be a perennial. If it later turned out to be a weed, I'd pull it then. Now I know the look, shape, and feel of our emerging flowers. It's important to get the spring weeds early with a hand cultivator or hoe. Then mulch the garden. You'll still have some weeds to pull, and you may need to renew the mulch in areas where weeds are coming through, but it will be far less work than the weeding that unmulched soil calls for. Don't put on the mulch, though, until you see that the perennials are growing well. Mulch insulates the soil and keeps it cool;

this can delay the emergence of some plants if you apply the mulch too soon. And mulch will smother young perennials if it's laid on too early and too thick.

A word is in order here about dandelions. I'm of two minds about this ubiquitous weed. I can see the point that its cheery yellow flowers relieve the colorless humdrum of late spring. But I also think that its common, bright color will overwhelm early spring color associations in the garden. *Doronicum caucasicum,* or leopard's bane, has a dandelion-like flower of a similar, if slightly finer, color. Doronicum completely gets lost in the garden if it's surrounded by mobs of yellow dandelions. If you're serious about presenting a fine perennials' display at dandelion time, you'd best keep these weeds out of the garden and lawn.

If you keep weeds down and out for several years, you'll notice they will become less of a problem. They'll never permanently disappear from your beds, for weed seeds are constantly carried in on the wind and in bird droppings, and they also lie dormant in the soil for many, many years until someone turns the soil and puts them in a position to germinate. Established gardens that have been well-mulched for years don't need a lot of digging and the weed problems subside.

Edging

Grass, we know, is invasive. Ordinary lawn grasses will strike out underground for new territory until they run into a barrier of some sort. They'll creep right into your beds or borders, too, if you don't stop them. There are commercial edgings available—

these are usually long plastic strips that are meant to be set on edge and prevent grass roots from crossing them. My grass tends to crawl right over the strips, so I've stopped using them.

Rows of rocks or bricks make a nice edging and, if wide enough, will keep the grass out of the garden. "Wide enough" is about 15 inches. Another alternative is to use an edger and keep the edge of the lawn sliced clean. Also, sometimes a tall, floppy plant will topple onto the grass, and the dense shade it makes will keep the grass there in check.

My personal recommendation for edging the garden is to use a couple of rows of bricks set in lengthwise and protruding a little above the soil surface. Grass can be mowed right up to the bricks, and miniature perennials will grow right up to the other side. Whatever method of edging you choose, grass must be kept from invading the flowers, for it competes heavily for nutrients and moisture. Flagstone or brick walks create their own edging.

Pests and Diseases

The kinds of perennials we grow are not usually prone to ailments or insects, but some of them will have trouble. A few always do in any area. My advice is to get rid of them. There are so many incredibly beautiful flowers that those with troubles can be eliminated from your garden without regret. Why spend your time spraying or nursing along plants that are unsuited to your conditions? If I must chase insects, I use pyrethrum and rotenone dusts.

If your phlox gets a fungus, you might try moving it to a drier, sunnier spot. Fungicides are among the most harmful horticultural chemicals; don't use them.

The foregoing advice may seem like short shrift in a big area, but I'm serious about eliminating plants that are vulnerable to pests in your area. We don't grow many roses in our garden for that reason; we grow only the cultivars that we find aren't attacked by diseases, fungi, and pests.

If you would like to delve into organic plant protection, Rodale Press publishes a book on that subject (*The Encyclopedia of Natural Insect and Disease Control*, edited by Roger B. Yepsen, Jr.). Your county agricultural extension agent will also be able to advise you on natural and chemical means of pest control.

Routine Care

Many perennials grow by means of spreading roots. These roots can sometimes be invasive, as are those of coreopsis and monarda, and tend to overrun their neighbors. Watch in the spring when perennials emerge, and if they are overstepping their bounds, dig up the extra roots and shoots. These can be replanted in another area, if you're expanding, but try to curb that tendency. As a perennial grower once told me, "A man should never have a garden larger than his wife can take care of." The compost pile is a perfectly suitable place for most or all of these extras, unless you want to pot them up and give them away as presents. If you do want to save the extra roots, replant them immediately, mixing some compost with the soil to give them a boost at the start.

Some perennials, such as asters, put on new growth around their peripheries each year. The second year is the strongest one for many of these plants. After that, there's a lessening of bloom and crowding of small shoots around the outside. The center of the clump turns woody and dies out. At this point, you need to divide the plant. Lift it with as much of the root ball intact as possible. Shake and tease out as much of the soil as you can, to expose the roots and their growing points. The roots are the truly perennial part of the plant—its heart, where it overwinters. Learn the shapes and textures of the roots of your perennials, just as you know their foliage and flowers, and you'll always know when they need division. Pull the clump apart into root pieces with several growing points, taking pieces from the outside of the clump for replanting, and discarding the worn-out, woody center part. Several divisions can be replanted in the same spot to renew the clump.

Plants with taproots, such as dictamnus, don't like to be moved, and they should not be. Other plants, such as kniphofia and hemerocallis, have fleshy, tuberous roots. Some perennials, such as campanula, have fibrous roots. When dividing plants, your job is to disentangle the roots and pull, slice, or pry the pieces off the clump. To pry apart a tough root ball, stick two spading forks into the middle of the clump, back to back, and, using them for leverage, push the handles in the opposite directions. For really tough, matted roots, use a hatchet.

Try to take divisions with enough roots and emerging foliage to make it through the shock of transplanting. Spindly little divisions with too few roots for too much foliage often fail. Just remember that the purpose of division is either to get more plants for expansion or to keep clumps uncrowded, fresh, and young.

Plants are usually divided in the spring before they bloom. The earliest bloomers are not to be disturbed, however, and division for them should be done right after bloom, as for *Dianthus* and *Primula* species.

Replant and water divisions immediately. Give them shade until their leaves perk up, and they appear to have settled in.

A more thorough look at propagation by division, stem cuttings, root cuttings, and other means of propagating plants is given in the next section of this chapter.

Routine care of perennials also involves keeping rampant growers in check. You may notice that some species of dianthus will produce a great deal of foliage during bloom, then look ratty after the flowers have gone. Cut them back halfway, and remove the dead flower heads to encourage more blooming.

Wander through the garden with a trowel and a knife and look for superfluous, weak growth. Delphiniums will often put up so many shoots after being cut back that they would be too small if all the shoots were allowed to grow. Cut out the weak ones and leave four or five of the strongest. Similarly, phlox will send up many shoots and benefits greatly from culling the weaker 50 percent.

Check for insects on plants and remove them, but leave garden spiders, who trap pests. Turn over an occasional leaf and see if there are neat clusters of insect eggs attached. Scrape them off with a thumbnail when you find them. Garden spiders, ladybugs, assassin bugs, and many other insects are beneficial friends, so don't think every bug you see is a pest.

As you make your garden rounds, pull a weed here, trim off an offending shoot there. Keep things generally spruced up. If there's a color combination you thought would work, but doesn't, mark it in your notebook to correct in the fall or spring, depending on which perennials are involved. Enter in your notebook combinations you really like, as well as those that don't work. Revamp the garden according to the notebook every spring, and it will continue to improve in grace and beauty through the years.

Propagation

Almost all your perennials will make babies, which allows you to expand the garden, to make potted plants for sales or gifts, and to renew clumps that have gotten old and woody. New plants can be grown from division, stem cuttings, root cuttings, and from seed.

Division

Several factors have to be considered when dividing perennials. First, don't divide in the hottest part of the year, or in the driest part. Also avoid the very late fall, when winter is approaching, or the roots won't have time to put out new fibrous feeder roots and will freeze out over winter. In the northern portion of the United States, most perennials will be best divided in spring when they are showing just a couple of inches of green growth. If the growth reaches 5 inches or more, successful division becomes less sure. Plants that bloom in April and May should be divided after bloom.

In the more temperate parts of the United States, north of the Sun Belt but south of the cold northern tier of states, division

Perennials That Need Dividing Every Year or Two	
Most of these perennials will benefit from being divided yearly, although they can go two years before division. All need to be divided at least every two years.	
Achillea spp.	*Eupatorium* spp.
Anthemis spp.	*Helenium* spp.
Artemisia lactiflora	*Helianthus* spp.
Aster novae-angliae	*Lysimachia* spp.
Aster novi-belgii	*Physostegia* spp.
Boltonia asteroides	*Primula* spp.
Cerastium tomentosum	*Rudbeckia* spp.
Chrysanthemum spp.	*Solidago* spp.

works well in spring and in early fall. At both these times the weather is cool and the ground moist. If there's drought in the fall, thoroughly water the plants to be divided the day before you plan to move them, and water the spot where you'll be putting them. After division and replanting in this moist soil, water deeply once again and keep the soil moist if the rains don't come.

In the milder parts of the country, such as the Gulf Coast and the West Coast, division in autumn is best, since winters tend to be mild and wet, and the roots will make fibrous growth over winter and be up and going as temperatures rise in late winter.

Check plants for broken, elongated, and scraggly roots and prune these off. A little root trimming on heavily matted plants will stimulate them to put out lots of new fibrous roots, which makes for strong growth.

When dividing plants with foliage, cut back the tops to about one-third of their

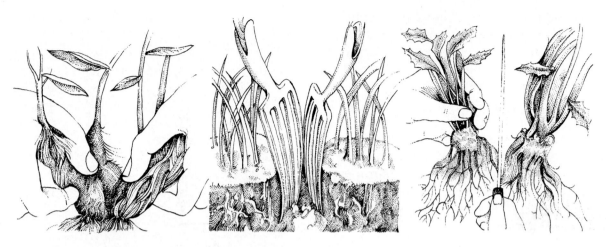

Three ways to divide perennials (left to right): pulling apart clumps by hand, as for asters; prying apart a thick clump of daylilies with two pitchforks or spades; and cutting apart a dense clump, such as astilbe, with a knife.

full length, leaving about a third of the leaves.

Late-blooming plants like chrysanthemums and asters must be divided in spring. If you wait until they've finished blooming, they won't have time to settle in before the ground freezes, and you could well lose your plants.

When dividing, keep a pail of water handy and soak any divisions that have lost their soil. This prevents the roots from drying out—and dried roots are usually dead roots.

Fall-divided perennials that don't seem to be sturdily established should be covered with mulch and perhaps evergreen boughs to keep drying winds from the crowns.

Crowns are the growing points of the plant, and in most perennials new ones appear on roots pushing out from the base of the plant. These fresh roots with new crowns are taken as root divisions. For a full mass of bloom in summer after spring division, keep roots with from three to five crowns.

You can, however, pull the roots apart into single crowns. These small divisions are chancier to reestablish than larger clumps, but you get more of them.

A few plants like their crowns set about an inch lower in the soil than where they were growing when you started dividing. Peonies, coral bells (*Heuchera*), and bearded iris are perennials that like to be set slightly below their previous soil level. With almost every other perennial, crowns should be planted at the level they were growing, or so their growing points are at or just above soil level. For these, setting the crowns too low promotes rot.

Never divide a plant when it is getting ready to bloom, for then all its energy is going toward reproduction, not growth. Dividing at this time produces divisions that are confused, sulky, and prone to die out.

Try to divide plants on overcast mornings when it will remain cloudy all day. In fact, if the weather report says that you're in for a three-day period of cloudy, wet weather, get out there and divide plants before the rain starts. Divisions will be much happier recovering in a cool, low-light rain than baking in the hot sun.

When dividing a plant, choose the strongest-looking parts and discard any weak parts.

Some plants may have a strong-growing central root mass that defies efforts to pry it apart. You can reduce the size of such plants by pulling off new crowns that have formed around the outside or by trimming back the edges with a spade. The central root mass can then be replanted. These plants like constricted roots. Examples are acanthus, agapanthus, kniphofia, hemerocallis, and Siberian iris.

Although it's most common to divide plants into pieces with several crowns, there are those that like to be completely divided into single crowns. Liriope, aquilegia, gerbera, convallaria, bergenia, and members of the aster and chrysanthemum groups are examples.

Quite a few perennials grow fresh roots around their periphery, and from these roots little rosettes of new leaves emerge. To divide these plants, simply cut off the roots with rosettes near the old portion of the clump. Look over the fresh root pieces carefully, and replant only the plump-looking, healthy ones. You'll find that asters, alchemilla, pachysandra, ajuga, achillea, filipendula, heuchera, *Phlox paniculata,* primula, and many others have this easy-to-work-with habit.

And many perennials grow from underground runners. To divide these, simply spade out a shovelful of earth with the runners in it, and replant elsewhere at the same depth. Water well. If divided in early spring,

---

Hard-to-Transplant Perennials Propagated by Potting Up Pieces of Root

Some plants that resent being disturbed can be propagated by pulling soil away from one side of the plant to expose one or more of the medium-sized fleshy roots, then cutting off the exposed parts. These are cut into 2-inch pieces and planted in moist compost about a half inch beneath the soil surface, slanting downward at a 45-degree angle. Make sure they are planted with the same orientation as they grew; that is, the part of the root that grew deepest on the parent plant is placed deepest in the propagating bed. These cuttings are generally taken in the fall, and the bed covered with mulch when frosts come on. In the spring, these will show new green growth and can be moved to spots in the garden. Some may bloom that year, but most will bloom the second year.

Anemone japonica or *A.* × *hybrida*	*Gypsophila paniculata*
Asclepias tuberosa	*Limonium latifolia*
Baptisia australis	*Papaver orientale*
Dicentra spectabilis	*Stokesia laevis*
Echinops ritro	*Thermopsis caroliniana*
Eryngium amethystinum	*Yucca filamentosa*

---

the runners will hardly know they've been moved. Creeping perennials and ones that form carpets, such as low-growing veronicas, and some plants with taller stems, such as monarda, solidago, lythrum, and coreopsis, grow from underground runners.

If you have an old plant that still looks healthy but is just getting too big, hack it apart into several clumps and replant the best-looking one. It will benefit from the division and be stimulated to produce new fibrous roots.

There are exceptions, of course. Some plants intolerant of division are aconitum, asclepias, baptisia, dictamnus, euphorbia, gypsophila, *Helleborus niger,* limonium, oriental poppies, platycodon, and thermopsis. On the other hand, some perennials divide easily and love it. Hostas and hemerocallis, for instance, simply need to be spaded apart and replanted, then watered in.

Stem Cuttings

Plants with tough stems, such as achillea, make good candidates for propagation by stem cuttings. Always choose the handsomest specimen for cutting stock. Slips— or cuttings—are usually taken in spring well before bloom, or from new vegetative growth after bloom. Cuttings shouldn't be taken when the plant is about to bloom, for, again, its energy is going toward flower production and not vegetative growth. Gypsophila and phlox are two plants that propagate best by cuttings taken after bloom.

The technique of propagating from cuttings is simple. Cut the slip with sharp shears or a knife. Take the top 6 or 8 inches of the stem. Remove any leaves that are near the cut and that would be under the soil after replanting. Leave the top three or four pairs of leaves. Many gardeners replant these slips into pots placed in a cool, shady area. We have a north-facing bed of moist, rich soil in which we root the slips. If there's any question about their rooting ability, we cover them with plastic, gallon-size milk jugs with the bottoms cut out. The jugs keep the environment moist and protect the cuttings from the wind.

Some Perennials to Propagate from Stem Cuttings	
Achillea spp.	Heuchera spp.
Alchemilla spp.	Lupinus spp.
Aster spp.	Monarda spp.
Campanula spp.	Oenothera spp.
Chrysanthemum spp.	Potentilla spp.
Erigeron spp.	Salvia nemorasa
Euphorbia spp.	Sedum spectabile
Geranium spp.	Sidalcea spp.
Geum spp.	Solidago spp.
Helenium spp.	Veronica spp.

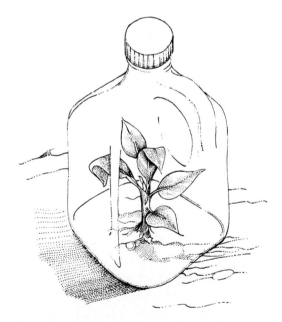

New transplants can be protected from cold weather by covering them with a bottomless plastic milk jug during their first few days in the garden. The top can be removed if the plant is in full sun and starts to show heat stress.

Make sure when you plant each slip that you firm the soil so it's in contact with the stem. Plant the cutting so that about 2½ to 3 inches of the stem are buried, and a couple of inches, with small leaves, protrude. The soil must be kept constantly moist. Keep these cuttings shady. Roots will sprout along the buried part of the stem.

Root Cuttings

The procedure described on page 194, in the section on division of plants that grow new roots around their peripheries, is root cutting. The roots are simply cut off and replanted. Make sure they are replanted with the upper part of the root still facing up.

Seeds

Many perennials self-sow, and your main problem will be how to get rid of all the seedlings that spring up around the mother plant each year. (Here's another good reason to dead-head plants, or pull off the spent flowers and flower stalks.) If you want to propagate from seed, you can replant the volunteer seedlings, or you can gather from the seed heads enough seed to sow in flats in the spring. Remember that most second-generation plants will not reproduce the parent's flower color or size.

Purchased seed is best planted according to the directions given on the seed packet. Each plant will have different needs, but there are some general rules to follow.

First, don't sprout plants in pots on windowsills. There is rarely enough light in late winter to make strong plants. Your seedlings will be long and leggy, weak, and prone to fall over and rot. Start your seeds in a stand with fluorescent "grow" lights or a combination of warm and cool fluorescent lights, in banks of three tubes. Give seedlings lots of light indoors when they germinate. Keep the potting soil in the trays or flats moist. A good potting soil can be made from 50 percent finished compost and 50 percent peat or vermiculite. If the soil dries out, the tender young seedlings will die. When the little plants show their first three or four true leaves (the first two leaves are called cotyledons and are the seed leaves), transplant them to pots or into an outside bed if the air temperature is averaging 65°F.

Plants started in the house must be hardened off before you plant them outside. This process takes about a week. Bring the plants outside during the day when the weather is mild, then back into the house at night. Increase the outside exposure from a few hours the first day to ten hours by the fifth day. On the sixth and seventh days, if nighttime temperatures don't go below 50° or 55°F, let the plants stay out overnight. During the hardening-off procedure, keep the soil moist.

You can also plant seeds in flats or pots outside in spring when the temperatures rise. Keep the soil moist and the containers in a shady spot until the plants have developed several true leaves, then transplant to the nursery bed or garden. When planting in flats, thin the seedlings to an inch apart when they emerge, so they aren't crowded. If nights threaten to be too cold, move the young plants into a cold frame or into a cool part of the house.

A separate nursery bed is ideal for most perennials. This is a bed with fine, carefully prepared soil. Locate the nursery in a shady spot and keep the bed moist during germination time. Thin out the weak seedlings, and when the strongest have four or five leaves, transplant them to the garden. You can also let the plants grow in the nursery bed for the first year and transplant to the garden in the fall or the following spring.

Always hold seedlings by the leaves to transplant them; don't handle the stems. If you break a leaf, the plant can grow a new one. If you damage the stem, there goes the plant.

Alternatively, you can plant seeds right in the garden where you want them to grow. This is a dangerous procedure, as you will be stepping around in the garden, weeding, mulching, and generally doing big, rough tasks that don't mix well with stands of delicate seedlings. Besides, most plants—except those with taproots—like to be transplanted at least once when they're small. It stimulates their root growth.

Few perennials will bloom the first year. They'll spend that first year after being transplanted into their permanent place making good foliage and root growth, and getting ready for a floral spectacular the next year.

Planting Nursery Stock

There are two kinds of nursery stock—bare-rooted perennials sent to you by mail order, generally in the spring, and nursery-bought plants in pots.

The bare-rooted stock requires the most care. When it arrives, plant it as soon as possible. Don't let it sit in the package. If you can't plant it within three days, take it out of the package and bury the roots in a trench full of sand and thoroughly moist peat moss until you can get to it. Don't hold plants this way for more than a few days.

At planting time, carefully remove the packing material and soak the roots in a pail of water for five minutes. If the garden is dry, water the planting area deeply the night before. With shears or a knife, trim off any rotted, moldy, broken, or elongated roots. Plant the stock in the soil so that the crown is just above soil level and the roots can ray out from the crown at a 45-degree downward angle. It may help to make a mound of earth in the bottom of the planting hole and spread the roots over it. You may also want to mix some bone meal and compost with the garden soil for plants that like it rich. Even plants that like poor soil may benefit from a little bone meal.

Cover the roots with soil and press down firmly all around, so you're sure all the roots, especially those in the area under the crown, are in contact with soil. Slightly depress the soil around the crown to catch water, and gently water the plant well until the soil is wet all the way down. Spread some mulch around the new plant and put a peach basket or cardboard box over it. Hold down the box or basket with a board or a weight, so the wind doesn't blow it off. The plant can stay in this dark, protected shelter for three to six days.

After three to six days, remove the box or basket and water again, if necessary. The plant should now be breaking dormancy and putting out new growth. If hot, drying winds arrive at this time, you may want to cover the plant again until they subside.

If you purchased potted plants from a nursery, remove each plant from the pot by holding it upside down, with the foliage protruding between your fingers. Give the pot a sharp rap with the heel of your hand. That should knock the plant loose. If it doesn't, hit it against a sturdy fence post or

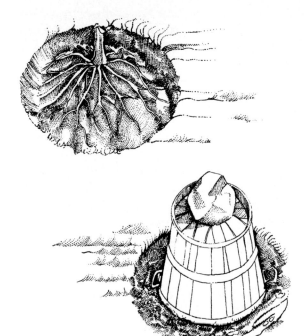

When planting bare-rooted perennials, it is often a good idea to make a mound of earth in the bottom of the planting hole and gently spread the roots over it. Protect the new plant for the first three to six days by covering it with a basket.

piece of wood. If that still doesn't work, run a knife around the inside edge of the pot, then rap it again. And if that doesn't work, force out the plant by pushing something through the drainage hole in the bottom of the pot (this can damage roots, so do it only as a last resort).

With shears or scissors, trim off the white roots that are encircling the root ball and plant. Add some compost and bone meal to the planting hole and set in the plant so that the root ball's soil surface is the same level as the garden soil surface. Firm the soil well around the root ball. Water thoroughly. Usually potted plants have plenty of roots and don't need to go under the protective box for more than a day or two, if at all.

Fine-tuning the Color Harmonies

Experience will be your best teacher in refining color harmonies. You need to know the physical look and texture of the color of a flower. For instance, red geum has a particularly waxy look that I think of as crayon red. The same red looks quite different on the soft petals of a bee balm. As you progress with perennial gardening, you'll come to know the flowers as individuals, not just as names. It's then that the real fine-tuning comes in, as you arrange flowers in the bed or border to suit your educated, refined taste.

In our own gardens we've chosen from catalogs plants that we thought would work in harmonious groups, only to find that they are not what we thought they were. For example, the gypsophila is not a white mass—from a distance it's more like a light wash of white film over darker foliage, and up close it's a constellation of tiny flowers. Liatris has lavender spikes, all right, but they were lower-growing than I first expected, and they have a strawberry-pink aspect to their lavenderness that was unexpected. Just as each person has a personality, so does each plant. *Campanula glomerata* is a prickly sort of plant that does not invite one to touch it. Monkshood is a deep violet-flowered plant with dark green leaves. When you get to know it, there's a bit of menace about it. As you become familiar with the personalities and psychological aspects of your plants, groups can be more than just pleasing color associations. You may find that lily-of-the-valley and bleeding heart suggest the Victorian age to you, as they do to me, and look for other flowers that have an antique appeal to add to this spring group.

Putting the Garden to Bed for the Winter

If the garden is visible from the house, you may not want to cut down the stalks of dead plants after the frosts settle in for good. They, and the permanent compositional features of the garden such as coniferous and broad-leaved evergreen shrubs, can work together with such garden additions as grasses to keep a display during the winter, subdued to its bare bones though it may be.

If you do let stalks and plumes of summer greenery persist over the winter, remove them when the snow melts off in the spring, so the bed or border will be ready for new growth as temperatures rise.

If you're growing perennials in their northernmost zones or in a zone in which they aren't perfectly hardy, you can mulch them deeply (cover with 3 feet of hay or leaves) and probably bring most of them through the winter. I've grown globe artichokes here in eastern Pennsylvania, and I know of fig trees that survive in Montreal and Boston, because they are covered with mulch over the winter. I've also seen liriope, usually said not to be hardy much above Philadelphia, growing well in Kennebunkport, Maine. Liriope, by the way, should

have its dead leaves cut back to 2 inches in spring before growth begins, or else it looks ratty.

Some plants may need special attention. Kniphofia, the red-hot poker, needs to have its leaves tied up over its crowns in the fall in our area, or they will turn to rotten mush.

Also, any transplants or divisions that may have been made in the fall will benefit from a mulch to keep the winds from drying them out. Mulching in the fall is good practice, as it keeps winter rains from eroding soil, keeps the crowns at an even temperature—rather than the alternate thawing and freezing that heaves roots and damages plants—and decays in the spring into a weed-free, soil-conditioning, fertilizing humus.

The best mulch to use is dry leaves. When loose, these tend to blow. They can be kept in check by attaching chicken wire to stakes set in around the garden's edges, but this is costly. An alternative is to get some bales of spoiled hay to set around the edges of the garden to act as a wall. Or you can pull the bales apart into 2-inch-thick pads that can be tossed on top of the leaves to weight them down.

Don't apply this winter mulch to hardy plants until the soil is frozen. If the mulch is thick, remove most of it in the spring so it doesn't smother emerging perennials or delay their emergence by holding the frost in the ground. What's left of the mulch will decay and look good, as I've said.

Look at Nature's perennials—the woodland plants that die back and reappear each year. She showers them over with a light mulch of tree leaves. For most hardy perennials, that's just what you should do.

CHAPTER 7

A Guide to Garden Perennials

We have designed the following chart to include the information American gardeners need to design perennial gardens suitable for their regions. We've chosen 154 genera, selected for the wide availability of their various species and cultivars within those species. You'll be able to find these cultivars in one or more of the mail-order firms listed in the appendix that follows the chart.

We chose this format to help gardeners select plants primarily by season of bloom, height, flower color, and growing needs—the factors gardeners must consider when designing gardens.

How to Use the Chart

We'd like to give you some guidelines for using the chart, and the best way to do that is to explain what all the column headings mean, and what sort of information you'll find under each one. There are ten headings in the chart. Let's look at them one by one.

Name of Plant

Each genus is listed in boldface, with its pronunciation alongside it in brackets. Next to the pronunciation, you'll find the common name of the genus (where there is a common name that applies to the genus as a whole). Example: **MONARDA** (genus name); [moan-AR-duh] (pronunciation); Bee Balm (common name).

Then we list the species (the types of plants within the genus, which is given in italics) along with a cultivar (listed in single quotes), chosen for its wide availability and beauty, plus its good horticultural qualities. Example: *M. didyma* (*M.* stands for *Monarda* and *didyma* is the species name) 'Cambridge Scarlet' (the particular cultivar described under the other nine headings in the chart). Where different species within a genus carry different common names, we list these under the name of each species.

Since species often have many cultivars that differ by color and sometimes height, we have listed under the heading of "Other cultivars" some other cultivars of the given species that may interest the grower and that are widely available. Information given after the names of these other cultivars is limited to those characteristics that differ from the featured cultivar. If, for instance, we look at "Other cultivars" under *Monarda didyma*, we find "'Croftway Pink', pink flowers" as the first entry. 'Croftway Pink' thus differs from 'Cambridge Scarlet' only in its flower color. All the other information given in the chart for 'Cambridge Scarlet' applies to 'Croftway Pink' as well.

In some cases, botanists differ from the mail-order catalogs in naming plants. Where there are variations, we have tried to give both the name found in the catalogs and the name favored by botanical taxonomists.

Zones

The numbers under this heading refer to the U.S. Department of Agriculture's growing zones, shown in the map on page xiii. We give both the coldest zone in which the plant is hardy and the warmest zone in which it will grow. For instance, for *Monarda didyma* we find Zones 4–9, meaning that the plant will grow as far north as Zone 4 and as far south as Zone 9, plus all the zones in between.

Season of Bloom

Since bloom time will vary—beginning earlier in the southern range of the plant's habitat and later in the north—we give bloom times based on flowering at about 40 degrees north latitude. The entire season of bloom is given. For instance, under *Monarda didyma* 'Cambridge Scarlet' season of bloom is given as "July–Aug." This means that it begins to bloom in July and continues into August. Exact dates cannot be specified, since every garden varies not only in latitude but also in microclimatic conditions.

Height

The height given for the featured cultivar applies to "Other cultivars" also, except where specified after the other cultivar's name. Because plants are individuals and growing conditions vary according to climate, site, and soil fertility, plant heights in your garden may differ somewhat from those given in the chart. The heights given in the chart are assumed to be an average height, attained by a plant grown with adequate moisture and soil fertility, without heavy competition from weeds or other plants.

Flower Color

The colors listed in the chart refer to the dominant color impression given by each flower, so that you can more quickly identify plants within a color range. *Monarda didyma,* for instance, is listed as red, but it is really more accurately described as scarlet. Where the flower color is exceptional, we describe it more fully under "Plant Description."

Where a plant's flowers come in many colors, you'll find that noted under "Flower Color." Where flowers contain two or more colors, we list them as "Bicolor."

Plant Description

The information in this column will help you visualize the plant. When you design your perennial gardens, this descriptive information will make it easier for you to mix flower and foliage types to create varying textures in the garden. Where no mention is made of foliage, the leaves are inconspicuous in the garden setting.

Light Requirements

Full sun means just that—the plant needs a sunny location that allows it to receive at least six hours of direct sunlight a day. And that should be overhead sunlight rather than the weaker rays of morning or late afternoon sun. Some plants that like full sun will tolerate partial shade, which we define as from one to six hours of sun a day. Shade or full shade means that only dappled sunlight, if any at all, reaches the plant, which prefers an absence of direct sunlight.

The plant's preferences are given in order; that is, "Full sun to partial shade" means that the plant likes full sun but will tolerate partial shade, especially bright shade or an area that gets close to six hours of sun a day. "Partial shade to shade," on the other hand, means that the plant prefers partial shade, but will tolerate full shade.

Soil Requirements

The ideal soil conditions for each plant are given in this column of the chart. Many flowering perennials will do well in a range of soil conditions that vary from the ideal. Average soil refers to deeply dug earth that has been liberally enriched with finished compost. Where plants have special soil needs, these are given.

Propagation

General guidelines for dividing plants are given. "Cuttings" refers to stem cuttings. Root cuttings are always specified as such in this chart. Cuttings should be taken from herbaceous plants when they are in their elongating, growing phase, before flowering gets underway. Cuttings from woody plants (which we don't really get into in the book) should be taken before growth starts in the spring, so that root growth and leaf area keep apace. They can be taken later in the year, but not when plants are in flower or fruit. "Seed" means that the plants can be easily started from seed, either purchased or collected from ripened flower heads. Planting distances are a general recommendation and will help you to visualize the size of the full-grown plant when you are putting in small seedlings or started plants.

Remarks

We used this heading as a catchall category to mention something extraordinary or important about each plant or genus.

This kind of chart could not begin to list all the perennial species and cultivars available to North American gardeners. But we hope it will serve as a handy reference to some of the more popular and widely available plants, and we hope it will make your garden planning easier.

155 Perennial Genera

NAME OF PLANT	ZONES	SEASON OF BLOOM	HEIGHT	FLOWER COLOR	PLANT DESCRIPTION
ACANTHUS [a-*KAN*-thus] Bears'-Breech					
A. perringii	8–10	June–Aug.	18 in.	Red	Rose red, snapdragon-like flowers in regular rows on compact spikes. Deeply toothed, grey-green leaves.
ACHILLEA [a-kill-*EE*-ah] Yarrow					
A. ageratifolia	3–8	May–June	6–12 in.	White	1-in., daisy-like blossoms. Feathery, silver-green foliage.
A. filipendulina 'Coronation Gold'	3–8	June–Aug.	3 ft.	Yellow	3-in., flat-topped cluster of small, mustard yellow flowers. Feathery, grey-green foliage.
Other cultivars: 'Gold Plate', 4 ft. tall, golden yellow flowers; 'Parkers Variety', 3½ ft. tall, golden yellow flowers.					
A. millefolium 'Fire King'	2–8	June–Sept.	18 in.–2 ft.	Red	3-in., rosy red flower heads above mounds of ferny, sea green leaves.
Other cultivars: 'Red Beauty', 8 in. tall, bright red flowers; 'White Beauty', 20 in. tall, white flowers.					
A. ptarmica 'Angels' Breath' (Sneezewort)	2–8	June–Sept.	2 ft.	White	Double flowers; narrow, smooth, dark green leaves.
Other cultivars: 'The Pearl', 18 in. tall, very double, white flowers.					
A. taygetea 'Moonshine'	2–8	June–Sept.	18 in.–2 ft.	Yellow	3-in., light yellow flower heads above neat, feathery, grey-green foliage.
A. tomentosa 'King Edward'	2–8	June–Aug.	6 in.	Yellow	1–2 in., light yellow flower heads. Woolly, grey-green leaves form ground-covering mats.

LIGHT REQUIREMENTS	SOIL REQUIREMENTS	PROPAGATION	REMARKS
Full sun to partial shade	Rich, moist soil	Division in spring. Seed. Plant 2 ft. apart.	Good specimen plant. *A. mollis* 'Latifolius' grows 4–5 ft.
Full sun	Average to poor, dry soil	Division in early spring or fall. Plant 12 in. apart.	Early blooming; good in the rock garden.
Full sun	Average to poor, dry soil	Division in spring every 3 or 4 years. Plant 18 in. apart.	The standard golden yarrow, developed by Alan Bloom. Best for dried flowers.
Full sun	Average to poor, dry soil	Division in spring or fall. Plant 12–18 in. apart.	Can be invasive; needs dividing every other year.
Full sun	Average to poor, dry soil	Division. May need dividing every year to check spreading. Plant 12 in. apart.	Common name, sneezewort, refers to old practice of using the powdered root for snuff.
Full sun	Average to poor, dry soil	Division in spring or fall. Plant 18 in. apart.	Flowers fade to a beautiful pale yellow.
Full sun	Average to poor, dry soil	Division. Plant 8–10 in. apart.	Good rock garden plant. Smallest of the tomentosa, or woolly, yarrow.

(continued)

155 Perennial Genera—*Continued*

NAME OF PLANT	ZONES	SEASON OF BLOOM	HEIGHT	FLOWER COLOR	PLANT DESCRIPTION
ACONITUM [ak-o-*NY*-tum] Monkshood					
A. carmichaelii or *A. fischeri*	2–7	Sept.–Oct.	3 ft.	Blue	Spikes of helmet-shaped, dark blue flowers. Glossy, deep-fingered leaves.
A. napellus	2–7	July–Aug.	3–4 ft.	Blue	Foliage more finely divided than *A. carmichaelii.*
Other cultivars: 'Alba', 3–4 ft. tall, white flowers; 'Bicolor', 4 ft. tall, blue and white flowers.					
ADENOPHORA [ay-den-*AH*-for-uh] Ladybells					
A. confusa or *A. farreri*	3–9	July–Aug.	2½ ft.	Blue	Spires of nodding, bell-shaped flowers.
AEGOPODIUM [ee-go-*PO*-dee-um] Goutweed					
A. podagraria 'Variegatum'	3–9	May–June	6 in.	White (not snowy)	Mats of white-edged, green foliage form attractive ground cover.
AETHIONEMA [*EETH*-ee-o-*NE*-ma] Persian Candytuft					
A. × *warleyense* 'Warley Rose'	3–9	Apr.–May	6 in.	Pink	Small, pink umbels cover blue-green, needlelike leaves.
AJUGA [a-*JU*-gah] Bugleweed					
A. genevensis	2–8	May–June	8–12 in.	Blue	Deep blue flower spikes on mat-forming, glossy green leaves.
Other cultivars: 'Rosea', pink flowers.					
A. pyramidalis	2–8	May–June	12 in.	Blue	Tallest of the ajugas. Forms a compact clump. Deep blue flowers.

LIGHT REQUIREMENTS	SOIL REQUIREMENTS	PROPAGATION	REMARKS
Partial shade to full sun if soil is kept moist	Rich, moist, deep soil	Tuberous roots are best divided in fall, but prefer not to be disturbed. Plant 12–18 in. apart.	All aconitums are poisonous. Wash hands after planting or cutting.
Partial shade to full sun	Rich, moist, deep soil	Slow to colonize and prefer to be left where they are. Division in fall. Plant 12–18 in. apart.	Aconitums are useful in the back border as a blue vertical accent.
Full sun to partial shade	Rich, moist soil	Resents being moved. Cuttings or seed are easiest. Plant 12 in. apart.	Nice source of blue for the middle border in late summer.
Full sun to shade	Poor or rich soil	Division. Plant 12 in. apart.	Very invasive, but useful as a ground cover in difficult areas. Plant where mower or pavement can confine its growth.
Full sun	Sandy, well-drained, alkaline soil	Cuttings taken from new growth after flowering. Plant 8 in. apart.	A gem for rock gardens. In colder areas, mulch.
Partial shade to full sun	Average, well-drained soil	Division. Plant 8 in. apart.	Does not spread as fast as A. reptans.
Partial shade to full shade	Average or rich soil	Division. Plant 8 in. apart.	Many people prefer A. pyramidalis because it's not as invasive as A. reptans.

155 Perennial Genera—*Continued*

NAME OF PLANT	ZONES	SEASON OF BLOOM	HEIGHT	FLOWER COLOR	PLANT DESCRIPTION
AJUGA (continued)					
A. reptans 'Burgundy Glow'	2–8	May–June	6 in.	Blue	Deep blue flowers, variegated foliage of burgundy, white, and green.
Other cultivars: 'Alba', white flowers.					
ALCHEMILLA [al-kem-*ILL*-ah] Lady's-Mantle					
A. vulgaris	3–9	June–July	18 in.	Chartreuse	Foamy sprays of small flowers. Fan-shaped, grey-green leaves resemble a woman's cape, hence the common name.
ALLIUM [*AL*-ee-um]					
A. aflatunense	4–8	May–June	3 ft.	Lilac	Star-shaped florets create a 4-in. ball atop thick, hollow stalks. Strap-shaped leaves.
A. giganteum	4–9	June–July	4 ft.	Lilac	Huge, bright lilac flower balls, 5 in. across, on tall stalks above basal clumps of strap-shaped leaves.
A. moly	4–9	May–June	15 in.	Yellow	3-in. clusters of starlike flowers above 1-in.-wide, grey-green leaves.
A. neapolitanum 'Grandiflorum'	6–9	Apr.–May	18 in.	White	Fragrant, 3-in. umbels of starlike flowers with dark eyes.
ALTHAEA [al-*THEE*-ah] Hollyhock					
A. rosea 'Singles'	3–8	July	6–8 ft.	Red, yellow, pink, white	Tall stalks bearing many large-cupped flowers.
Other cultivars: 'Chater's Doubles', mixed colors, double flowers; 'Powder Puff', subdued colors, large, fluffy flowers.					

LIGHT REQUIREMENTS	SOIL REQUIREMENTS	PROPAGATION	REMARKS
Partial shade to shade	Average or rich soil	Division. Plant 8 in. apart.	Rapid growth from stolons. *A. reptans* makes an excellent ground cover, especially where soil is acid and grass won't grow.
Full sun to partial shade	Likes humusy soil	Division or seed. Plant 12 in. apart.	Dew in cupped leaves sparkles like jewels. Used as a low-growing foliage plant.
Full sun	Rich, moist, well-drained soil	Divide bulblets from parent in fall. Seed. Plant 8 in. deep and 12 in. apart.	Decorative relative of the onion with a dramatic effect in late spring.
Full sun	Rich, moist, well-drained soil	Divide bulblets from parent in fall. Seed. Plant 8 in. deep and 12 in. apart.	Spectacular in the back border. Plant in groups of 3–5.
Full sun	Rich, moist, well-drained soil	Divide bulblets from parent in fall. Seed. Plant 4 in. deep and 3 in. apart.	Like all alliums, this one is easy to grow. Best planted in masses.
Full sun	Rich, moist, well-drained soil	Divide bulblets from parent in fall. Seed. Plant 3 in. deep and 3 in. apart.	This allium has a sweet fragrance and makes a good cut flower.
Full sun	Rich, deep soil	Reseeds. Treat as biennial for best bloom. Plant 12 in. apart.	Background plant. Will need staking if not planted against a fence or wall. Reclassified into genus *Alcea*.

155 Perennial Genera—*Continued*

NAME OF PLANT	ZONES	SEASON OF BLOOM	HEIGHT	FLOWER COLOR	PLANT DESCRIPTION
ALYSSUM [ah-*LISS*-um] Basket of Gold					
A. saxatile 'Compactum'	3–9	Apr.–May	8–10 in.	Yellow	Large clouds of small, bright yellow flowers cover grey-green leaves.

Other cultivars: 'Citrum', pale yellow flowers; 'Flore Pleno', double, bright yellow flowers; 'Sunny Border Apricot', delicate, apricot flowers.

AMSONIA [am-*SONE*-ee-uh] Bluestar					
A. tabernaemontana	3–8	June	3 ft.	Blue	Starry, pale blue flowers on willowlike leaves.
ANAPHALIS [an-*AFF*-al-iss] Pearly Everlasting					
A. cinnamomea or *A. yedoensis*	3–7	July–Sept.	2 ft.	White	Buttonlike flowers on woolly, silver-grey stems and leaves.
ANCHUSA [an-*SHUZ*-ah] Bugloss					
A. azurea 'Royal Blue'	3–8	June–Aug.	3 ft.	Blue	Intense blue, forget-me-not-type flowers on branching spikes. Hairy, coarse leaves.

Other cultivars: 'Dropmore', 4 ft. tall, blue flowers; 'Little John', compact, 12 in. tall, blue flowers; 'Lodden Royalist', blue flowers.

ANEMONE [ah-*NEM*-oh-nee]					
A. japonica or *A. × hybrida* 'September Charm' (Japanese Anemone)	5–8	Sept.–Oct.	2½ ft.	Pink	Single, 2-in., saucer-shaped, silvery pink flowers on well-branched stems. Foliage forms an attractive mound of 3-lobed, toothed, dark green leaves.

Other cultivars: 'Alba', 20 in. tall, single, white flowers; 'Margarette', 20 in. tall, double, rosy pink flowers; 'Max Vogel', 20 in. tall, semidouble, rosy pink flowers; 'Prince Henry', 20 in. tall, double, rose red flowers.

LIGHT REQUIREMENTS	SOIL REQUIREMENTS	PROPAGATION	REMARKS
Full sun	Average, well-drained soil	Easily grown from seed in spring or fall, or cuttings taken in summer. Plants apt to get leggy—should be cut back after flowering. Plant cuttings 8–12 in. apart.	Charming when it spills over dry walls. Bold masses of color for the rock garden or border's edge.
Full sun to partial shade	Average soil, moist or dry	Division in spring. Seed. Plant 18 in. apart.	A carefree plant. Flowers are not showy, but foliage stays nice all year.
Full sun to partial shade	Average, well-drained soil	Division in spring. Plant 12 in. apart.	Excellent for dried flower arrangements. Looks good with Japanese anemones in the garden. Also known as *A. margaritacea.*
Full sun	Deep, well-drained soil	Self-sows. Plants need division every 2–3 years, spring or fall. Plant 18 in. apart.	A true blue color for the back border. Cut back to encourage second blooming.
Partial shade to full sun	Rich, humusy, well-drained soil	Root cuttings or division in fall. Plant 18 in. apart.	Among the best for fall bloom. Mulch in colder climates.

155 Perennial Genera—*Continued*

NAME OF PLANT	ZONES	SEASON OF BLOOM	HEIGHT	FLOWER COLOR	PLANT DESCRIPTION
ANEMONE (continued)					
A. pulsatilla (Pasque Flower)	4–8	Apr.–May	8–12 in.	Violet	Bell-shaped, deep violet flowers are followed by unusual, fuzzy seed heads. Attractive, ferny foliage.
Other cultivars: 'Alba', white flowers; 'Rubra', burgundy red flowers.					
A. sylvestris (Snowdrop Anemone)	2–7	May–June	12 in.	White	Large, fragrant flowers similar to the Japanese anemone but smaller.
A. vitifolia 'Robustissima' (Grape-Leaf Anemone)	5–8	Aug.–Oct.	2½ in.	Pink	2-in., saucer-shaped flowers with leaves like grape leaves.
ANTENNARIA [an-ten-*NAR*-ee-ah] Pussytoes					
A. dioica 'Rosea'	2–8	May–June	3–4 in.	Pink	Silver-green foliage grown as a ground cover. Small, clustered flower heads are rose pink and woolly.
ANTHEMIS [*AN*-them-iss] Golden Marguerite					
A. biebersteiniana or *A. marschalliana*	4–9	May–June	10–12 in.	Yellow	Golden yellow, daisy-like flowers with yellow button centers. Feathery, silver foliage.
A. tinctoria 'Moonlight'	4–9	June–Aug.	2 ft.	Yellow	Feathery, green foliage with masses of single, 2-in., pale yellow, daisy-like flowers.
Other cultivars: 'Beauty of Grallagh', deep golden yellow flowers; 'E. C. Buxton', white flowers with yellow centers.					
AQUILEGIA [ah-kwill-*EE*-jee-ah] Columbine					
A. caerulea	3–8	May–June	2 ft.	Blue and white	Flowers with long spurs carried on long stems. Graceful, blue-green foliage.

LIGHT REQUIREMENTS	SOIL REQUIREMENTS	PROPAGATION	REMARKS
Full sun to partial shade	Rich, gritty, well-drained soil (likes lime)	Self-sows; difficult to remove once they are established. Plant 8 in. apart.	One of the early harbingers of spring. Good for a rock garden, front border, or bed.
Partial shade to full sun	Rich, humusy, well-drained soil	Same as *A. japonica.*	Quickly forms a fine clump.
Partial shade to full sun	Rich, humusy, well-drained soil	Same as *A. japonica.*	Earliest of the fall anemones to bloom. Prefers morning sun with afternoon shading.
Full sun	Thrives in poor, dry soil	Division in early spring. Seed. Plant 6–8 in. apart.	Useful ground cover in dry, difficult spots. Good for rock gardens.
Full sun	Average, well-drained soil	Division in spring. Seed. Plant 12 in. apart.	Also called alpine chamomile. Thrives in hot, dry soil where other plants fail.
Full sun	Average, well-drained soil	Division in spring every other year, as clumps tend to develop dead spots in the middle. Seed. Plant 15 in. apart.	Foliage is aromatic. Flowers are good for cutting.
Partial shade to full sun	Moist, well-drained soil	Seed. Plant 12 in. apart.	These are the Rocky Mountain columbines with 2–3-in., sky blue and white flowers.

155 Perennial Genera—*Continued*

NAME OF PLANT	ZONES	SEASON OF BLOOM	HEIGHT	FLOWER COLOR	PLANT DESCRIPTION
AQUILEGIA (continued)					
A. canadensis	2–8	Apr.–May	18 in.–2 ft.	Red and yellow	Small, nodding flowers with cheerful red spurs surrounding bright yellow centers.
A. ×hybrida 'McKana Hybrids'	3–8	May–June	2–3 ft.	Red, pink, purple, yellow, blue, white	Large flowers with long spurs come in exquisite color variations.

Other cultivars: 'Biedermeier', 8 in. tall, neat, compact mounds of foliage; 'Nora Barlow', 2 ft. tall, reddish pink, fully double, spurless flowers; 'Spring Song', 2 ft. tall, multicolored, long, spurred, almost double flowers.

NAME OF PLANT	ZONES	SEASON OF BLOOM	HEIGHT	FLOWER COLOR	PLANT DESCRIPTION
ARABIS [ah-*RAB*-iss] Rock Cress					
A. procurrens	3–7	Apr.–June	6–8 in.	White	Very fine flowers on mats of creeping, dark green foliage.
ARENARIA [ar-en-*AIR*-ee-ah] Sandwort					
A. montana	4–9	May–June	2–4 in.	White	Compact, evergreen, mosslike plant that carpets the ground with small flowers.
ARMERIA [ar-*MER*-ee-ah] Sea Pink					
A. maritima 'Laucheana'	3–8	May–June	6 in.	Pink	Deep rose pink, globular flower heads on stiff stems. Foliage is neat, grasslike tufts.

Other cultivars: 'Alba', white flowers; 'Dusseldorf Pride', crimson flowers.

NAME OF PLANT	ZONES	SEASON OF BLOOM	HEIGHT	FLOWER COLOR	PLANT DESCRIPTION
ARTEMISIA [ar-tem-*EE*-zee-ah] Wormwood					
A. abrotanum (Southernwood, Old Man)	4–8	Foliage only	3–5 ft.		Soft, grey-green, feathery, aromatic leaves. Stems are woody.
A. lactiflora (White Mugwort)	4–8	Aug.–Sept.	4–5 ft.	White	Plumes of creamy white flowers on leaves that are deep green above and silvery beneath.

LIGHT REQUIREMENTS	SOIL REQUIREMENTS	PROPAGATION	REMARKS
Partial shade to full sun	Average, well-drained soil	Self-sows freely if it likes its spot. Plant 8–12 in. apart.	Beautiful planted with alyssum and myosotis.
Partial shade to full sun	Average, well-drained soil	Self-sows but hybrid colors are lost. Replace with commercial seed. Plant 12 in. apart.	Plant them everywhere for a garden flecked with their subtle colors.
Full sun	Gravelly, well-drained soil	Division in spring. Seed. Plant 8–12 in. apart.	More compact and delicate than *A. alpina* and *A. caucasica* species. Colonizes readily in the rock garden.
Partial shade	Moist, well-drained soil	Division in spring. Plant 6–12 in. apart.	Looks nice between paving stones. Shallow roots need water during dry spells.
Full sun	Sandy, dry soil	Divide clumps every 3 years or when center foliage starts to die out. Plant 8–12 in. apart.	Excellent for the rock garden, between cracks in terraces, or along stone walls. Looks lovely with veronica.
Full sun	Average to poor, well-drained soil	Cuttings. Plant 18 in. apart.	Pungent, aromatic leaves used as a moth repellent.
Full sun	Average to poor, well-drained soil	Division in spring. Plant 18 in. apart.	Best grouped with colored flowers. Used to separate areas of contrasting color schemes.

155 Perennial Genera—*Continued*

NAME OF PLANT	ZONES	SEASON OF BLOOM	HEIGHT	FLOWER COLOR	PLANT DESCRIPTION
ARTEMISIA (continued)					
A. ludoviciana var. *albula* 'Silver King'	4–8	Foliage only	2–3 ft.		Silver-grey leaves with pleasing aromatic scent.
A. schmidtiana 'Silver Mound'	4–8	Foliage only	12 in.		Mounds of fine silver foliage about 12 in. high and 18 in. across.
ARUNCUS [uh-*RUNK*-uss] Goat's Beard					
A. dioicus or *A. sylvester*	5–9	June–July	6 ft.	White	Showy plumes of creamy white flowers on broad-toothed leaves.
Other cultivars: 'Kneiffii', 3 ft. tall.					
ASARUM [as-*AR*-um] Wild Ginger					
A. europaeum	4–8	Foliage only	6 in.		Glossy, deep green, kidney-shaped foliage forms a low ground cover.
ASCLEPIAS [as-*KLEE*-pee-us] Butterfly Weed					
A. tuberosa	3–8	July–Aug.	2 ft.	Orange	This native looks much like the common milkweed. Its clusters of bright orange flowers are pollinated by the monarch butterfly.
ASPERULA [as-*PER*-oo-lah] Sweet Woodruff					
A. odorata or *Galium odoratum*	4–8	Apr.–May	6–8 in.	White	Small, star-shaped flowers above whorls of thin, pale green leaves.

LIGHT REQUIREMENTS	SOIL REQUIREMENTS	PROPAGATION	REMARKS
Full sun	Average to poor, well-drained soil	Plants spread quickly; need division every year to keep them where you want them. Plant 12 in. apart.	Provides a contrasting silver foliage in the border or bed.
Full sun	Average to poor, well-drained soil	Cuttings. Plant 18 in.–2 ft. apart.	If stems flop over or centers tend to die out, soil is too rich. Wonderful in the rock garden or as an edging plant.
Partial shade to full sun	Rich, moist soil	Division in spring. Frequent division is not necessary. Plant 2 ft. apart.	Handsome specimen for the back border or the center of an island bed.
Full shade to partial shade	Rich, moist, humusy, well-drained soil	Division in spring. Plant 12 in. apart.	Though grown for its beautiful foliage, asarum has brown, tube-shaped flowers hidden under its leaves in May.
Full sun	Poor, well-drained soil	Seed. Or root cuttings in early spring. Taproot makes division difficult. Plant 12 in. apart.	This hardy, well-behaved plant needs little attention. It is slow to appear in spring, so mark it well.
Partial shade	Moist, humusy, well-drained soil	Division in spring or fall. Plant 6–12 in. apart.	An excellent ground cover for shaded spots. Dried leaves used to flavor May wine.

155 Perennial Genera—*Continued*

NAME OF PLANT	ZONES	SEASON OF BLOOM	HEIGHT	FLOWER COLOR	PLANT DESCRIPTION
ASTER [*AS*-ter] Michaelmas Daisy					
A. × *frikartii* 'Wonder of Staffa'	5–9	June–Sept.	2½– 3 ft.	Lavender	2½ in., lavender-blue, daisy-like flowers with golden centers. Stiff stems with lancelike leaves.
A. novae-angliae 'Harrington's Pink'	4–9	Aug.–Oct.	3–4 ft.	Pink	A profusion of light pink flowers on tall, wiry stems.

Other cultivars: 'Alma Potschke', warm pink flowers; 'September Ruby', ruby red flowers; 'Treasurer', lilac flowers.

A. novi-belgii 'Crimson Brocade'	4–9	Sept.–Oct.	3–4 ft.	Red	Semidouble, crimson red flowers with yellow centers.

Other cultivars: 'Eventide', semidouble, deep blue flowers; 'Fellowship', double, light pink flowers; 'Mount Everest', single, white flowers; 'Alert', dwarf, 12–15 in. tall, crimson red flowers; 'Jenny', dwarf, 12–15 in. tall, violet-purple flowers; 'Melba', dwarf, 12–15 in. tall, semidouble, rose pink flowers; 'Royal Opal', dwarf, 12–15 in. tall, pale lilac-blue flowers; 'Snow Flurry', dwarf, 12–15 in. tall, white flowers.

ASTILBE [as-*TILL*-bee]					
A. × *arendsii* 'Rhineland'	4–8	June–July	2 ft.	Pink	Showy, rose pink plumes rise above attractive, semiglossy foliage.

Other cultivars: 'Europe', early blooming, light pink flowers; 'Gladstone', early, white flowers; 'Deutschland', early, white flowers; 'Bridal Veil', midseason, white flowers; 'Fanal', midseason, bright red flowers; 'Peach Blossom', midseason, salmon pink flowers; 'Amethyst', late blooming, lilac flowers; 'Intermezzo', late, deep pink flowers; 'Red Sentinel', late, deep red flowers.

A. chinensis 'Pumila'	4–8	Aug.–Sept.	15 in.	Pink	Dwarf variety with lavender-pink flowers. Creeping habit forms a nice ground cover.
A. taquetii 'Superba'	4–8	Aug.–Sept.	3–4 ft.	Pink	Plumes of rosy purple, blooming later than *A. arendsii*.
AUBRIETA [aw-*BREE*-tah] Purple Rock Cress					
A. deltoidea 'Giant Superbissima'	4–7	Apr.–June	4–6 in.	Lilac, purple, rose, red	Myriads of 1–in. flowers bloom atop grey-green, mat-forming foliage.

LIGHT REQUIREMENTS	SOIL REQUIREMENTS	PROPAGATION	REMARKS
Full sun	Average, well-drained soil	Division in spring every year. Plant 18 in. apart.	A long-blooming aster; produces flowers throughout the year in frost-free climates.
Full sun	Average, well-drained soil	Division in spring every other year. Or seed. Plant 12 in. apart.	Flowers close at night. In colder climates do not pinch—they may not have time to flower.
Full sun	Average, well-drained soil	Division in spring every other year. Plant 12–18 in. apart.	More compact and refined looking than *A. novae-angliae*. Pinch shoots once or twice before midsummer to stimulate branching.
Partial shade	Moist, humusy soil	Division in early spring. Plant 12–18 in. apart.	Astilbes come in a variety of colors, both early and late blooming, and provide a staggered season of bloom.
Partial shade	Moist, humusy soil	Division in spring. Plant 12 in. apart.	Nice for the front edge of a shady border or bed.
Partial shade	Moist, humusy soil	Division in spring. Plant 12–18 in. apart.	Will tolerate full sun as long as roots have adequate moisture.
Partial shade to full sun	Sandy, well-drained soil	Division in spring. Cuttings. Seed. Plant 6–8 in. apart.	A cool, moist soil is ideal. Where summers are hot, plants are apt to be short-lived.

155 Perennial Genera—*Continued*

NAME OF PLANT	ZONES	SEASON OF BLOOM	HEIGHT	FLOWER COLOR	PLANT DESCRIPTION
BAPTISIA [bap-*TEEZ*-ee-ah] Blue Wild Indigo					
B. australis	3–8	June	4 ft.	Blue	Racemes of pealike flowers followed by black seed pods. Blue-green foliage stays nice all year.
BELAMCANDA [bell-am-*CAN*-duh] Blackberry Lily					
B. chinensis	5–10	July	3 ft.	Orange	Clusters of 2-in., star-shaped flowers with iris-like leaves. Flowers are orange with red dots.
BERGENIA [ber-*JEEN*-ee-ah] Heart-Leaved Bergenia					
B. cordifolia	3–8	Apr.–May	12 in.	Pink	Clumps of large, glossy, cabbage-shaped leaves produce clusters of bell-shaped, rose pink flowers on thick stems.
Other cultivars: 'Alba', white flowers; 'Perfecta', lilac-red flowers; 'Rotblum', red flowers.					
BOLTONIA [bol-*TONE*-ee-ah] White Boltonia					
B. asteroides 'Snowbank'	3–8	Aug.–Sept.	4–5 ft.	White	Masses of 1-in., white, daisy-like flowers on tall, branching stems. Small leaves.
BRUNNERA [brewn-*ERR*-ah] Siberian Bugloss					
B. macrophylla	3–8	Apr.–May	18 in.	Blue	Bold, heart-shaped leaves bear delicate, forget-me-not flowers.
CAMPANULA [kam-*PAN*-you-lah] Bellflower					
C. carpatica 'Blue Chips' (Carpathian Harebell)	3–8	June–Sept.	8 in.	Blue	1½-in., blue, cup-shaped flowers on mounds of heart-shaped leaves.

Other cultivars: 'China Doll', lavender-blue flowers; 'Wedgewood Blue', violet-blue flowers; 'Wedgewood White', white flowers; 'White Star', free-flowering, with large white flowers.

LIGHT REQUIREMENTS	SOIL REQUIREMENTS	PROPAGATION	REMARKS
Partial shade to full sun	Moist, humusy soil (lime-free)	Seed works best since deep taproot can be difficult to divide. Root cuttings. Plant 2 ft. apart.	A noninvasive, hardy specimen for the middle or back border. Give it a permanent location.
Full sun	Rich, sandy soil	Seed. Or tubers divided in spring. Plant 1 in. deep and 6 in. apart.	Flowers are followed by pods, which, upon ripening, open to reveal glossy black seeds resembling blackberries.
Partial shade to full sun	Average soil, moist or dry	Division in spring. Plant 12 in. apart.	In colder regions, foliage turns a handsome bronze in fall.
Full sun	Average soil, moist or dry	Division in spring. Plant 12 in.–2 ft. apart.	These tall plants bloom the same time as asters, and the two make an interesting background hedge if planted close together.
Partial shade to full sun	Rich, moist soil	Division in spring. Plant 12 in. apart.	Some would call these flowers true blue. In any case, they're beautiful.
Full sun to partial shade	Average, moist, well-drained soil	Easily raised from seed. Plant 10–12 in. apart.	Delightful in the front border or rock garden.

155 Perennial Genera—*Continued*

NAME OF PLANT	ZONES	SEASON OF BLOOM	HEIGHT	FLOWER COLOR	PLANT DESCRIPTION
CAMPANULA (continued)					
C. glomerata 'Superba' (Clustered Bellflower)	3–8	June–July	18 in.	Purple	Showy, tight clusters of intense purple flowers. Leaves are rough and hairy.
Other cultivars: 'Alba', white flowers; 'Acaulis', amethyst-violet flowers; 'Joan Elliott', deep violet-blue flowers.					
C. lactiflora 'Superba'	5	June–July	3 ft.	Blue	Violet-blue, bell-shaped flowers held in loose panicles on stiff stems.
Other cultivars: 'Loddon Anna', soft pink flowers.					
C. persicifolia 'Caerulea' (Peach-Leaved Bellflower)	3–8	June–Aug.	2 ft.	Blue	Nodding, bright blue, cup-shaped flowers held aloft on slender stems from basal rosettes of peach-leaf–shaped foliage.
Other cultivars: 'Alba', white flowers; 'Blue Gardenia', double, deep silver-blue flowers; 'White Pearl', double, pure white flowers.					
C. poscharskyana	3–8	June–Frost	12 in.	Blue	Star-shaped sprays of light blue flowers on compact foliage.
C. rotundifolia 'Olympica' (Bluebells-of-Scotland)	3–8	June–Sept.	12–18 in.	Blue	Lavender-blue, drooping, bell-shaped blossoms on slender, wiry stems.
CATANANCHE [cat-uh-*NAN*-chee] Cupid's-Dart					
C. caerulea	5–9	June–Aug.	18 in.–2 ft.	Blue	Daisy-like flowers of lavender-blue held on wiry stems, which arise from clumps of grey-green, grassy leaves.

LIGHT REQUIREMENTS	SOIL REQUIREMENTS	PROPAGATION	REMARKS
Full sun to partial shade	Average, well-drained soil	Division every other year to keep plants where you want them. Plant 2 ft. apart.	A striking plant that harmonizes with the lighter pinks and blues of the June garden.
Full sun to partial shade	Average, moist, well-drained soil	Division in spring. Plant 12 in. apart.	An easy-to-grow campanula.
Full sun to partial shade	Average, well-drained soil	Division in spring every 2 or 3 years. Plant 18 in. apart.	Can naturalize in out-of-the-way places.
Partial shade to full sun	Sandy soil	Division in spring. Seed. Plant 12 in. apart.	Vigorous creeper, making large but neat mats. Especially suited for rock gardens, dry walls, and sandy slopes.
Full sun to partial shade	Average, well-drained soil	Division in spring. Seed. Plant 8–12 in. apart.	Blooms all summer. Good in between rock crevices.
Full sun	Average, well-drained soil	Seed sown in spring. Root cuttings in fall. Plant 12 in. apart.	Best planted in masses. Especially nice with artemisia. Good for cut flowers and dried flower arrangements.

155 Perennial Genera—*Continued*

NAME OF PLANT	ZONES	SEASON OF BLOOM	HEIGHT	FLOWER COLOR	PLANT DESCRIPTION
CENTAUREA [sen-*TAW*-ree-ah] Perennial Cornflower					
C. dealbata	3–8	June–Aug.	2 ft.	Red-violet	2-in., thistlelike flowers, white in center, surrounded by striking, rosy red-violet. Handsome foliage is coarsely cut, dark green above and silvery underneath.
C. macrocephala	3–9	July	4 ft.	Yellow	3-in., thistlelike flowers on stiff stems. Large, ragged, oval leaves.
C. montana	4–8	May–July	2 ft.	Blue	Deep violet-blue, 3-in., fringed flowers on slender stems that may need staking. Silver-grey foliage.
CENTRANTHUS [sent-*RANTH*-us] Red Valerian					
C. ruber	5–9	July–Aug.	3 ft.	Red	Dense, terminal clusters of fragrant flowers above rich green foliage.
CERASTIUM [sih-*RAS*-tee-um] Snow-in-Summer					
C. tomentosum	2–8	June	6 in.	White	Masses of pure white, star-shaped flowers. Silver-grey foliage forms dense mat.
CERATOSTIGMA [sir-at-oh-*STIG*-ma] Plumbago					
C. plumbaginoides	6–9	Aug.–Oct.	6–8 in.	Blue	Intense gentian blue flowers have attractive leathery foliage that turns a deep mahogany in fall.

LIGHT REQUIREMENTS	SOIL REQUIREMENTS	PROPAGATION	REMARKS
Full sun	Average, well-drained soil	Division in spring every 3 years. Plant 18 in. apart.	Its beautiful magenta can be noisy near more subtle colors.
Full sun	Average, well-drained soil	Division in spring every 2–4 years. Plant 2 ft. apart.	Best planted individually as the foliage is large and coarse, making a bold statement. Short bloom period.
Full sun	Average, well-drained soil	Division in spring every 2 years. Spreads rapidly; self-sows. Plant 12 in. apart.	Cut back for a second bloom in September.
Full sun to partial shade	Average to poor, well-drained soil	Division in spring. Self-sows. Plant 18 in. apart.	Will grow in waste areas. Self-sown seedlings are a nuisance in the bed or border.
Full sun	Average to poor, well-drained soil	Seed. Or division in spring. Softwood cuttings taken in early summer. Plant 12 in. apart.	Spreading rapidly over dry slopes, cerastium can be invasive. Ideal for trailing over rock walls. *C. bierbersteinii* is similar but not as rampant.
Full sun to partial shade	Average, well-drained soil	Division in spring. Cuttings taken in early summer. Plant 12 in. apart.	A late-blooming ground cover adored for its intense blue.

155 Perennial Genera—*Continued*

NAME OF PLANT	ZONES	SEASON OF BLOOM	HEIGHT	FLOWER COLOR	PLANT DESCRIPTION
CHELONE [chell-*OWN*] Turtlehead					
C. lyonii	4–9	Aug.–Sept.	3 ft.	Pink	Shiny, dark green leaves on shoots ending in clusters of tubular, hooded flowers, resembling a turtle's head.
CHRYSANTHEMUM [kriss-*AN*-theh-mum]					
C. coccineum 'Robinson's Rose' (Pyrethrum or Painted Daisy)	4–9	June–July	2 ft.	Pink	3-in., daisy-like, rosy pink flowers with yellow centers on tall, single stems. Foliage is deeply cut and dark green.

Other cultivars: 'Album', single, white flowers; 'Robinson's Crimson', rich red, single flowers.

C. maximum 'Alaska' (Shasta Daisy)	4–9	June–Aug.	2 ft.	White	The classic, large, showy, single daisy. Leaves are long, narrow, and glossy.

Other cultivars: 'Aglaya', 2½ ft. tall, very double, 5-in. flowers; 'Cobham Gold', creamy yellow, double flowers; 'Little Miss Muffet', 12–15 in. tall, semidouble, white flowers.

C. × morifolium 'Allure' (Garden or Hardy Mum, Cushion Type)	4–8	Sept.–Frost	14 in.	Yellow	Free-blooming, compact plants, literally covered with hemispherical flowers in fall.

Other cultivars: 'Crackerjack', pearly white flowers with yellow centers; 'Glamour', orchid-lavender flowers; 'Red Dandy', scarlet flowers; 'Spotless', white flowers.

C. × morifolium 'Autumn Royal' (Garden or Hardy Mum, Decorative Type)	4–8	Sept.–Frost	2 ft.	Purple	4-in., double, showy flowers, growing taller and more open than cushion mums.

Other cultivars: 'Chapel Bells', white flowers; 'Cheyenne', red flowers; 'Chiquita', lemon yellow flowers; 'Confetti', pink flowers; 'Nutmegger', orange flowers.

C. × morifolium 'Daisy Red' (Garden or Hardy Mum, Single Type)	4–8	Sept.–Frost	20 in.	Red	3-in., vermilion, daisy-like flowers with yellow centers.

Other cultivars: 'Joan Helen', 15 in. tall, reddish purple flowers; 'My Love', 18 in. tall, apricot flowers; 'Sleigh Ride', 2 ft. tall, white flowers; 'Yellow Marguerita', 26 in. tall, yellow flowers.

LIGHT REQUIREMENTS	SOIL REQUIREMENTS	PROPAGATION	REMARKS
Partial shade to full shade	Rich, moist soil	Division in spring. Seed. Cuttings taken in summer. Plant 18 in. apart.	Hardy native that thrives in swampy areas, along a stream, or edge of a pond.
Full sun	Average, well-drained soil	Division in spring or fall. Seed. Plant 12 in. apart.	Best planted in groups of 3 to 5. They make wonderful cut flowers. Reclassified as *Tanacetum collineum*.
Full sun	Rich, well-drained soil	Division every other year to keep plants flowering. Seed. Plant 12 in. apart.	Especially free-flowering plant for border or bed. Remove spent flowers for extended bloom. Excellent for cutting. Reclassified as *Leucanthemum maximum*.
Full sun	Rich, well-drained soil	Division in spring every year. Plant 12 in. apart.	Doesn't need pinching or staking. Cushion mums come in all colors except blue.
Full sun	Rich, well-drained soil	Division in spring every year. Plant 18 in. apart.	Decorative types need pinching in early summer to produce good bloom. Needs staking.
Full sun	Rich, well-drained soil	Division in spring every year. Plant 12 in. apart.	All single types have conspicuous yellow centers. Needs staking and pinching.

155 Perennial Genera—*Continued*

NAME OF PLANT	ZONES	SEASON OF BLOOM	HEIGHT	FLOWER COLOR	PLANT DESCRIPTION
CHRYSANTHEMUM (continued)					
C. × *morifolium* 'Dew Drops' (Garden or Hardy Mum, Pompon Type)	4–8	Sept.–Frost	2 ft.	Pink	Light pink, 1½-in., ball-shaped flowers appear in clusters on tall stems with open foliage.
Other cultivars: 'Good Humor', 22 in. tall, creamy white flowers; 'Hawaii', 18 in. tall, orange-red flowers; 'Red Gold', 20 in. tall, deep golden yellow flowers; 'Sarah', 20 in. tall, peach flowers; 'Sprite', 18 in. tall, deep purple flowers.					
C. × *morifolium* hybrids 'Baby Tears' (Garden or Hardy Mum, Button Type)	4–8	Sept.–Frost	12 in.	White	Very tight, 1-in., ball-like flowers that completely cover foliage in neat mounds.
Other cultivars: 'Ann Fulton', pink flowers with deep rose centers; 'Brown Eyes', bronze flowers with mahogany centers; 'Ethel', red flowers; 'Purple Button', purple flowers.					
C. parthenium (Feverfew)	6–10	June–Oct.	12 in.–3 ft.	White	1-in., short-petaled, daisy-like flowers with large, pale yellow centers. Foliage is pungent.
CHRYSOGONUM [kriss-*OGG*-oh-num] Golden Star					
C. virginianum	6–9	May–Oct.	8 in.	Yellow	Dainty, star-shaped flowers with spooned leaves. Makes a dense ground cover.
CIMICIFUGA [sim-ih-*SIFF*-you-guh] Snakeroot					
C. racemosa	3–9	July–Aug.	6 ft.	White	Tall wands of creamy white florets glow above bold, very dark green foliage.

LIGHT REQUIREMENTS	SOIL REQUIREMENTS	PROPAGATION	REMARKS
Full sun	Rich, well-drained soil	Division in spring every year. Plant 12 in. apart.	Pompons need pinching in early summer. Stake.
Full sun	Rich, well-drained soil	Division in spring every year. Plant 12 in. apart.	Stands up well to rain and does not need staking. All garden mums were reclassified into genus *Dendrathema.*
Full sun	Average to poor, well-drained soil	Self-sows readily. Plant 12 in. apart.	In Zones 3–5, treat as an annual. Use for filling in between major colors—in the garden or bouquets.
Partial shade to full shade	Rich, moist soil	Division in spring or fall. Plant 12 in. apart.	This wildflower blooms all summer in a shaded spot. Dislikes dry soil in summer.
Partial shade to full shade	Rich, moist soil	Division in spring only if more plants are wanted. Plant 12 in. apart.	One of the most dramatic verticals for the back border.

155 Perennial Genera—*Continued*

NAME OF PLANT	ZONES	SEASON OF BLOOM	HEIGHT	FLOWER COLOR	PLANT DESCRIPTION
CLEMATIS [*KLEM*-uh-tiss]					
C. heracleifolia var. *davidiana* (Blue Tube Clematis)	4–9	Aug.–Sept.	3 ft.	Blue	Fragrant clusters of deep blue flowers, resembling hyacinths. Leaves are coarse, toothed, and broad.
C. integrifolia 'Caerulea' (Solitary Clematis)	4–9	June–Aug.	2 ft.	Blue	1½-in., single, porcelain blue, bell-shaped flowers on thin stems.
C. recta 'Mandshurica' (Ground Clematis)	4–9	June–July	3 ft.	White	Branching sprays of fragrant, ¾-in., tubular flowers above feathery foliage.
CONVALLARIA [kon-vall-*AIR*-ee-ah] Lily-of-the-Valley					
C. majalis	2–8	May–June	8 in.	White	Perfumed, waxy white bells hang from racemes that emerge from broad, fluted leaves.
COREOPSIS [kor-ee-*OP*-sis] Tickseed					
C. auriculata 'Nana'	4–9	June–Aug.	6 in.	Orange-yellow	1½-in., daisy-like flowers with jagged edges. Foliage forms ground-covering mats.
C. grandiflora 'Sunburst'	4–9	June–Aug.	20 in.	Yellow	Bright yellow, 2-in., semidouble, daisy-like flowers above narrow, lancelike foliage.

Other cultivars: 'Badengold', 3 ft. tall, large, 3-in., golden yellow flowers; 'Goldfink', 9 in. tall, golden yellow flowers; 'Mayfield Giant', 2½ ft. tall, rich, orange-yellow flowers.

C. lanceolata	4–9	June–Frost	2 ft.	Yellow	Looks like *C. grandiflora*, but flower centers may be brownish.
C. verticillata 'Moonbeam'	4–9	July–Frost	15 in.	Yellow	Masses of starry, pale yellow, daisy-like flowers on mound of fine filigree foliage.

Other cultivars: 'Golden Shower', golden, 2-in. flowers.

LIGHT REQUIREMENTS	SOIL REQUIREMENTS	PROPAGATION	REMARKS
Full sun to partial shade	Rich, well-drained soil	Division in spring or cuttings taken in early summer.	Prefers a slightly acid soil. Needs staking.
Full sun to partial shade	Rich, well-drained soil	Division in spring or cuttings taken in early summer. Plant 18 in.–2 ft. apart.	Requires staking or a wall to tumble over.
Full sun to partial shade	Rich, well-drained soil	Division in spring or cuttings taken in early summer. Plant 18 in. apart.	Plant along a path for fragrance.
Partial shade to full shade	Rich, moist, well-drained soil	Division of pips in spring or fall. Plant 8–12 in. apart.	A long-lived, old-fashioned favorite that naturalizes easily. Divide when flowers get sparse, and enrich soil with compost.
Full sun	Average to poor, well-drained soil	Division in spring every three years. Seed. Plant 10 in. apart.	Plant in rock garden or front edge of bed or border.
Full sun	Average to poor, well-drained soil	Seed. Plant 12 in. apart.	Free-blooming and drought resistant. Plants are short-lived but self-sow readily.
Full sun	Average to poor, well-drained soil	Division every 3 years. Plant 12 in. apart.	Known as perennial coreopsis, these plants are long-lived. Often confused with *C. grandiflora*.
Full sun to partial shade	Average to poor, well-drained soil	Division in spring from spreading roots. Seed. Plant 12 in. apart.	Excellent cultivar that blooms all summer. Unusually fine leaves are nice accompaniment to broad-leaved neighbors.

NAME OF PLANT	ZONES	SEASON OF BLOOM	HEIGHT	FLOWER COLOR	PLANT DESCRIPTION
CORYDALIS [kor-*ID*-al-iss] Fumitory					
C. lutea	3–8	May–Aug.	12 in.	Yellow	Sprays of tubular flowers and lacy, fernlike foliage.
CYPRIPEDIUM [sip-rih-*PEED*-ee-um]					
C. acaule (Pink Lady's Slipper)	3–8	May–June	12 in.	Pink	Leafless stems bear single, pouchlike blossoms from 2 oblong leaves.
C. calceolus (Yellow Lady's Slipper)	3–8	May–June	15 in.	Yellow	Leafy stems make a nice clump and bear 1 or 2 slippers.
DELPHINIUM [del-*PHIN*-ee-um] Larkspur					
D. ×*belladonna* 'Bellamosa' (Garland Delphinium)	3–7	June–July	3–4 ft.	Blue	Single, dark blue florets cover 4-ft. spikes. Foliage is finer cut than *D. elatum*.
Other cultivars: 'Casa Blanca', white flowers; 'Cliveden Beauty', light blue flowers.					
D. elatum Connecticut Yankee strains (Candle Delphinium)	3–7	June–July	2½ ft.	White, blue, purple	Looks like a dwarf, single-flowered, Pacific Coast type.
D. elatum Pacific Coast strains (Candle Delphinium)	3–7	June–July	5–6 ft.	White, blue, mauve, purple	Majestic spires carry 2- to 3-in. florets that may be single or double. Leaves are coarse and deeply divided.
D. elatum hybrids Blackmore and Langdon strains (Candle Delphinium)	3–7	June–July	5–6 ft.	White, blue, purple	Large flowers cover tall flower spikes. Deeply lobed leaves are larger at the base.
D. grandiflorum (Chinese or Siberian Delphinium)	3–7	June–Aug.	18 in.	White, blue, purple	1-in., spurred flowers cluster loosely on a branched spike. Foliage, deeply divided, keeps low.

LIGHT REQUIREMENTS	SOIL REQUIREMENTS	PROPAGATION	REMARKS
Partial shade to full sun	Rich, moist, well-drained soil	Division in spring. Plant 8–10 in. apart.	At home in the shaded rock garden.
Partial shade to full shade	Rich, moist, humusy, well-drained soil	Plants don't transplant easily.	A thrill to find blooming along the woodland path. They like a leaf mulch, preferably oak leaves.
Partial shade	Rich, moist soil	Division in spring or fall. Plant 12 in. apart.	Easiest of the orchids to establish. Makes a nice specimen plant in a sheltered spot.
Full sun to partial shade	Rich, well-drained, slightly alkaline soil	Division in spring. Cuttings. Seed. Plant 18 in. apart.	Summer mulch benefits all delphiniums, as does dead-heading, which encourages later bloom. Needs staking.
Full sun to partial shade	Rich, well-drained, slightly alkaline soil	Division in spring. Seed. Plant 2 ft. apart.	Smaller, more compact plants may not need staking.
Full sun to partial shade	Rich, well-drained, slightly alkaline soil	Division in spring. Seed. Plant 2½ ft. apart.	A regal plant in the back of the border. Lasts only 2 years. Plants need staking.
Full sun to partial shade	Rich, well-drained, slightly alkaline soil	Division in spring. Seed. Plant 2–2½ ft. apart.	More perennial than Pacific Coast strains. All forms of *D. elatum* have contrasting centers called bees. Needs staking.
Full sun to partial shade	Rich, well-drained, slightly alkaline soil	Division in spring. Seed. Plant 12 in. apart.	Will bloom all summer if spent blooms are cut back. Does not need staking.

NAME OF PLANT	ZONES	SEASON OF BLOOM	HEIGHT	FLOWER COLOR	PLANT DESCRIPTION
DIANTHUS [di-*AN*-thus]					
D. × *allwoodii* hybrids 'Helen'	4–8	May–June	12 in.	Salmon pink	Lots of little carnations on graceful, grassy foliage.
Other cultivars: 'Blanche', white flowers; 'Doris', salmon pink flowers with deeper pink eyes.					
D. caryophyllus 'English Giants' (Carnation)	6–7	June–July	2 ft.	White, pink, red	Various shades of double carnation blossoms. Narrow, greyish leaves tend to sprawl.
D. deltoides 'Brilliant' (Maiden Pinks)	4–8	May–June	4–6 in.	Pink	Low-growing, semievergreen foliage is covered with single blossoms.
Other cultivars: 'Alba', white flowers; 'Flashing Light', bright crimson flowers.					
D. gratianopolitanus 'Petite' (Cheddar Pinks)	3–8	May–June	3 in.	Pink	Masses of miniature flowers on blue-grey, mat-forming foliage. Dainty.
Other cultivars: 'Tiny Rubies', 4 in. tall, rosy red, double flowers.					
D. plumarius 'Spring Beauty' (Cottage Pinks)	4–8	May–June	12–15 in.	White, pink, red	Double, mixed flowers in various shades of rose, salmon, pink, and white on tufts of blue-green foliage.
DICENTRA [di-*SENT*-ruh] Bleeding-Heart					
D. cucullaria (Dutchman's-Breeches)	2–7	Apr.–May	10 in.	White	Delicate, pantaloon-shaped flowers dangle above the grey-green, fernlike foliage.
D. eximia (Fringed Bleeding-Heart)	3–7	Apr.–Sept.	12 in.	Pink	Handsome, greyish green, fernlike foliage with sprays of deep rose pink, heart-shaped flowers.
D. formosa (Pacific Bleeding-Heart)	3–7	May–Sept.	12 in.	Pink	Similar to *D. eximia* with coarser leaves and creeping, underground rhizomes.

LIGHT REQUIREMENTS	SOIL REQUIREMENTS	PROPAGATION	REMARKS
Full sun	Average, well-drained, slightly alkaline soil	Cuttings taken in summer. Seed. Plant 8–12 in. apart.	Created by Montague Allwood of England, these charming, dainty hybrids bloom all summer along a border's edge if spent flowers are cut.
Full sun	Average, well-drained, slightly alkaline soil	Cuttings taken in summer. Seed. Plant 12 in. apart.	In Zones 8–10 treat as biennials; in Zones 5 and colder, as annuals.
Full sun	Sandy, well-drained, alkaline soil	Divide into small clumps and plant 8 in. apart. Seed.	Bright pink carpets making intense spots of color, often escaping into the lawn.
Full sun	Sandy, well-drained, alkaline soil	Cuttings taken in summer. Plant 8 in. apart.	Needs excellent drainage. Good for the rock garden.
Full sun	Average, well-drained, alkaline soil	Cuttings taken in summer. Plant 12 in. apart.	Nice for a border's edge in a sunny spot.
Partial shade	Rich, moist soil	Divide right after bloom before foliage dies back. Plant 8 in. apart.	This woodland native is a delight tucked among rocks. Foliage dies back early. *D. canadensis* (squirrel corn) shares same habitat.
Partial shade to full sun	Rich, moist soil	Division in spring every 3 years. Self-seeds.	Ever-blooming, starting with spring bulbs and flowering right on through with campanulas.
Partial shade	Rich, moist soil	Division. Plant 12 in. apart.	Given a cool, moist, humusy spot, they will naturalize readily.

NAME OF PLANT	ZONES	SEASON OF BLOOM	HEIGHT	FLOWER COLOR	PLANT DESCRIPTION
DICENTRA (continued)					
D. spectabilis (Common Bleeding-Heart)	3–7	May–June	2½ ft.	Pink	Graceful racemes dripping with ornate flowers, resembling valentine hearts. Foliage dies back in summer.
Other cultivars: 'Alba', white flowers.					
DICTAMNUS [dik-*TAM*-nuss] Gas Plant					
D. alba or *D. fraxinella*	3–8	June	2½ ft.	White	Lemon-scented flowers on large, terminal spikes. Flowers exude volatile oils whose gas can be ignited.
Other cultivars: 'Rubra', rose pink flowers.					
DIGITALIS [did-je-*TAL*-iss] Foxglove					
D. ambigua or *D. grandiflora*	4–8	June–July	3 ft.	Yellow	Full spires of drooping, creamy yellow, tubular flowers spotted with brown.
D. × mertonensis hybrids	4–8	June–Aug.	3 ft.	Pink	Flowers are unusual, crushed-strawberry color.
DORONICUM [dor-*AHN*-ik-um] Leopard's Bane					
D. caucasicum or *D. cordatum*	4–7	Apr.–May	18 in.	Yellow	2-in., bright yellow, daisy-like flowers above ragged, heart-shaped foliage.
DRABA [*DRAY*-buh] Willow Grass					
D. sibirica	3–8	Apr.–May	2 in.	Yellow	A creeping, grasslike mat with clusters of flowers.

LIGHT REQUIREMENTS	SOIL REQUIREMENTS	PROPAGATION	REMARKS
Partial shade to full sun	Rich, moist soil	Division in spring. Root cuttings. Self-seeds. Plant 2 ft. apart.	Every garden should have a spot for this romantic, old-time favorite.
Full sun	Rich, well-drained soil	Established plants have deep roots and resent being transplanted. Seed. Plant 3 ft. apart.	Although bloom is short, attractive seed pods follow. Foliage stays nice throughout season.
Partial shade	Rich, moist, well-drained, acid soil	Division in spring. Seed.	Although not as showy as common foxglove, *D. purpurea* (a biennial), it makes a fine vertical accent.
Partial shade	Rich, moist, well-drained soil	Division after flowering. Seed. Plant 12 in. apart.	This is a hybrid of *D. grandiflora* and *D. purpurea.*
Full sun to partial shade	Rich, moist soil	Division in spring or Aug. while plant is dormant. Seed. Plant 12 in. apart.	Foliage goes dormant in summer.
Full sun	Average, well-drained soil	Divide after plant flowers.	Useful in the rock garden.

155 Perennial Genera—*Continued*

NAME OF PLANT	ZONES	SEASON OF BLOOM	HEIGHT	FLOWER COLOR	PLANT DESCRIPTION
ECHINACEA [ek-in-*AY*-see-uh]					
E. purpurea 'Bright Star'	3–9	July–Sept.	3 ft.	Pink	Rosy pink, 4-in., daisy-like flowers have prominent center cone surrounded by skirt of petals. Leaves are dark green.
Other cultivars: 'White Luster', white flowers.					
ECHINOPS [*EK*-in-ops] Globe Thistle					
E. ritro 'Taplow Blue'	4–9	July–Sept.	4–5 ft.	Blue	3-in., prickly, steel blue globes on coarse, thistlelike foliage.
EPIMEDIUM [ep-ih-*MEED*-dee-um] Bishop's Hat					
E. alpinum var. *rubrum*	4–7	May–June	12 in.	Red and yellow	Dainty, airy flowers above asymmetrical, heart-shaped leaves.
ERIGERON [ee-*RIDGE*-er-on] Fleabane					
E. speciosus 'Prosperity'	4–8	June–Sept.	18 in.	Blue	2-in., mauve-blue, daisy-like flowers with central yellow disks.
Other cultivars: 'Pink Jewel', pink flowers with yellow eyes.					
ERYNGIUM [eh-*RINJ*-ee-um] Sea Holly					
E. amethystinum	4–7	July–Aug.	2 ft.	Blue	Spiky, steel blue petals surround teasel-like centers. Leaves are as prickly looking as the flowers.
EUPATORIUM [you-pah-*TOR*-ee-um]					
E. coelestinum (Hardy Ageratum)	5–8	Aug.–Frost	2 ft.	Lavender	Clusters of light lavender puffs on slender purple stems with widely spaced, triangular leaves.

LIGHT REQUIREMENTS	SOIL REQUIREMENTS	PROPAGATION	REMARKS
Full sun	Rich, sandy, well-drained soil	Division in spring. Seed. Plant 12 in. apart.	This striking plant is long-lived and noninvasive.
Full sun	Average to poor, well-drained soil	Division or root cuttings in spring. Seed. Plant 2 ft. apart.	Its bold globes make an unusual accent in the back border. *E. tournefortii* has white flowers.
Partial shade	Average, well-drained soil	Division in spring or fall. Plant 8–10 in. apart.	A graceful and hardy ground cover. *E. pinnatum* has yellow flowers; *E. × youngianum* 'Niveum', white.
Full sun	Light, sandy, well-drained soil	Division in spring or fall. Seed. Plant 12 in. apart.	Bushy little plants resemble asters but bloom earlier.
Full sun	Poor, sandy, well-drained soil	Root cuttings taken in spring. Deep taproot resents moving. Plant 2 ft. apart.	Slowly covers itself with bloom. Best grown as a single specimen. Excellent in dried arrangements.
Full sun to partial shade	Light, humusy soil	Division in spring. Plant 2 ft. apart.	Weedy but wonderful for the late fall display.

155 Perennial Genera—*Continued*

NAME OF PLANT	ZONES	SEASON OF BLOOM	HEIGHT	FLOWER COLOR	PLANT DESCRIPTION
EUPHORBIA [you-*FOR*-bee-ah] Spurge					
E. cyparissias (Cypress Spurge)	4–8	May–June	12 in.	Lime green bracts	Tiny forests of slender-leaved foliage end in lime green bracts.
E. epithymoides (Cushion Spurge)	4–8	May–June	12 in.	Yellow-green bracts	Hemispherical hedge of dark green foliage ending in bright yellow-green bracts.
E. myrsinites (Myrtle Spurge)	5–8	May–June	6 in.	Yellow-green bracts	Bluish green, fleshy stems end in yellow-green bracts.
FILIPENDULA [fill-ih-*PEN*-dyoo-luh] Meadowsweet					
F. palmata 'Elegans' (Siberian Meadowsweet)	3–9	June–July	15 in.	Pink	Clusters of tiny, pale pink flowers fade to white. Large, glossy green leaves form handsome clump.
F. rubra 'Venusta' (Queen-of-the-Prairie)	3–9	June–July	4–6 ft.	Pink	Fragrant, deep pink, feathery plumes bloom on stalks with large, coarse, jagged leaves.
F. ulmaria 'Flore Pleno' (Queen-of-the-Meadow)	3–9	June–July	4 ft.	White	Flowers are similar to *F. rubra* but are white.
F. vulgaris or *F. hexapetala* 'Flore Pleno' (Dropworth)	3–9	June–July	2 ft.	White	Double flowers in loose panicles above fine, fernlike foliage.
GAILLARDIA [gay-*LAR*-dee-ah] Blanket Flower					
G. × grandiflora 'Goblin'	3–9	June–Frost	12 in.	Red and yellow	Large, deep red, daisy-like flowers, tipped with gold, bloom profusely on mounds of grey-green, lance-shaped foliage.

Other cultivars: 'Burgundy', 2½ ft. tall, wine red flowers; 'Dazzler', 2 ft. tall, maroon flowers tipped with gold; 'Yellow Queen', 2½ ft. tall, pure golden yellow flowers.

LIGHT REQUIREMENTS	SOIL REQUIREMENTS	PROPAGATION	REMARKS
Full sun to partial shade	Average, well-drained soil	Division in spring or fall. Plant 12 in. apart.	Invasive. Don't plant in the garden; a barren bank suits it just fine.
Full sun	Average, sandy, well-drained soil	Division in spring. Cuttings. Seed. Plant 18 in. apart.	Foliage turns red in the fall.
Full sun	Average, sandy, well-drained soil	Division in spring. Seed. Plant 12–18 in. apart.	This low-growing trailer looks decorative on a sunny bank or spilling over a wall.
Full sun	Rich, moist soil	Division in spring. Plant 18 in. apart.	Smallest of the filipendulas.
Full sun	Rich, moist soil	Division in spring. Seed. Plant 3 ft. apart.	This native of the prairies is a rampant spreader in damp soil.
Full sun to partial shade	Rich, moist soil	Division in spring. Plant 2 ft. apart.	This European native carries beautiful foliage before and after flowering.
Full sun to partial shade	Average soil, moist or dry	Division in spring. Seed. Plant 12 in. apart.	Ferny tufts make a good ground cover.
Full sun	Average to poor, well-drained soil	Division in spring. Seed. Root cuttings. Plant 8 in. apart.	Crowns tend to die out, especially in heavier soils, but in spring it returns in nearby spots from persistent roots. Dig and replant.

155 Perennial Genera—*Continued*

NAME OF PLANT	ZONES	SEASON OF BLOOM	HEIGHT	FLOWER COLOR	PLANT DESCRIPTION
GENTIANA [gent-*SHEE*-anna] Gentian					
G. asclepiadea (Willow Gentian)	4–8	July–Sept.	18 in.	Blue	Graceful, arching stems with spear-point leaves have stalkless, intense blue, trumpetlike flowers in their axils.
G. septemfida	4–8	July–Aug.	18 in.	Blue	Intense deep blue, trumpetlike blossoms with white throats, on trailing foliage.
GERANIUM [jer-*AIN*-ee-um] Cranesbill, Hardy Geranium					
G. cinereum 'Ballerina'	4–9	May–Sept.	8 in.	Pink	Saucer-shaped flowers with purple red veining and centers bloom all summer above neat, deeply cut, grey-green leaves.
G. endressii 'Wargrave Pink'	4–9	June–Sept.	15 in.	Pink	Masses of clear pink flowers on deeply divided, light green leaves.
Other cultivars: 'Johnson's Blue', lavender-blue flowers.					
G. himalayense or *G. grandiflorum*	4–9	May–June	15 in.	Blue	Intense violet-blue flowers with delicate veining over dense tuffets of dainty leaves.
G. sanguineum (Bloody Cranesbill)	4–9	May–Sept.	12 in.	Pink	Livid magenta-pink flowers bloom on mounds of deeply cut leaves all summer.
Other cultivars: 'Album', 12 in. tall, white flowers; 'Lancastriense', 6 in. tall, salmon pink flowers; 'Prostratum', 6 in. tall, carmine-red flowers.					

LIGHT REQUIREMENTS	SOIL REQUIREMENTS	PROPAGATION	REMARKS
Partial shade	Rich, moist, acid soil	Resents transplanting. Seed works best. Plant 12 in. apart.	Gentians have a reputation of being hard to grow. This is one of the easiest, especially in the East.
Partial shade	Rich, moist, well-drained soil	Seed. Plant 8 in. apart.	Another easy-to-grow gentian. Give it a special spot.
Full sun	Average, well-drained soil	Division in spring or fall. Plant 8 in. apart.	Often confused with the popular bedding geraniums, whose genus name is *Pelargonium.*
Full sun	Average, well-drained soil	Division in spring or fall. Plant 12 in. apart.	This old-time favorite makes an excellent ground cover.
Full sun	Average, well-drained soil	Division in spring or fall. Plant 12 in. apart.	Rivals delphinium in the quality of its intense blue.
Full sun	Average, well-drained soil	Division in spring or fall. Plant 12 in. apart.	Foliage turns reddish in the fall.

155 Perennial Genera—*Continued*

NAME OF PLANT	ZONES	SEASON OF BLOOM	HEIGHT	FLOWER COLOR	PLANT DESCRIPTION
GEUM [*JEE*-um] Avens					
G. ×*borisii*	4–8	May–June	12 in.	Orange	Pure orange flowers on hairy stalks that stand above dense clumps of hairy leaves.
G. quellyon or *G. chiloense* 'Lady Stratheden'	4–8	May–June	2 ft.	Yellow	Golden yellow flowers on long stems contrast with the dark green, toothed leaves.

Other cultivars: 'Fire Opal', fiery red-orange flowers; 'Mrs. Bradshaw', crimson flowers; 'Princess Juliana', orange flowers.

G. rivale 'Leonard's Variety'	4–8	May–June	12 in.	Pink	Coppery rose, buttercup-like flowers with reddish stalks bloom above small clump of hairy leaves.
GYPSOPHILA [jip-so-*FIL*-ah] Baby's Breath					
G. paniculata 'Bristol Fairy'	4–8	June–Aug.	3 ft.	White	Fluffy clouds of tiny, double flowers float above inconspicuous grey-green foliage.

Other cultivars: 'Perfecta', white, extra-large flowers; 'Flamingo', double, clear pink flowers.

C. reptens 'Alba'	4–8	June–Aug.	6 in.	White	Spreading, low-growing form of baby's breath, whose flowers fade to pink.

Other cultivars: 'Rosea', pink flowers.

HELENIUM [hel-*EEN*-ee-um] Helen's Flower					
H. autumnale 'Butterpat'	3–9	Aug.–Oct.	3 ft.	Yellow	2-in., daisy-like flowers with prominent centers bloom profusely on many-branched stems.

Other cultivars: 'Bruno', 4 ft. tall, rich mahogany red flowers; 'Crimson Beauty', 3 ft. tall, deep bronze-red flowers; 'Riverton Beauty', 4 ft. tall, yellow flowers with maroon eyes.

LIGHT REQUIREMENTS	SOIL REQUIREMENTS	PROPAGATION	REMARKS
Full sun to partial shade	Humusy, well-drained soil	Division in spring. Plant 12 in. apart.	Geums are known for their pure, shiny colors.
Full sun	Humusy, well-drained soil	Division in spring. Plant 12 in. apart.	This Chilean type is less hardy than other geums and needs winter mulch where the soil freezes hard.
Full sun	Humusy, well-drained soil	Division in spring. Plant 12 in. apart.	The cupped flowers have an orange cast. Foliage stays low.
Full sun	Light, well-drained, alkaline soil	Cuttings. Seed. Long taproots resent moving. Plant 12 in. apart.	Good succession plant to follow spring bloomers. Contrasts well with large-leaved plants. Excellent for cut or dried flowers.
Full sun	Light, well-drained, alkaline soil	Division. Cuttings. Seed.	Good for the rock garden or trailing over a dry wall.
Full sun	Rich, moist soil	Division in spring every other year. Plant 2 ft. apart.	Free-flowering daisies bloom throughout the fall.

155 Perennial Genera—*Continued*

NAME OF PLANT	ZONES	SEASON OF BLOOM	HEIGHT	FLOWER COLOR	PLANT DESCRIPTION
HELIANTHEMUM [heel-ee-*ANTH*-ih-mum] Rock Rose					
H. nummularium 'Rose Glory'	5–9	June–July	10 in.	Pink	Low-growing, evergreen shrub. Grey-green foliage covered with flimsy, 5-petaled flowers.

Other cultivars: 'Buttercup', golden yellow flowers; 'Dazzler', crimson red flowers; 'Peach', apricot-peach flowers; 'Pumkin', pumpkin orange flowers; 'St. Mary's', pure white flowers.

NAME OF PLANT	ZONES	SEASON OF BLOOM	HEIGHT	FLOWER COLOR	PLANT DESCRIPTION
HELIANTHUS [he-lee-*AN*-thus] Sunflower					
H. × multiflorus 'Loddon Gold'	3–9	Aug.–Sept.	6 ft.	Yellow	4-in., double, golden yellow, dahlia-like flowers with sturdy-looking foliage.

NAME OF PLANT	ZONES	SEASON OF BLOOM	HEIGHT	FLOWER COLOR	PLANT DESCRIPTION
HELIOPSIS [hell-ee-*OP*-sis] Hardy Zinnia					
H. scabra 'Incomparabilis'	3–9	June–Sept.	3½ ft.	Yellow	3-in., semidouble, daisy-like flowers with pointed leaves along tall stems.

Other cultivars: 'Golden Plume', double yellow flowers; 'Gold Greenheart', double yellow flowers with emerald green centers; 'Karat', large, single yellow flowers.

NAME OF PLANT	ZONES	SEASON OF BLOOM	HEIGHT	FLOWER COLOR	PLANT DESCRIPTION
HELLEBORUS [hel-eh-*BOR*-iss] Hellebore					
H. niger (Christmas Rose)	4–8	Jan.–Mar.	12 in.	White	Sturdy stems bear 2–4-in., greenish white flowers with showy golden centers. Foliage is saw-toothed and evergreen.
H. orientalis (Lenten Rose)	4–8	Mar.–May	18 in.	Pink	2-in. flowers varying from white to deep plum, often spotted with rosy purple. Leaves are lighter green than *H. niger*.

NAME OF PLANT	ZONES	SEASON OF BLOOM	HEIGHT	FLOWER COLOR	PLANT DESCRIPTION
HEMEROCALLIS [hem-er-oh-*KALL*-iss] Daylily					
H. flava or *H. lilioasphodelus* (Lemon Daylily)	3–8	June–July	2 ft.	Yellow	Pure yellow blossoms open on tall stalks above gracefully arching, lance-shaped leaves.

LIGHT REQUIREMENTS	SOIL REQUIREMENTS	PROPAGATION	REMARKS
Full sun	Light, well-drained, alkaline soil	Cuttings work best. Plant 12 in. apart.	Cut back after flowering. Delightful for the rock garden or above a rock wall.
Full sun	Average, well-drained soil	Division in spring every other year. Plant 2 ft. apart.	These invasive, vigorous growers with their rough appearance give a bright yellow in the back of the border.
Full sun	Rich, moist, well-drained soil	Division in spring every other year. Plant 2 ft. apart.	Blooms all summer.
Partial shade to full shade	Rich, moist, well-drained soil	A long-lived perennial that resents division. Transplanting of nearby seedlings works best. Plant 18 in. apart.	Given a sheltered spot, hellebores cheerfully brave the winter weather.
Partial shade to full shade	Rich, moist, well-drained soil	Faster and easier to grow than *H. niger.* Self-sows prolifically. Plant 18 in. apart.	Hellebores do best in deciduous shade, as their evergreen leaves need winter sun.
Full sun to partial shade	Average, well-drained soil	Division in spring or fall. Plant 2 ft. apart.	An early bloomer with delightful fragrant blossoms.

155 Perennial Genera—*Continued*

NAME OF PLANT	ZONES	SEASON OF BLOOM	HEIGHT	FLOWER COLOR	PLANT DESCRIPTION
HEMEROCALLIS (continued)					
H. fulva (Tawny Daylily)	3–8	June–July	3 ft.	Orange	Large orange flowers with reddish brown throats.
H. hybrids	3–8	May–Sept.	12 in.–4 ft.	All colors except white and true blue	In color and shape, they are variations on the theme expressed by *H. flava.*
HESPERIS [*HESS*-purr-iss] Sweet Rocket					
H. matronalis	3–8	June–Aug.	3 ft.	Purple, white, mauve	Fragrant, phlox-like flowers on tall, branching stems.
HEUCHERA [*HEW*-kerr-uh] Coral Bells					
H. sanguinea 'Chatterbox'	3–8	May–July	18 in.	Pink	Stiff stems carry sprays of dainty, bell-shaped flowers. Foliage is glossy, evergreen, and clump forming.
Other cultivars: 'Chartreuse', soft chartreuse flowers; 'Firebird', 2½ ft. tall, deep red flowers; 'Freedom', 2½ ft. tall, rose pink flowers; 'June Bride', pure white flowers.					
HEUCHERELLA [*HEW*-kerr-*EL*-uh]					
H. alba 'Bridget Bloom'	3–8	May–July	12 in.	Pink	Sprays of tiny, light pink flowers, resembling tiarella, above foliage that resembles heuchera.
HIBISCUS [hi-*BIS*-kiss] Rose Mallow					
H. moscheutos 'Mallow Marvels'	5–9	July–Oct.	4–6 ft.	Red, pink, white	Dramatic flowers up to 6–10 in. across in showy colors on tall, sturdy stems with broad leaves.

LIGHT REQUIREMENTS	SOIL REQUIREMENTS	PROPAGATION	REMARKS
Full sun to partial shade	Average, well-drained soil	Division in spring or fall. Plant 2 ft. apart.	This is the common roadside daylily.
Full sun to partial shade	Average, well-drained soil	Division in spring or fall. Plant 2 ft. apart.	Breeders have produced almost infinite variations on the daylily. See chapter 5 for more information.
Full sun to partial shade	Moist, well-drained, alkaline soil	Seed. Plant 18 in. apart.	Short-lived perennials that reseed themselves readily.
Full sun to partial shade	Rich, moist, well-drained soil	Division in spring every 3 years. Seed. Plant 12 in. apart.	Neat little clumps for edging or filling in here and there. Keep spent flowers cut for longer bloom.
Partial shade to full sun	Rich, moist, well-drained soil	Division in spring. Plant 12 in. apart.	This is a hybrid between *Heuchera* and *Tiarella*.
Full sun to partial shade	Rich, moist soil	Division in spring. Cuttings. Seed. Plant 3 ft. apart.	Native to marshes of the southern U.S., this is the largest-flowered herbaceous perennial.

NAME OF PLANT	ZONES	SEASON OF BLOOM	HEIGHT	FLOWER COLOR	PLANT DESCRIPTION
HOSTA [*HAHS*-tuh] Plantain Lily					
H. albomarginata or *H. sieboldii*	3–8	Aug.	12 in.	Lavender	4–6-in., oblong, sage green leaves with white margins. Bell-shaped flowers are pale lilac.
H. decorata	3–8	Aug.	18 in.	Lavender	4-in., rounded, blunt, dark green leaves with white margins that run all the way down the stem.
H. fortunei 'Aureomarginata'	3–8	Aug.–Sept.	2 ft.	Lavender	9-in., dark green leaves with gold edges that hold their color through the season.
H. lancifolia	3–8	Aug.	18 in.	Lavender	6-in., glossy, narrow leaves form dense clumps in arching, tiered layers.
H. plantaginea 'Grandiflora' (August Lily)	3–8	Aug.	2 ft.	White	9-in., broad, heart-shaped, bright green leaves form a large, loose clump. Large, trumpet-shaped flowers are deliciously fragrant.
H. sieboldiana 'Frances Williams'	3–8	July	2½ ft.	Lavender	12-In., striking, seersuckered leaves of metallic blue-green are edged with golden margin that deepens as summer progresses. Creamy lavender flowers.
Other cultivars: 'Elegans', solid blue-green foliage, prefers full shade.					
H. undulata	3–8	July–Aug.	15 in.	Lavender	8-in., twisting, undulating, broad, oval leaves carry green margins and white centers.
H. ventricosa	3–8	Aug.–Sept.	18 in.	Violet	8-in., broad, heart-shaped leaves of shiny dark green form attractive clumps.
H. venusta	3–8	June–July	8 in.	Lavender	1½-in., soft green leaves form a mound 4 in. high.

LIGHT REQUIREMENTS	SOIL REQUIREMENTS	PROPAGATION	REMARKS
Partial shade to full shade	Average, humusy, well-drained soil	Division in spring or fall. Plant 12 in. apart.	Hostas are grown mostly for foliage, although height listed here refers to flowers held above leaves on taller scapes.
Partial shade to full shade	Average, humusy, well-drained soil	Division in spring or fall. Plant 18 in. apart.	Like most hostas, spreads by underground rhizomes. One of the earliest to appear in the spring.
Partial shade to full shade	Average, humusy, well-drained soil	Division in spring or fall. Plant 18 in. apart.	Leaves of related cultivar, 'Aureomaculata', begin gold but turn green over the summer.
Partial shade to full shade	Average, humusy, well-drained soil	Division in spring or fall. Plant 12 in. apart.	Makes superb edging for walkways, beds, and borders in shady spots.
Partial shade to full sun	Average, humusy, well-drained soil	Division in spring or fall. Plant 2 ft. apart.	Grown primarily for its flowers, which perfume the night air.
Partial shade to full shade	Average, humusy, well-drained soil	Division in spring or fall. Plant 18 in. apart.	Unusual in size, color, and texture, *H. sieboldiana* is a conversation piece of the shade garden.
Partial shade to full shade	Average, humusy, well-drained soil	Division in spring or fall. Plant 8–12 in. apart.	Brightens up a shady spot.
Partial shade to full shade	Average, humusy, well-drained soil	Division in spring or fall. Plant 18 in. apart.	All hostas, especially this one, make excellent ground covers.
Partial shade to full shade	Average, humusy, well-drained soil	Division in spring or fall. Plant 12 in. apart.	One of the smallest hostas. A real treasure for a shaded rock garden.

252

155 Perennial Genera—*Continued*

NAME OF PLANT	ZONES	SEASON OF BLOOM	HEIGHT	FLOWER COLOR	PLANT DESCRIPTION
IBERIS [*EYE*-burr-iss] Candytuft					
I. sempervirens 'Purity'	3–9	May–June	8 in.	White	Low mounds of dark, glossy, evergreen foliage, covered with 2-in. clusters of pure white flowers.

Other cultivars: 'Autumn Snow', 9 in. tall, white flowers bloom again in fall; 'Pygmea', 4 in. tall, white flowers.

INCARVILLEA [in-car-*VILL*-ee-ah] Hardy Gloxinia					
I. delavayi	6–9	May–June	2 ft.	Pink	Clusters of 3-in., deep pink, trumpet-shaped flowers with yellow throats above glossy green, deeply divided foliage.
INULA [*IN*-you-luh] Sunray Flower					
I. ensifolia	3–9	July–Sept.	16 in.	Yellow	2-in., daisy-like flowers on wiry stems above neat clumps of narrow leaves.
IRIS [*EYE*-riss] Flag					
I. cristata (Crested Iris)	3–8	May	5 in.	Lilac-blue	Surprisingly large, 4-in. blossoms nestle among short, spiky leaves.
I. × *germanica* (Bearded Iris)	4–8	May–June	9 in.–4 ft.	Every color	Several elegant flowers open successively on tall stalks that emerge among fans of swordlike leaves.
I. kaempferi (Japanese Iris)	3–8	June–July	3 ft.	Blue, purple, red, white	Large, velvety, infinitely graceful, orchid-like flowers, displayed above ribbed, sword-shaped leaves.
I. pseudacorus (Yellow Flag)	5–8	June–July	3 ft.	Yellow	Rich yellow, fleur-de-lis blossoms on stalks tightly held by bright green leaves.

LIGHT REQUIREMENTS	SOIL REQUIREMENTS	PROPAGATION	REMARKS
Full sun	Rich, well-drained soil	Cuttings taken after flowering. Seed. Plant 12 in. apart.	Actually a sub-shrub; cut back half-way after flowering to promote new growth.
Full sun to partial shade	Sandy, humusy, well-drained soil	Seed. Fleshy roots resent being disturbed. Plant 12 in. apart.	Can be grown in Zones 4–5 with winter protection.
Full sun	Average, well-drained soil	Division in spring. Seed. Plant 12 in. apart.	Flowers are long-lasting.
Partial shade to full sun	Rich, moist, acid soil	Divide 6 weeks after flowering. Plant 8–12 in. apart.	A native American iris, considered the best of the dwarfs for low maintenance.
Full sun	Average, well-drained soil	Divide every 3 years 6 weeks after bloom. Plant 12 in. apart.	Standard garden iris comes in every imaginable color and many sizes. The "beard" is fuzzy tongue that emerges from flower's throat.
Full sun	Rich, moist, acid soil	Division in spring. Plant 12 in. apart.	Perfect for moist, sunny spot. Will not tolerate limy or alkaline soils.
Full sun	Rich, wet soil	Division in early spring. Plant 18 in. apart.	Primarily for edges of streams or ponds. Can be grown in garden if kept constantly moist.

155 Perennial Genera—*Continued*

NAME OF PLANT	ZONES	SEASON OF BLOOM	HEIGHT	FLOWER COLOR	PLANT DESCRIPTION
IRIS (continued)					
I. sibirica (Siberian Iris)	3–8	June–July	3 ft.	Blue, purple, red, white	Lots of dainty blossoms appear among tips of dense clumps of narrow-leaved foliage.
KNIPHOFIA [niff-*FOE*-fee-ah] Tritoma, Red Hot Poker					
K. uvaria 'Royal Standard'	5–9	Aug.–Sept.	3 ft.	Red and yellow	Long, narrow, spiky leaves surround striking, stiff pokers. Tightly packed red buds turn yellow as they open from bottom up.
Other cultivars: 'Earliest of All', 2½ ft. tall, coral-rose flowers; 'Goldmine', 2½ ft. tall, orange flowers; 'Primrose Beauty', yellow flowers; 'White Giant', white flowers.					
LAMIASTRUM [lay-me-*ASS*-trum] Yellow Dead-Nettle					
L. galeobdolon 'Variegatum'	4–9	May–June	12 in.	Yellow	Spreading, green and silver mottled leaves with dense whorls of snapdragon-like flowers.
LAMIUM [*LAY*-mee-um] Dead-Nettle					
L. maculatum	4–9	Apr.–Aug.	8–12 in.	Pink	Crinkly green leaves, striped with light silver-grey, make a hardy, sprawling ground cover. Purplish pink, 1-in. flowers, resembling snapdragons, bloom in dense whorls throughout the summer.
Other cultivars: 'Alba', white flowers.					
L. maculatum 'Beacon Silver'	4–9	Apr.–Aug.	6 in.	Pink	Light silver-grey foliage edged in green; rose pink flowers.

LIGHT REQUIREMENTS	SOIL REQUIREMENTS	PROPAGATION	REMARKS
Full sun to partial shade	Average, well-drained soil	Divide 6 weeks after flowering. Plant 18 in. apart.	Hardy, trouble-free, easy to grow.
Full sun	Rich, moist, well-drained soil	Division in spring. Plant 18 in. apart.	For the flamboyant gardener, a bold accent. In winter, tie leaves together to protect crowns from rotting.
Partial shade to full shade	Average, well-drained soil	Division in spring. Plant 12 in. apart.	Like lamium, which it resembles, useful for covering spent spring bulb foliage.
Partial shade to full sun	Average soil	Division in spring or fall. Plant 8–12 in. apart.	Useful for covering spent spring bulb foliage.
Full shade	Average soil	Division in spring or fall. Plant 8–12 in. apart.	Not as rank as the species. Superb ground cover whose silver leaves glow in the shade.

NAME OF PLANT	ZONES	SEASON OF BLOOM	HEIGHT	FLOWER COLOR	PLANT DESCRIPTION
LATHYRUS [*LATH*-riss] Perennial Pea					
L. latifolius	4–9	July–Sept.	9 ft.	Pink	A climbing, scrambling vine with grey-green foliage and clusters of 1½-in., pealike blossoms.
LAVANDULA [la-*VAN*-dyoo-lah] Lavender					
L. angustifolia 'Hidcote'	5–9	June–Aug.	18 in.	Violet-blue	Long wands end in fragrant florets. Silver-grey, needlelike leaves yield fresh, clean smell when crushed.
Other cultivars: 'Jean Davis', pale pink flowers; 'Munstead Dwarf', 12 in. tall, rosy purple flowers; 'Twickel Purple', deep blue flowers.					
LIATRIS [lye-*AY*-triss] Gay-Feather					
L. pycnostachya (Kansas Gay-Feather)	3–8	Aug.–Sept.	4 ft.	Lavender	Tall spikes of dense, fuzzy blossoms open first at top, then downward. Leaves are dark green, grasslike tufts.
L. scariosa 'September Glory' (Tall Gay-Feather)	3–8	Aug.–Sept.	4–6 ft.	Purple	Similar to *L. pycnostachya*, except for the deep purple flower spikes that open simultaneously.
L. spicata 'Kobold' (Spike Gay-Feather)	3–8	July–Sept.	18 in.	Rosy lavender	Spires form above narrow-leaved plants.
LIGULARIA [lig-you-*LAR*-ee-ah]					
L. dentata 'Desdemona'	4–8	July–Aug.	3–4 ft.	Orange	Large, elephant-ear leaves are reddish underneath. Daisy-like flowers in late summer.
L. stenocephala 'The Rocket'	4–8	Aug.–Oct.	5–6 ft.	Yellow	Tall, black-stemmed racemes, profusely covered with small florets. Broad, toothed foliage makes a decorative mound.

LIGHT REQUIREMENTS	SOIL REQUIREMENTS	PROPAGATION	REMARKS
Full sun	Average, well-drained soil	Long-lived perennial. Seed. Plant 2 ft. apart.	Needs a support, such as a fence, trellis, or rock pile, or just let it sprawl down a steep bank.
Full sun	Light, sandy, alkaline soil	Cuttings taken in spring. Plant 12 in. apart.	Useful in the herb garden, rock garden, or edging along the perennial bed or border. Mulch in colder climates.
Full sun	Rich, moist, well-drained soil	Division in spring or fall. Seed. Plant 18 in. apart.	Showiest when massed in groups. Flowers excellent for cutting or drying.
Full sun	Rich, moist, well-drained soil	Division in spring or fall. Seed. Plant 18 in. apart.	'White Spires' is related cultivar with pure white flowers.
Full sun	Rich, moist, well-drained soil	Division in spring or fall. Seed. Plant 12 in. apart.	Compact cultivar that adds strong vertical interest to front of the border.
Partial shade	Rich, constantly moist soil	Cuttings. Division. Seed. Plant 2 ft. apart.	Wonderful waterside plant, primarily for foliage contrast.
Partial shade	Rich, moist soil	Division in spring. Plant 3 ft. apart.	More of a garden habitué than L. dentata; perfect for August focal point.

155 Perennial Genera—*Continued*

NAME OF PLANT	ZONES	SEASON OF BLOOM	HEIGHT	FLOWER COLOR	PLANT DESCRIPTION
LILIUM [*LIL*-ee-um] Lily					
Division I, Asiatic Hybrids	3–8	June–July	2–5 ft.	Lavender, orange, pink, red, yellow, white	Asiatic hybrids have upright, outward-facing or pendent flowers from 4–6 in. across.
Division II, Martagon Hybrids	3–8	June–July	3–6 ft.	Brown, lavender, orange, red, yellow, white	3–4-in., pendent flowers with recurving petal tips.
Division III–V not generally available					
Division VI, Aurelian Hybrids	3–8	July	4–6 ft.	Apricot, pink, yellow, white	6–10-in., fragrant blossoms of trumpet, bowl, pendent, or star-shaped flowers.
Division VII, Oriental Hybrids	3–8	Aug.	2–7 ft.	Red, pink, purple, white	6–12-in., fragrant, spectacular lily blossoms in trumpet, bowl, flat, or recurved forms.
Division VIII not generally available					
Division IX, Species Lilies *L. canadense* (American Meadow Lily)	3–8	July–Aug.	4–7 ft.	Yellow-orange	Lots of 2–3-in. nodding bells on graceful masses of branched, sturdy stems.
L. candidum (Madonna Lily)	3–8	June–July	2–4 ft.	White	Clusters of upturned, 4-in., trumpet-shaped flowers with golden stamens.
L. tigrinum (Tiger Lily)	3–8	July–Aug.	3–5 ft.	Salmon red	3–5-in. flowers heavily dotted with purple-brown spots.

LIGHT REQUIREMENTS	SOIL REQUIREMENTS	PROPAGATION	REMARKS
Full sun to partial shade	Average, humusy, well-drained soil	Divide bulb scales in spring. Or plant leaf axil bulbils. Plant 8 in. apart.	An early-blooming group of lilies.
Partial shade	Average, humusy, well-drained soil	Division of bulbs in spring. Or plant leaf axil bulbils. Plant 8 in. apart.	This division includes many compact lilies preferring afternoon shade.
Full sun to partial shade	Average, humusy, well-drained soil	Divide bulb scales in fall, or transplant stem bulblets in second year. Plant 3 ft. apart.	Tall, large-flowered, dramatic lilies for the back border.
Full sun to partial shade	Humusy, well-drained soil	Divide bulb scales in fall, or transplant stem bulblets in second year. Plant 3 ft. apart.	Largest and latest flowering of the lilies.
Partial shade	Moist or wet bog soil	Seed or scales. Transplant stem bulblets in fall. Plant 3 ft. apart.	Will readily naturalize in damp areas or wet meadows.
Full sun	Average, humusy, well-drained soil	Scales or stem bulblets are transplanted in fall. Plant 3 ft. apart.	Especially pretty planted in groups of 3 or more with blue delphiniums.
Full sun to partial shade	Average, humusy, well-drained soil	Offsets. Scales. Bulbils. Plant 3 ft. apart.	Super-hardy variety that produces 12–20 blossoms per plant. Can carry mosaic infection to nearby Asiatic types.

155 Perennial Genera—*Continued*

NAME OF PLANT	ZONES	SEASON OF BLOOM	HEIGHT	FLOWER COLOR	PLANT DESCRIPTION
LIMONIUM [lih-*MOAN*-ee-um] Statice					
L. latifolium	3–8	July–Sept.	18 in.	Lavender-blue	Small, papery blossoms on stiffly branched stems create a billowy mass above flat rosette of leathery leaves.
LINUM [*LYE*-num] Flax					
L. flavum (Golden Flax)	5–9	June–Aug.	15 in.	Yellow	Profusion of bright yellow, waxy flowers. Foliage is greener than the blue flaxes.
L. narbonense (Narbonne Flax)	5–9	May–June	2 ft.	Blue	Azure blue flowers with white eyes.
L. perenne (Perennial Flax)	5–9	May–Aug.	2 ft.	Blue	Delicate, pale blue flowers on graceful, arching, blue-green foliage.
Other cultivars: 'Alba', white flowers.					
LIRIOPE [lir-*EYE*-oh-pee] Lilyturf					
L. muscari 'Majestic'	6–9	Aug.–Sept.	15 in.	Lavender	Evergreen tufts of grasslike foliage produce spikes of tiny, belled flowers, followed by blackberry-like seeds.
L. spicata	4–9	Aug.–Sept.	12 in.	Lavender	Not as showy as *L. muscari* but hardier.
LOBELIA [low-*BEE*-lee-ah]					
L. cardinalis (Cardinal Flower)	4–8	July–Sept.	3–4 ft.	Red	Tall spikes, topped with striking scarlet, tubular flowers, arise from basal rosette of leaves.

LIGHT REQUIREMENTS	SOIL REQUIREMENTS	PROPAGATION	REMARKS
Full sun	Light, sandy, well-drained loam	Long-lived perennial that resents being moved. Root cuttings or seed. Plant 18 in. apart.	Excellent for cut flowers or dried winter bouquets.
Full sun	Light, average, well-drained soil	Cuttings. Seed. Plant 18 in. apart.	A low-growing flax for front of border.
Full sun	Light, average, well-drained soil	Cuttings. Seed. Plant 18 in. apart.	Excellent with pink and magenta companions.
Full sun	Light, average, well-drained soil	Cuttings. Seed. Plant 18 in. apart.	Gives light, airy effect in the garden.
Partial shade	Average, well-drained soil	Division in spring. Plant 12 in. apart.	Outstanding ground cover or border plant; will tolerate deep shade to full sun.
Partial shade	Average, well-drained soil	Division in spring. Plant 12 in. apart.	In northern climates, where leaves get winter burn, cut back to ground in spring.
Partial shade to full sun	Rich, moist, humusy soil	Division in spring. Reseeds itself. Plant 12 in. apart.	Well-loved native of the eastern U.S.; often found along streams or in damp meadows. Makes a wonderful intense red accent.

155 Perennial Genera—*Continued*

NAME OF PLANT	ZONES	SEASON OF BLOOM	HEIGHT	FLOWER COLOR	PLANT DESCRIPTION
LOBELIA (continued)					
L. siphilitica (Great Blue Lobelia)	4–8	Aug.–Sept.	2–3 ft.	Blue	Bright blue, tubular flowers bloom in leaf axils on stiff, leafy stalks.
LUPINUS [loo-*PINE*-us] Lupine					
L. polyphyllus 'Russell's Hybrids'	4–8	June–July	3–5 ft.	Blue, lavender, pink, red, white, yellow, bicolor	Huge racemes of pealike flowers come in wide range of beautiful pastel colors and bicolors.
LYCHNIS [*LICK*-niss]					
L. chalcedonica (Maltese Cross)	3–8	June–July	2½ ft.	Red	Dense heads of small, scarlet, crosslike flowers on stiff stems.
L. coronaria (Rose Campion)	3–8	June–July	2 ft.	Magenta pink	Intense magenta pink flowers on wide-branching, silver stems make a striking combination.
L. viscaria (German Catchfly)	3–8	May–July	18 in.	Red	Clusters of rose red blossoms above tufts of grasslike foliage.
LYSIMACHIA [lye-sim-*ACK*-ee-ah] Loosestrife					
L. clethroides (Gooseneck Loosestrife)	5–8	July–Aug.	3 ft.	White	White, curving racemes create a "gooseneck" appearance above leafy stems.
L. nummularia (Creeping Jennie)	5–8	June–Aug.	1–2 in.	Yellow	Cup-shaped flowers above deep green, rounded leaves.
L. punctata (Yellow Loosestrife)	5–8	June–July	2½ ft.	Yellow	Lemony flowers with brown throats bloom from leaf axils whorling around stiff stems.

LIGHT REQUIREMENTS	SOIL REQUIREMENTS	PROPAGATION	REMARKS
Partial shade to full sun	Rich, moist, humusy soil	Division in spring. Reseeds itself. Plant 12 in. apart.	Also an eastern native, known for its medicinal uses. Reseeds itself here and there but is not invasive.
Full sun to partial shade	Deep, rich, well-drained, acid soil	Resents transplanting when established. Renew every 4 years by cuttings or seed. Plant 18 in. apart.	Lupines thrive in cool, moist areas like the Pacific Northwest. Mulch to keep roots cool.
Full sun	Average, moist, well-drained soil	Division in spring. Seed. Plant 12 in. apart.	Intense spots of color; best used as an accent.
Full sun	Average, moist, well-drained soil	Division in spring. Seed. Plant 12 in. apart.	Intense color doesn't easily mix in the garden. Great as a specimen plant.
Full sun	Average, well-drained soil	Division in spring. Seed. Plant 12 in. apart.	More subdued in color than its sister species. Hardy and long-lived.
Partial shade	Average, moist soil	Division in spring. Plant 12 in. apart.	Nice naturalized along a wood's edge. Too invasive for the garden unless divided frequently.
Partial shade	Average, moist soil	Division in spring. Plant 12 in. apart.	They don't call her creeping Jennie for nothing, so keep her retained.
Partial shade to full sun	Average, moist, well-drained soil	Division in spring. Plant 12 in. apart.	Has naturalized in the eastern U.S. Can be invasive.

264

155 Perennial Genera—*Continued*

NAME OF PLANT	ZONES	SEASON OF BLOOM	HEIGHT	FLOWER COLOR	PLANT DESCRIPTION
LYTHRUM [*LITH*-rum] Purple Loosestrife					
L. salicaria 'Morden Pink'	3–8	June–Aug.	3 ft.	Pink	Tall spires of clear pink flowers on well-branched, bushy plants.

Other cultivars: 'Dropmore Purple', rich purple flowers; 'Fire Candle', rosy red flowers; 'Happy', 18 in. tall, dark pink flowers; 'Morden Gleam', bright carmine flowers.

MACLEYA [mack-*LEE*-ah] Plume Poppy, Boccania					
M. cordata	4–9	July–Aug.	6–8 ft.	White	Large, scalloped leaves, grey-green above and silvery white beneath, form tall stalks, topped with creamy white plumes.

MAZUS [*MAY*-zus]					
M. reptans	4–8	May–June	2 in.	Blue	Mats of small, bright green leaves bear a profusion of lovely, purplish blue, lobelia-like flowers.

MERTENSIA [mer-*TEN*-zee-ah] Virginia Bluebells					
M. virginica	3–8	Apr.–May	18 in.–2 ft.	Blue	Clusters of pink buds open as heavenly blue bells. Broad, pale green leaves disappear by summer.

MONARDA [moan-*AR*-duh] Bee Balm					
M. didyma 'Cambridge Scarlet'	4–9	July–Aug.	3 ft.	Red	Ragged flower heads contain whorls of many tubular blossoms. Erect, square stems carry aromatic leaves.

Other cultivars: 'Croftway Pink', pink flowers; 'Mahogany', mahogany flowers; 'Snow White', white flowers; 'Violet Queen', violet flowers.

LIGHT REQUIREMENTS	SOIL REQUIREMENTS	PROPAGATION	REMARKS
Partial shade to full sun	Average, moist, well-drained soil	Division in spring. Plant 2 ft. apart.	This gorgeous plant is found wild in the northeastern U.S., making its cultivars excellent for naturalizing.
Full sun to partial shade	Rich, moist, well-drained soil	Division in spring. Root cuttings. Seed. Plant 3–4 ft. apart.	Robust grower. Plant where invasive roots can be contained. Nice as specimen in front of wall or dark hedge.
Full sun to partial shade	Rich, moist soil	Division in spring. Plant 8–12 In. apart.	A gem between flagstones. Will spread rapidly. *M. japonicus* 'Albiflorum' has white flowers.
Partial shade	Rich, moist, humusy soil	Reseeds itself readily in moist, woodland conditions. Plant 12 in. apart.	One of the loveliest and most welcome of spring flowers.
Partial shade to full sun	Rich, moist, humusy soil	Division in spring every 3–4 years. Plant 12 in. apart.	Delightful summer flower whose tubular flowers perfectly fit a hummingbird's beak. Good for naturalizing.

155 Perennial Genera—*Continued*

NAME OF PLANT	ZONES	SEASON OF BLOOM	HEIGHT	FLOWER COLOR	PLANT DESCRIPTION
MYOSOTIS [my-oh-*SO*-tis] Forget-Me-Not					
M. alpestris 'Victoria' (Alpine Forget-Me-Not)	2–8	May–June	8 in.	Blue	Compact tufts of little leaves, covered with small, dark blue forget-me-nots.
M. scorpioides or *M. palustris* (True Forget-Me-Not)	3–8	May–Aug.	12 in.	Blue	Sprays of dainty, sky blue flowers, sometimes pink with yellow eyes, appear on ends of sprawling stems.
M. sylvatica (Woodland Forget-Me-Not)	5–8	May–June	2 ft.	Blue	Mists of sky blue flowers above open, grey-green foliage.
NEPETA [*NEP*-eh-tuh] Catmint					
N. ×faassenii	3–8	June–Aug.	18 in.	Lavender	Sprays of small, lavender-blue flowers on aromatic, bushy, grey-green plants.
OENOTHERA [ee-no-*THEE*-rah] Sundrops					
O. missourensis (Ozark Sundrop, Evening Primrose)	4–9	June–Aug.	10 in.	Yellow	Showy, 4-in., cuplike flowers, followed by large, winged seed pods. Dark green, leafy stems lie along ground.
O. tetragona 'Fireworks' (Common Sundrop)	4–9	June–Aug.	18 in.	Yellow	Bright, 2-in. blossoms contrast nicely with reddish buds and leathery bronze leaves.
OPUNTIA [oh-*PUN*-shee-ah] Prickly Pear					
O. humifusa	6–10	June–July	10 in.	Yellow	Flat, prickly cactus pads (stems) are covered with 3-in., rose-like blossoms, followed by 1-in., dark red fruits.

LIGHT REQUIREMENTS	SOIL REQUIREMENTS	PROPAGATION	REMARKS
Partial shade	Moist, humusy, well-drained soil	Division in late summer. Cuttings. Seed. Plant 8 in. apart.	These are lovers' plants and charming in any garden.
Partial shade	Wet, gravelly soil	Division in spring. Cuttings. Seed. Plant 12 in. apart.	Often naturalized along woodland streams. Will thrive in a constantly moist soil.
Partial shade	Moist, humusy, well-drained soil	Annual from Zone 4 north, biennial from Zone 5 south, where seed is sown in early fall for spring bloom. Plant 12 in. apart.	While it's a biennial in most regions, it reseeds itself freely, providing perennial bloom. Plant with spring bulbs.
Full sun	Average, sandy, well-drained soil	Division in spring. Plant 12 in. apart.	Its cool colors act as a foil for warmer tones, especially pinks. Cut after blooming to encourage new growth.
Full sun	Average, well-drained soil	Division in spring every 3–4 years. Plant 12 in. apart.	A nice trailer for the front border or rock garden. Seed pods used for dried bouquets. Blooms in evening.
Full sun	Average, well-drained soil	Division in spring every 3–4 years. Plant 12–15 in. apart.	Often confused with a similar species, *O. fruticosa*. Both day-bloomers, their bright yellow is good for accent.
Full sun	Sandy, well-drained soil	Pads are easily rooted in sand. Plant 12 in. apart.	A hardy cactus that adds variety to the northern rock garden. Can be rampant in the South.

155 Perennial Genera—*Continued*

NAME OF PLANT	ZONES	SEASON OF BLOOM	HEIGHT	FLOWER COLOR	PLANT DESCRIPTION
PACHYSANDRA [pack-ee-*SAND*-rah]					
P. terminalis 'Green Carpet'	4–8	Apr.–May	8 in.	White	Glossy, dark, evergreen leaves carpet the ground from stoloniferous roots. Short, white flower spikes are not particularly showy.
PAEONIA [pee-*OHN*-yuh] Peony					
P. lactiflora (Chinese Peony)	3–8	June	2–4 ft.	Pink, red, white	Sumptuous flowers up to 10 in. across, from single to very double forms, are borne profusely at tips of dense stands of leafy stalks.
P. officinalis 'Rubra Plena' (Memorial Day Peony)	3–8	May–June	2 ft.	Red	Double, deep red blooms on ferny foliage.
P. tenuifolia (Fernleaf Peony)	3–8	May	18 in.– 2 ft.	Red	3-in., cup-shaped, dark crimson flowers contrast beautifully with lacy, ferny, deep green foliage.
PAPAVER [pah-*PAVE*-er] Poppy					
P. orientale 'Helen Elizabeth' (Oriental Poppy)	3–8	June	3–4 ft.	Salmon pink	Large, showy, crepe-paper flowers on long stems emerge from coarse, toothed foliage.

Other cultivars: 'Big Jim', deep carmine-red flowers; 'Harvest Moon', orange-red flowers; 'White King', white flowers.

NAME OF PLANT	ZONES	SEASON OF BLOOM	HEIGHT	FLOWER COLOR	PLANT DESCRIPTION
PELTIPHYLLUM [pelt-ih-*FILL*-um] Umbrella Plant					
P. peltatum	5–8	Apr.	3 ft.	Pink	Clusters of starry, ½-in. flowers bloom atop leafless stalks, followed by large, tropical-looking leaves.

LIGHT REQUIREMENTS	SOIL REQUIREMENTS	PROPAGATION	REMARKS
Partial shade	Rich, moist, acid soil	Division or cuttings taken in summer. Plant 8 in. apart.	Perfect ground cover for deep shade, even under trees. The silver-edged leaves of 'Variegata' brighten a shaded spot.
Full sun	Rich, humusy, well-drained soil	Long-lived. Divide in late August only to increase plantings. Plant 18 in. apart.	Hundreds of cultivars available. Heavy, flowered forms need staking. The blooms are as short-lived as the plants are long-lived.
Full sun	Rich, humusy, well-drained soil	Long-lived. Divide in late August only to increase plantings. Plant 18 in. apart.	Native to Europe and common in gardens since the 16th century.
Full sun	Rich, humusy, well-drained soil	Divide in late August every 3 years. Plant 18 in. apart.	Foliage disappears by late summer.
Full sun	Average, well-drained soil	4-in. root cuttings taken in August when plants are dormant. Seed. Plant 18 in. apart.	These flamboyant beauties make bold accents. Foliage dies back in July, then reemerges in September.
Partial shade to shade	Rich soil, moist or wet	Division. Plant 2 ft. apart.	This Oregon native bog plant makes a bold statement along streams or ponds.

155 Perennial Genera—*Continued*

NAME OF PLANT	ZONES	SEASON OF BLOOM	HEIGHT	FLOWER COLOR	PLANT DESCRIPTION
PENSTEMON [*PEN*-stih-min] Beard Tongue					
P. barbatus 'Rose Elf'	5–9	June–Aug.	18 in.	Pink	Spires of 1-in., tubular, coral pink blossoms hang on slender, leafy stems.
Other cultivars: 'Elfin Pink', 12 in. tall, clear pink flowers; 'Prairie Dusk', rose-purple flowers; 'Prairie Fire', orange-red flowers.					
P. gloxinioides 'Ruby King'	7–10	June–Aug.	2 ft.	Red	Very showy, 2-in., red trumpets cluster atop slender-leaved plants.
P. heterophyllus 'True Blue'	5–9	June–Aug.	15 in.	Blue	Slim stems sprout a profusion of true blue, tubular flowers.
PEROVSKIA [per-*AWV*-skee-ah] Russian Sage					
P. atriplicifolia	3–9	July–Aug.	3 ft.	Blue	A many-branched sub-shrub, whose leaves are covered with silvery hairs, bursts into a mist of small, lavender-blue flowers in summer.
PHLOX [*FLOX*]					
P. carolina 'Miss Lingard' (Early Phlox)	3–8	June–July	3 ft.	White	Large clusters of flowers top tall, leafy stems.
P. divaricata 'Laphamii' (Wild Blue Phlox)	3–8	May–June	15 in.	Blue	Loose clusters of lavender-blue, 1-in., star-shaped flowers top 10-in. stems with small leaves.
Other cultivars: 'Fullers White', white flowers.					
P. paniculata 'Brighteyes' (Summer Phlox)	3–8	July–Aug.	3 ft.	Pink	Ballooning, 6-in. clusters of fragrant, 1-in., pale pink petals with crimson eyes.
Other cultivars: 'Amethyst', lavender flowers; 'Progress', light blue flowers with purple eyes; 'Thundercloud', red flowers; 'Orange Perfection', orange flowers; 'World Peace', white flowers.					

LIGHT REQUIREMENTS	SOIL REQUIREMENTS	PROPAGATION	REMARKS
Full sun	Light, gravelly, well-drained soil	Division in spring. Cuttings. Seed. Plant 12 in. apart.	Needs winter protection north of Zone 5.
Full sun	Light, gravelly, well-drained soil	Cuttings. Plant 12 in. apart.	A popular flower in the Gulf states and coastal California.
Full sun	Light, gravelly, well-drained soil	Cuttings. Seed. Plant 12 in. apart.	This California native adds a blue note in the primarily red genus *Penstemon*.
Full sun	Average to dry, well-drained soil	Cuttings. Plant 18 in. apart.	Cut to the ground each spring to promote strong, young growth with abundant bloom.
Full sun to partial shade	Rich, moist, humusy, well-drained soil	Division in spring or fall every 3–4 years. Plant 2 ft. apart.	Useful old favorite, blooms a month earlier than summer phlox and is mildew resistant.
Partial shade to full sun	Rich, humusy, well-drained soil	Divide after flowering. Plant 12 in. apart.	Naturalizes well among spring bulbs.
Full sun to partial shade	Rich, humusy, well-drained soil	Division in spring or fall every 3–4 years. Plant 2 ft. apart.	Needs plenty of room to avoid mildew. Thin stems to 4–5 per plant. Seedlings don't come true to color. Cut spent blossoms.

155 Perennial Genera—*Continued*

NAME OF PLANT	ZONES	SEASON OF BLOOM	HEIGHT	FLOWER COLOR	PLANT DESCRIPTION
PHLOX (continued)					
P. stolonifera 'Blue Ridge' (Creeping Phlox)	3–8	May–June	6 in.	Blue	Fragrant, nodding clusters of clear blue flowers. Glossy, rounded, evergreen leaves lie flat on ground.
P. subulata 'Emerald Blue' (Moss Pinks)	3–8	May–June	4–6 in.	Blue	Carpeting the ground, mosslike, evergreen foliage is covered with myriads of ½-in. flowers.

Other cultivars: 'Brilliant', rich, deep red flowers; 'Exquisite', pink flowers; 'Millstream Jupiter', blue flowers with yellow eyes; 'White Delight', pure white flowers.

PHYSALIS [*FISS*-al-iss] Chinese Lantern					
P. alkekengi or *P. franchetii*	2–7	Showy seed husks appear in September.	2 ft.		Not grown for its flowers but rather the bright orange, 2-in., inflated seed husks that dangle from stems like paper lanterns.

PHYSOSTEGIA [fy-so-*STEEJ*-ee-ah] Obedient Plant					
P. virginiana 'Bouquet Rose'	2–8	Aug.–Oct.	3 ft.	Pink	Spires of shell pink flowers densely packed in neat rows. Individual florets, when moved to either side, stay in bent position, hence the common name. Leaves are dark green and willowlike.

Other cultivars: 'Summer Glow', rosy crimson flowers; 'Summer Snow', white flowers; 'Variegata', variegated foliage with pink flowers.

LIGHT REQUIREMENTS	SOIL REQUIREMENTS	PROPAGATION	REMARKS
Partial shade	Rich, humusy, acid soil	Division in spring or fall. Plant 8–12 in. apart.	Excellent ground cover in a shaded spot.
Full sun	Rich, sandy, alkaline soil	Divide in spring after flowering. Cuttings. Plant 8–12 in. apart.	Intense spots of color for the midspring rock garden.
Full sun to partial shade	Rich, moist, well-drained soil	Division in spring. Seed. Plant 12 in. apart.	Used in dried bouquets. This hardy spreader is quite invasive. Best given its own spot outside the garden.
Partial shade to full sun	Average, moist soil	Division in spring every other year to keep in bounds. Plant 18 in. apart.	A vigorous spreader; good for rough places. Stands out among the yellows of late summer.

155 Perennial Genera—*Continued*

NAME OF PLANT	ZONES	SEASON OF BLOOM	HEIGHT	FLOWER COLOR	PLANT DESCRIPTION
PLATYCODON [plat-ee-*KO*-dun] Balloon Flower					
P. grandiflorus 'Blue'	3–8	July–Aug.	2 ft.	Blue	Ballooning buds open into shallow, star-shaped cups. Tall, slender stems have grey-green foliage.
Other cultivars: 'Albus', white flowers; 'Apoyama', 10 in. tall, violet-blue flowers; 'Shell Pink', pale pink flowers; 'Mariesii', 15 in. tall, deep violet-blue flowers.					
POLEMONIUM [po-li-*MOAN*-ee-um] Jacob's Ladder					
P. caeruleum (Jacob's Ladder)	3–8	May–June	2½ ft.	Blue	Clear blue clusters of bell-shaped blossoms atop stiff stems. Common name refers to the fernlike leaves, resembling rungs on a ladder.
Other cultivars: 'Album', white flowers.					
P. reptans (Creeping Jacob's Ladder)	3–8	Apr.–June	8–12 in.	Blue	Pale blue, bell-shaped flowers clustered atop thin stems give sprawling appearance. Foliage is neat tuft of fernlike leaves.
POLYGONATUM [polly-go-*NAY*-tum] Solomon's Seal					
P. biflorum (Small Solomon's Seal)	3–8	May–June	2–3 ft.	White	Delicate, greenish white, bell-shaped flowers are hung along graceful, arching stems with very ornamental leaves.
POTENTILLA [po-ten-*TILL*-ah] Cinquefoil					
P. nepalensis 'Miss Willmott'	5–8	June–Frost	12 in.	Rose	Sprays of carmine-rose, cup-shaped flowers bloom on well-branched stems. Strawberry-like leaves.

LIGHT REQUIREMENTS	SOIL REQUIREMENTS	PROPAGATION	REMARKS
Full sun to partial shade	Average, well-drained soil	Resents moving. Root cuttings taken when shoots are 1 in. high. Seed. Plant 15 in. apart.	Excellent low-maintenance perennial. Intense blue glows at dusk. Plants late to emerge in the spring.
Partial shade to full sun	Rich, moist, well-drained soil	Division in spring or fall. Cuttings. Seed. Plant 18 in. apart.	Well-behaved plant giving accents of blue.
Partial shade	Rich, moist, well-drained soil	Division in spring. Plant 8–12 in. apart.	Naturalizes well in shady nooks. Charming companion to bleeding-hearts.
Partial shade to full shade	Rich, humusy, well-drained soil	Division in spring. Seed. Plant 12 in. apart.	This native wildflower adds a graceful note. Will tolerate dry soil. Mix with ferns and hostas.
Full sun to partial shade	Average, well-drained soil	Division in spring. Seed. Plant 12 in. apart.	Good for the front of the border.

155 Perennial Genera—*Continued*

NAME OF PLANT	ZONES	SEASON OF BLOOM	HEIGHT	FLOWER COLOR	PLANT DESCRIPTION
POTENTILLA (continued)					
P. × tongeui	4–8	June–Frost	3 in.	Apricot	Apricot cups with crimson centers cover trailing mats. Strawberry-like leaves.
P. verna 'Aurea'	4–8	May–June	3 in.	Yellow	Single, rose-like flowers bloom amid trailing mats of strawberry-like leaves.
PRIMULA [*PRIM*-you-lah] Primrose					
P. auricula (Alpine Primrose)	3–8	Apr.–May	8 in.	Every color	Fragrant umbels of 1-in. flowers with contrasting eyes, borne on stiff stems above basal rosettes of evergreen leaves.
P. denticulata (Himalayan Primrose)	4–8	Apr.–May	12 in.	Purple, lavender, white	Charmingly toothed flowers form rounded ball above 10-in. stems. Leaves are crinkled.
P. japonica Candelabra Group (Japanese Primrose)	5–8	May–June	2 ft.	Red, pink, magenta, white	3-tiered whorls of 1-in. flowers are spaced along tall stalks.
P. × polyantha (Polyanthus Primrose)	3–8	May	10 in.	Every color	1½-in. flowers with golden eyes cluster above clumps of light green leaves.
PULMONARIA [pull-mun-*AIR*-ee-ah] Lungwort					
P. angustifolia 'Aurea' (Blue Lungwort)	3–8	Apr.–May	12 in.	Blue	Clusters of trumpet-shaped flowers opening pink soon turn blue. Foliage forms compact clumps of hairy, green leaves.

Other cultivars: 'Alba', white flowers; 'Lutea', sulfur yellow flowers; 'Salmon Glory', salmon flowers.

LIGHT REQUIREMENTS	SOIL REQUIREMENTS	PROPAGATION	REMARKS
Full sun to partial shade	Average, well-drained soil	Division in spring. Plant 15 in. apart.	Lovely trailing over garden walls.
Full sun to partial shade	Average, well-drained soil	Division in spring. Plant 10 in. apart.	Besides the herbaceous forms listed here, the shrubby potentilla, *P. fruticosa,* is common in gardens as hedges.
Partial shade	Rich, moist soil	Divide after flowering. Seed. Plant 12 in. apart.	Has been bred into varied, subtle colors. Mulch prevents heaving of shallow roots.
Partial shade	Rich, moist soil	Divide after flowering. Seed. Plant 12 in. apart.	Flowers before leaves fully emerge.
Partial shade	Rich, moist soil	Reseeds easily. Plant 12–18 in. apart.	Needs constantly moist soil.
Partial shade	Rich, moist soil	Divide after flowering. Seed. Plant 8–12 in. apart.	Most widely grown of the primroses. Fine for edging the path.
Partial shade to full shade	Rich, moist, humusy soil	Division in early summer (keep well-watered after transplanting). Seed. Plant 12 in. apart.	Good ground cover under shrubs or along a shaded path.

155 Perennial Genera—*Continued*

NAME OF PLANT	ZONES	SEASON OF BLOOM	HEIGHT	FLOWER COLOR	PLANT DESCRIPTION
PULMONARIA (continued)					
P. saccharata 'Mrs. Moon' (Bethlehem Sage)	3–8	Apr.–May	12 in.	Blue	Large, pink flower buds turn gentian blue when fully open. Oval leaves are dark green, flecked with silver.
Other cultivars: 'Alba', white flowers; 'Bowles Red', red flowers; 'Pink Dawn', pink flowers.					
RHEUM [*REE*-um] Ornamental Rhubarb					
R. palmatum 'Atrosanguineum'	3–8	June–July	6 ft.	Red	Huge, coarsely cut leaves arrayed around base of tall, loosely branched panicles.
RODGERSIA [rod-*JAIR*-zee-ah]					
R. aesculifolia	5–8	June–July	4 ft.	White	5 large, poinsettia-like leaves, arranged around a leaf stalk, have unusual bronze sheen. Pyramidal clusters of creamy white to pink flowers.
R. tabularis	5–8	June–July	3 ft.	White	Large, rounded leaves resembling those of a mayapple but 2 ft. across. Creamy white panicles.
RUDBECKIA [rude-*BECK*-ee-ah] Black-Eyed-Susan					
R. fulgida 'Goldsturm'	3–9	July–Sept.	2 ft.	Yellow	Deep golden yellow petals surround blackish brown, conical centers. Flowers are 3–4 in. across and bloom profusely on many-branched stems.
R. laciniata 'Goldquelle'	3–9	Aug.–Sept.	3 ft.	Yellow	Double, golden yellow blossoms massed above branching stems with dark green foliage.

LIGHT REQUIREMENTS	SOIL REQUIREMENTS	PROPAGATION	REMARKS
Partial shade to full shade	Rich, moist, humusy soil	Division in early summer (keep well-watered after transplanting). Seed. Plant 12 in. apart.	Mottled leaves create handsome display.
Full sun	Rich, humusy soil	Division. Plant 5 ft. apart.	Massive leaves make bold statement, especially by waterside.
Partial shade to shade	Rich soil, moist or wet	Division. Plant 3 ft. apart.	Will thrive in marshy ground along shaded streams.
Partial shade to shade	Rich soil, moist or wet	Division. Plant 3 ft. apart.	Bold leaves make great contrast with fine-leaved foliage.
Full sun	Average, well-drained soil	Division in spring every 3 years. Plant 18 in. apart.	Dazzling display of optical yellow.
Full sun	Average, well-drained soil	Division in spring every 3 years. Plant 18 in. apart.	This cultivar is more compact and less invasive than *R. laciniata* 'Hortensia', or golden glow, which can reach 7 ft.

155 Perennial Genera—*Continued*

NAME OF PLANT	ZONES	SEASON OF BLOOM	HEIGHT	FLOWER COLOR	PLANT DESCRIPTION
RUTA [*ROO*-tuh] Rue					
R. graveolens 'Blue Beauty'	4–9	July–Aug.	2 ft.	Yellow	Bushy, compact plant with pungent, blue-green leaves. Flowers are mustard yellow and inconspicuous.
SALVIA [*SALV*-ee-ah] Meadow Sage					
S. haematodes	4–9	June–July	3 ft.	Blue	Loose panicles of lavender-blue flowers form basal rosette of dark green leaves.
S. jurisicii	4–9	June–Sept.	3 ft.	Blue	Small, spreading spikes of violet-blue flowers above tufted foliage.
S. officinalis 'Purpurea'	4–8	Foliage only	12 in.		Hardy sub-shrub with purple, pebbly-textured leaves, grown for its foliage.
Other cultivars: 'Golden Variegated', gold and green foliage; 'Tricolor', red, green, and white foliage.					
S. pitcheri or *S. azurea* var. *grandiflora*	4–9	Sept.–Frost	3½ ft.	Blue	Slender spikes of gentian blue flowers contrast nicely against silver-green leaves.
S. × superba or *S. nemorosa* 'East Friesland'	4–9	June–Aug.	18 in.	Blue	Erect spikes of intense violet-blue on well-branched stems.
SANGUINARIA [sang-gwin-*AIR*-ee-ah] Bloodroot					
S. canadensis	3–8	Apr.–May	6 in.	White	Tightly rolled, scalloped, grey-green leaves unfurl, revealing delicate, pure white flowers.

LIGHT REQUIREMENTS	SOIL REQUIREMENTS	PROPAGATION	REMARKS
Full sun	Average to poor, well-drained soil	Cuttings. Seed. Plant 12 in. apart.	Grown for its beautiful blue-green foliage.
Full sun	Average to poor, well-drained soil	Division. Cuttings. Seed. Plant 18 in. apart.	Short-lived perennial; often acts like a biennial. Comes easy from seed.
Full sun	Average to poor, well-drained soil	Division. Cuttings. Seed.	A dwarf form for the rock garden or front border.
Full sun	Average to poor, well-drained soil	Cuttings. Seed. Plant 12 in. apart.	Ornamental form of the aromatic garden sage.
Full sun	Average to poor, well-drained soil	Division. Cuttings. Seed. Plant 18 in. apart.	A welcome show for the autumn garden. Needs support.
Full sun	Average to poor, well-drained soil	Division. Cuttings. Seed. Plant 18 in. apart.	Blooms throughout the summer. Excellent for cutting.
Full sun to partial shade	Rich, humusy, acid soil	Division in early fall. Mark spot as foliage disappears by summer. Plant 8 in. apart.	Delightful double form of a native wildflower. Bloom is short and sweet.

155 Perennial Genera—*Continued*

NAME OF PLANT	ZONES	SEASON OF BLOOM	HEIGHT	FLOWER COLOR	PLANT DESCRIPTION
SANTOLINA [san-tow-*LEEN*-ah] Lavender Cotton					
S. chamaecyparissus	6–8	Aug.–Sept.	12 in.	Yellow	Shrubby, evergreen herb with aromatic, silver-grey, woolly leaves. Bears solitary, ¾-in., buttonlike flowers.
S. virens	6–8	Aug.–Sept.	12 in.	Yellow	This species has dark green leaves bearing pale yellow, solitary, ¾-in., buttonlike flowers.
SAPONARIA [sap-oh-*NAIR*-ee-ah] Soapwort					
S. ocymoides	2–8	May–June	4 in.	Pink	Vigorous, creeping mats of tiny, semievergreen leaves, covered with small, starry, deep pink flowers.
SCABIOSA [scab-ee-*OH*-suh] Pincushion Flower					
S. caucasica 'Blue Perfection'	3–8	June–Sept.	12 in.	Blue	Delicate, lavender-blue, tatted, pincushionlike flowers on tall stems. Foliage forms basal clumps.
SEDUM [*SEE*-dum] Stonecrop					
S. sieboldii 'Dragon's Blood'	3–9	June–Sept.	10 in.	Red	Succulent evergreen foliage sports bright red flowers all summer.
S. spectabile 'Autumn Joy'	3–9	Aug.–Frost	2 ft.	Pink	Tall stalks with fleshy leaves produce slightly rounded flower heads, opening pink and slowly turning to mahogany by frost.

LIGHT REQUIREMENTS	SOIL REQUIREMENTS	PROPAGATION	REMARKS
Full sun	Average to poor, sandy, well-drained soil	Cuttings. Seed. Plant 12 in. apart.	Often used as miniature hedge. Mainstay of formal, European knot gardens.
Full sun	Average to poor, sandy, well-drained soil	Cuttings. Seed. Plant 12 in. apart.	Prune back in spring to keep neat, compact growth.
Full sun	Average, sandy, well-drained soil	Division. Seed. Plant 18 in. apart.	Creates flowering masses of pink as it spills over rocks.
Full sun	Average, sandy, well-drained soil	Division in spring every 3 years. Discard older, woody roots. Seed. Plant 12–15 in. apart.	Sparse effect. Plant in groups of 3 or more. Beautiful and long-lasting cuttings.
Full sun	Average to dry, well-drained soil	Division. Plant 12 in. apart.	Dozens of low-growing sedums are available.
Full sun	Average, well-drained soil	Division. Cuttings. Plant 15 in. apart.	'Autumn Joy' is an aptly named classic for the fall garden.

155 Perennial Genera—*Continued*

NAME OF PLANT	ZONES	SEASON OF BLOOM	HEIGHT	FLOWER COLOR	PLANT DESCRIPTION
SEMPERVIVUM [sem-per-*VEEV*-um] Hen and Chicks					
S. tectorum	4–10	June–Aug.	12 in.	Pink	Compact rosettes of fleshy leaves. Flower stalks erupt from the center.
SHORTIA [*SHOR*-tee-ah] Oconee-Bells					
S. galaifolia	4–8	June–July	8 in.	White	Shiny evergreen leaves send up 1-in., daintily fringed, bell-shaped flowers.
SIDALCEA [sid-*AL*-see-ah] Prairie Mallow					
S. malviflora 'Elsie Heugh'	5–9	July–Sept.	2–3 ft.	Pink	Spikes of shell pink flowers, resembling those of hollyhock in miniature form.
SOLIDAGO [sol-ih-*DAY*-go] Goldenrod					
S. 'Goldenmosa'	4–10	Aug.–Sept.	3 ft.	Yellow	Plumed flower heads are arrayed with golden florets held on erect stems carrying slender leaves.
STACHYS [*STACK*-iss] Lamb's Ears					
S. byzantian or *S. lanata* 'Silver Carpet'	4–9	Foliage only	10 in.		Woolly, silver-grey leaves resembling the shape and texture of a lamb's ear.
STOKESIA [*STOKES*-ee-ah] Stokes' Aster					
S. laevis 'Blue Danube'	5–8	July–Frost	15 in.	Blue	Deep blue, solitary, aster-like flower heads up to 4 in. across. Straplike leaves.

Other cultivars: 'Blue Moon', silvery blue flowers; 'Silver Moon', white flowers.

LIGHT REQUIREMENTS	SOIL REQUIREMENTS	PROPAGATION	REMARKS
Full sun	Average to poor, well-drained soil	Small, outer rosettes that form from mother rosette. Plant 1–6 in. apart.	Ideal for growing in rock walls or crevices. There are many varieties; all need the same growing conditions. For more information see chapter 5.
Shade	Rich, humusy, acid soil	Division. Plant 12 in. apart.	Delightful at the base of azaleas and rhododendrons.
Full sun	Average, well-drained soil	Division in spring every 3 or 4 years. Plant 12–15 in. apart.	Cut back after flowering to promote new growth.
Full sun	Average to poor, well-drained soil	Division in spring every 3 years. Plant 18 in. apart.	A hybrid; makes a lovely combination with lavender and purple asters. Many other hybrids and cultivars available.
Full sun	Average to poor, well-drained soil	Division in spring. Seed. Plant 12 in. apart.	Indispensable ground cover for contrasting color and texture in the sunny front border.
Full sun	Average, well-drained soil	Division in spring every 4 years. Seed. Plant 15 in. apart.	Named for English botanical writer, Dr. Jonathan Stokes. American native; provides excellent cut flowers.

155 Perennial Genera—*Continued*

NAME OF PLANT	ZONES	SEASON OF BLOOM	HEIGHT	FLOWER COLOR	PLANT DESCRIPTION
TEUCRIUM [*TEW*-cree-um] Germander					
T. chamaedrys	5–9	July–Aug.	15 in.	Rose	Sub-shrub with glossy, oval, dark green leaves. If left untrimmed, will cover itself in small spikes of sweet-smelling flowers.
THALICTRUM [thal-*LICK*-trum] Meadow Rue					
T. aquilegifolium (Columbine Meadow Rue)	5–8	May–June	3 ft.	Lavender	Loose clusters of fluffy, ½-in. flowers atop clumps of columbine-like foliage.
T. delavayi or *T. dipterocarpum* (Yunnan Meadow Rue)	5–8	Aug.–Oct.	3–5 ft.	Lavender	Airy sprays of delicate flowers with prominent yellow centers. Feathery foliage.
T. rochebrunianum (Lavender Mist Meadow Rue)	4–8	July–Sept.	3–5 ft.	Lavender	Misty masses of florets with conspicuous yellow centers, borne on stems of airy foliage.
T. speciosissimum (Dusty Meadow Rue)	5–8	July–Sept.	3–5 ft.	Yellow	Beautiful blue-green foliage carries slightly fragrant, soft yellow plumes.
THERMOPSIS [ther-*MOP*-sis] False Lupine					
T. caroliniana (Carolina Lupine)	3–9	June–July	4–5 ft.	Yellow	12-in. tapering spires of pealike flowers, resembling those of a yellow lupine, above attractive, dark green foliage.
THYMUS [*TY*-mus] Thyme					
T. lanuginosus (Woolly Thyme)	4–9	June	2 in.	Pink	Minute, silver-grey carpet of leaves has tiny, rose pink flowers.
T. serpyllum (Mother-of-Thyme)	3–9	June	3 in.	Lavender	Charming evergreen mats of tiny, shiny leaves with minute flowers.

Other cultivars: 'Albus', white flowers; 'Carneus', pale, flesh-colored flowers; 'Coccineus', scarlet flowers; 'Rosea', pink flowers.

LIGHT REQUIREMENTS	SOIL REQUIREMENTS	PROPAGATION	REMARKS
Full sun	Average, well-drained soil	Division in spring. Root cuttings. Seed. Plant 15 in. apart.	Usually trimmed into miniature hedge for edging walks or traditional knot gardens.
Partial shade to full sun	Rich, humusy, well-drained soil	Division in spring. Seed. Plant 12 in. apart.	Their natural habitat is a woods' edge.
Partial shade to full sun	Rich, humusy, well-drained soil	Division in spring. Seed. Plant 2 ft. apart.	Lovely species from Yunnan Province in southwestern China. Good in cut flower arrangements.
Partial shade to full sun	Rich, humusy, well-drained soil	Division in spring. Seed. Plant 18 in. apart.	Hardiest and most ornamental of the meadow rues.
Partial shade to full sun	Rich, humusy, well-drained soil	Division in spring. Seed. Plant 18 in. apart.	Foliage is the feature in early spring; flowers in late summer.
Full sun	Sandy, humusy soil	Fresh seed sown in late summer. Taproots make division difficult. Plant 18 in. apart.	Although native from North Carolina to Georgia, it is a hardy, long-lived perennial throughout much of the U.S.
Full sun	Average to poor, well-drained soil (likes lime)	Division. Seed. Plant 8–12 in. apart.	At home in the rock garden, among paving stones, or along walkways.
Full sun	Average to poor, well-drained soil	Division. Seed. Plant 8–12 in. apart.	Who can resist its name or its superb ground-covering quality, to say nothing of its fragrance?

155 Perennial Genera—*Continued*

NAME OF PLANT	ZONES	SEASON OF BLOOM	HEIGHT	FLOWER COLOR	PLANT DESCRIPTION
TIARELLA [tee-ar-*EL*-ah]					
T. cordifolia (Foamflower)	3–8	May–June	12 in.	White	Mats of maple-like leaves send up little puffs of creamy white stars.
TRADESCANTIA [trah-des-*KANT*-shee-ah] Spiderwort					
T. × andersoniana 'Blue Stone'	4–9	June–Aug.	2 ft.	Blue	Succulent stems, sheathed in grasslike leaves, produce clusters of 3-petaled, 1-in. flowers lasting only 1 day. Florets close by afternoon and are replaced with fresh crop in the morning.

Other cultivars: 'J. C. Weguelin', pale blue flowers; 'Pauline', pale pink flowers; 'Purple Dome', purple flowers; 'Red Cloud', rosy red flowers; 'Snowcap', white flowers.

NAME OF PLANT	ZONES	SEASON OF BLOOM	HEIGHT	FLOWER COLOR	PLANT DESCRIPTION
TRILLIUM [*TRIL*-ee-um] Wake Robin					
T. erectum (Purple Trillium)	4–8	Apr.–May	12 in.	Maroon	Each plant has 3 erect leaves. Each flower has 3 sepals and 3 petals.
T. grandiflorum (Snow Trillium)	4–8	Apr.–May	15 in.	White	Pure white, 3-petaled flowers bloom just above handsome, rounded foliage.
TROLLIUS [*TROH*-lee-us] Globe Flower					
T. europaeus 'Superbus'	4–8	May–June	2 ft.	Yellow	2-in., very double, buttercup-like flowers are held well above deeply divided, dark green leaves.
T. ledebourii 'Golden Queen'	4–8	June–July	3 in.	Orange	Flowers more open than *T. europaeus*.

LIGHT REQUIREMENTS	SOIL REQUIREMENTS	PROPAGATION	REMARKS
Partial shade to full shade	Rich, humusy, acid soil	Division in spring. Plant 8 in. apart.	Effective in masses.
Full sun to partial shade	Average, well-drained soil	Division in spring to curb growth. Plant 18 in. apart.	By midsummer stems become weedy and tend to flop. Cut back for tidier appearance.
Full shade	Rich, moist, humusy, well-drained soil	Division. Plant 12 in. apart.	This woodland wildflower may naturalize in conditions close to its wild habitat.
Full shade	Rich, moist, humusy, well-drained soil	Division. Plant 12 in. apart.	One of the easiest to grow and showiest of the trilliums. Naturalizes slowly.
Full sun to partial shade	Rich, moist, humusy soil	Division in fall. Seed sown as soon as it ripens. Plant 12 in. apart.	At home in shade or sun as long as soil stays moist.
Full sun to partial shade	Rich, moist, humusy soil	Division in fall. Seed sown as soon as it ripens. Plant 12 in. apart.	Both varieties of trollius bring beauty to waterside plantings.

155 Perennial Genera—*Continued*

NAME OF PLANT	ZONES	SEASON OF BLOOM	HEIGHT	FLOWER COLOR	PLANT DESCRIPTION
TUNICA [*TOO*-nick-ah] Tunic Flower					
T. saxifraga or *Petrorhagia saxifraga* 'Pleniflora Rosea'	4–8	July–Aug.	8 in.	Pink	Grasslike tufts, covered with masses of dainty flowers resembling gypsophila.
VALERIANA [val-air-ee-*AN*-ah] Garden Heliotrope					
V. officinalis	4–8	July–Aug.	4 ft.	White	Sweet-smelling billows of white to pink flowers on hollow stalks with deeply divided foliage.
VERBASCUM [ver-*BAS*-cum] Mullein					
V. chaixii 'Album'	4–8	June–Sept.	3 ft.	White	Stately spires of white flowers with mauve eyes emerge from clumps of silver-green leaves.
VERBENA [ver-*BEE*-nah]					
V. rigida or *V. venosa* 'Glowing Violet' (Hardy Verbena)	6–10	May–Frost	6 in.	Purple	Broad mats of trailing foliage produce blossoms all season.
VERONICA [ver-*AHN*-ik-ah] Speedwell					
V. incana (Woolly Speedwell)	3–8	June–Aug.	18 in.	Blue	Slender spikes of lavender-blue florets contrast nicely with whitish, woolly, lancelike leaves.
V. latifolia or *V. teucrium* 'Crater Lake Blue' (Hungarian Speedwell)	3–8	June–July	18 in.	Blue	Gentian blue spires sprawl above narrow, dark green leaves.
V. longifolia var. *Subsessilis* (Clump Speedwell)	4–8	July–Aug.	2 ft.	Blue	Striking royal blue flowers above handsome clumps of rich green foliage.
V. prostrata 'Heavenly Blue' (Harebell Speedwell)	5–8	May–June	6 in.	Blue	Mat-forming variety with tiny, dark green, toothed leaves and blue spikes.

LIGHT REQUIREMENTS	SOIL REQUIREMENTS	PROPAGATION	REMARKS
Full sun	Average, well-drained soil	Cuttings. Seed. Plant 8–12 in. apart.	A fine wall or rock garden plant.
Full sun to partial shade	Average, moist, well-drained soil	Division. Seed. Plant 2 ft. apart.	Can be rather rank in the garden; nice along woodlands' edge. An old-fashioned favorite.
Full sun	Average, well-drained soil	Root cuttings in spring. Plant 18 in. apart.	Perennial form of the biennial ornamental mullein.
Full sun	Average, well-drained soil	Division. Seed. Plant 12 in. apart.	North of the Carolinas, needs winter protection. Often used as annual bedding plant.
Full sun	Average, sandy, well-drained soil	Division every 4 years. Plant 12 in. apart.	Silvery leaves look good before and after bloom. Likes a sunny, sandy place.
Full sun	Average, well-drained soil	Division every 4 years. Plant 12 in. apart.	Intense true blue in a vertical shape. May need staking.
Full sun	Average, well-drained soil	Division every 4 years. Plant 12 in. apart.	One of the tallest veronicas; adds an inspiring vertical accent to drifts of other flowers.
Full sun to partial shade	Average, well-drained soil	Division every 4 years. Plant 8–12 in. apart.	Early-blooming gem in the May garden.

155 Perennial Genera—*Continued*

NAME OF PLANT	ZONES	SEASON OF BLOOM	HEIGHT	FLOWER COLOR	PLANT DESCRIPTION
VERONICA (continued)					
V. spicata 'Blue Peter' (Spike Speedwell)	3–8	June–Aug.	15 in.	Blue	Strong, compact spikes of deep blue.
Other cultivars: 'Blue Fox', bright lavender-blue flowers; 'Red Fox', deep rose flowers; 'Snow White', 18 in. tall, white flowers.					
VINCA [*VINK*-ah] Periwinkle					
V. minor 'Bowlesii'	4–9	Apr.–May	8 in.	Blue	Trailing runners of glossy evergreen leaves sparkle with light violet-blue flowers.
Other cultivars: 'Mrs. Jekyll', white variety.					
VIOLA [vi-*OH*-luh] Pansy, Violet					
V. cornuta 'Chantreyland' (Tufted Pansy)	5–8	May–Sept.	8 in.	Apricot	Small tufts of heart-shaped leaves bloom all season with pansy-like flowers.
Other cultivars: 'Arkwright Ruby', red flowers; 'Jersey Gem', blue flowers; 'Lutea Splendons', yellow flowers; 'White Perfection', white flowers.					
V. odorata 'Royal Robe' (Violet)	5–8	Apr.–May	6 in.	Purple	Fragrant violets nestle above and amid tufted mounds of heart-shaped leaves.
Other cultivars: 'Red Giant', deep red flowers; 'Rosina', dusky pink flowers; 'White Czar', white flowers.					
V. tricolor (Johnny-Jump-Up)	4–8	Apr.–June	3–12 in.	Violet, yellow, white	Tiny pansies on thin, sprawling stems.
YUCCA [*YUCK*-uh] Desert Candle					
Y. filamentosa	4–10	July–Aug.	4–6 ft.	White	A spray of large, swordlike leaves send up a summer stalk that opens into creamy white flower bells.

293

LIGHT REQUIREMENTS	SOIL REQUIREMENTS	PROPAGATION	REMARKS
Full sun	Average, well-drained soil	Division every 4 years. Plant 12 in. apart.	Of the many cultivars available, most are crosses between *V. longifolia* and *V. spicata*.
Partial shade to full shade	Moist, humusy, well-drained soil	Division. Cuttings. Plant 12 in. apart.	One of the prettiest ground covers for shaded areas.
Partial shade	Average, well-drained soil	Seed. Plant 15 in. apart.	Free-flowering if spent blooms are picked.
Partial shade	Rich, moist, humusy soil	Root division in spring. Offsets. Seed. Plant 8–12 in. apart.	Has the sweet, familiar fragrance of childhood's bouquets.
Full sun to partial shade	Average, well-drained soil	Seed. Plant 6 in. apart.	A short-lived perennial that reseeds itself easily. Tends to jump up here and there.
Full sun	Sandy, dry soil	Transplanting of offsets (parent plants resent moving). Seed. Plant 18 in. apart.	Native desert plant that does well in all parts of the U.S. except the far North.

_____ APPENDIX _____

Mail-Order Sources for Perennial Plants

The following mail-order firms carry all the perennials listed in the chart in chapter 7, and almost every plant described in this book. Not every firm carries every perennial, but between them, all are carried.

Most of these firms charge a small amount for their catalogs.

For Varied Selections of Perennials

Bluestone Perennials Inc.
    7211 Middle Ridge Road
    Madison, OH 44057

Busse Gardens
    635 East 7th Street
    Rt. 2, Box 13
    Cokato, MN 55321

Carroll Gardens, Inc.
    444 East Main Street
    Box 310
    Westminster, MD 21157

The Crownsville Nursery
    1241 Generals Highway
    Crownsville, MD 21032

Garden Place
    6780 Heisley Road
    P.O. Box 388
    Mentor, OH 44061

International Growers Exchange, Inc.
    17142 Lahser Road
    Detroit, MI 48219

Lamb Nurseries
    East 101 Sharp Avenue
    Spokane, WA 99202

Milaeger's Gardens
    4838 Douglas Avenue
    Racine, WI 53402

Powell's Gardens
    Rt. 2, Box 86
    Princeton, NC 27569

Andre Viette Farm & Nursery
    Rt. 1, Box 16
    Fishersville, VA 22939

Wayside Gardens
    Hodges, SC 29695

White Flower Farm
    Litchfield, CT 06759

For Ornamental Grasses and Ground Covers

Kurt Bluemel, Inc.
    2543 Hess Road
    Fallston, MD 21047

INDEX

Page numbers in italic indicate entry in chart. Boldface page numbers indicate photographs and illustrations.

Published and distributed by

ISLAND HERITAGE™
P U B L I S H I N G
94-411 KŌʻAKI STREET, WAIPAHU HAWAIʻI 96797-2806
Orders: (800) 468-2800 • Information: (808) 564-8800
Fax: (808) 564-8877 • islandheritage.com

ISBN# : 0-89610-354-4

First Edition, Thirty - Fourth Printing - 2011

COP 111104

Limu
The Blue Turtle

Written by Kimo Armitage
Illustrated by Scott Kaneshiro

Dedications

To my mom, Ethel and my Grandma Betty

Kimo

To my mom, Charlene and my Grandma Marlene

Scott

Every year, thousands of baby turtles climb out of their sandy nests and make their way to the ocean.

2

This year, out popped another
baby turtle -- but, this one was *blue!*

The tiny blue turtle opened its big eyes, shook the sand off its head, and started to make its way to the ocean.

When all the other turtles saw the blue turtle, they started to laugh. They pointed their flippers at the poor turtle and teased him.

"No one likes me," the blue turtle said.

He dunked his head under the surf and rode out to sea.

Growing up in the sea, Limu the Blue Turtle would meet other turtles.
But, after looking at Limu, the other turtles would laugh and swim away.
"No one wants to be my friend," Limu said.

7

But, growing up was not all bad.
Limu would bodysurf in the big waves . . .

8

. . . and he would chase colorful fishes into the coral.

One day, when he was eating his favorite seaweed off some rocks, he heard someone crying.
When Limu looked up, he saw a little 'opihi.

"Why are you crying?" asked Limu.

"I am so sad. I miss my sister who lives far away," cried the little 'opihi.

"I can take you," said the blue turtle. "I can swim really fast and we will be there in no time."

"You are such a nice turtle!" said the 'opihi. "My name is Nani."

"My name is Limu. Hop on my back and we'll leave right now," said the blue turtle.

The 'opihi jumped on Limu's back. She hung on tight as the blue turtle swam under the water.

They swam near the surface and they swam in the deep part of the water.

They laughed with a family of seals playing in the water.

All of a sudden, the water became black. Nani was very **scared.**

"What is it, Limu?" she cried.

When Limu looked up, he saw that he had bumped into a **big whale.**

The whale was crying.
"What's wrong?" Limu asked.
"I was swimming in the deep water near a sunken ship and I got a big piece of wood stuck in my flipper!" the whale cried. "It hurts so much!"

"Maybe I can help . . . " said Limu.
Limu bit onto the piece of wood and pulled with all his might.
He pulled and pulled and pulled!
"You can do it!" yelled Nani.
Suddenly, PLOP! The wood came out!

16

"How can I ever thank you?" asked the whale. "My flipper is as good as new!"

"Glad I could help! My name is Limu," the blue turtle said.

"My name is Jonah," replied the whale. "You are a good-hearted turtle, Limu. Thanks again!"

After a day of traveling, the blue turtle and the little 'opihi could see the beautiful bay where Nani's sister lived. Many different kinds of colorful fish lived in the reef.

Limu looked at all the different types of seaweed. There was so much food to eat!

"There is my sister's home!" cried Nani. "I am so happy! How can I ever thank you, Limu?"

"I am happy that I could help," said Limu.

They pulled closer to the water's edge where Nani's sister lived.

Nani let out a big yell, "HŪI! L-A-N-I!"

Lani saw Nani and cried tears of joy, for she was happy to see her sister, too.

Nani jumped off Limu's back and hugged
her sister.

"Thank you so much, Limu," said Lani. "You are a great friend to my sister and me. I am so glad to see Nani. You have a big heart."
Then she told Limu, "Please eat some seaweed!"

Limu ate and ate.

He had never seen so many different types of seaweed! He was so busy eating, that he did not see how far he had drifted from the rocky shore.

All of a sudden, he saw two beady eyes looking at him.

Then he saw a LOT of beady eyes and big, dark shapes . . . and Limu became very afraid.

"You look good -- good enough to *eat!*" said one of the dark shapes.

When it moved closer, Limu saw
that it was a **shark!**

"You will make a delicious lunch,"
said another shark. "We have never
eaten a **blue turtle** before!"

25

Just then, a big black shadow covered Limu!
The big black shadow started to flip the sharks
high into the sky, one by one. The other sharks were
afraid, and swam away as fast as they could.

"It looked like you needed some help, Limu," said the whale.
"Oh, thank you, Jonah!" said Limu. "You saved my life!"
"That's what friends are for. See you later, Limu!" said the whale as he swam away.

Limu swam back to Lani's home.
He was so happy because he was in a beautiful place with his friends -- and he knew that no matter what he looked like on the outside, others liked him because of the good turtle he was on the inside.

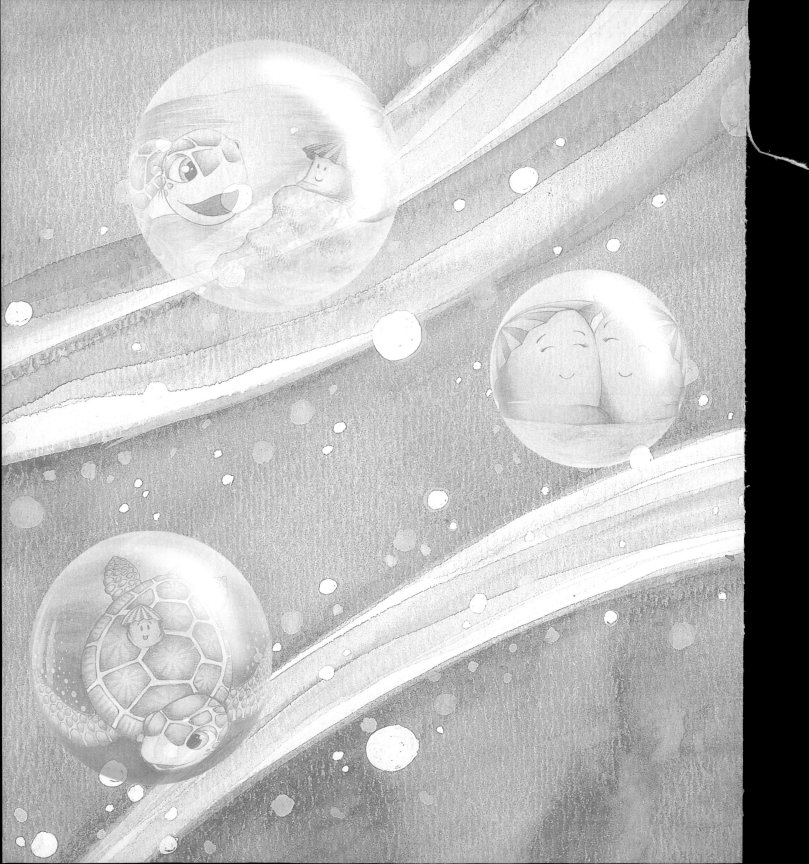